sponsored by

Supported by

CW00327257

the good
Employment
guide
for the voluntary sector

by Wendy Blake Ranken

voice of the voluntary sector

The National Council for Voluntary Organisations (NCVO) is the umbrella body for the voluntary sector in England, with sister councils in Wales, Scotland and Northern Ireland. NCVO has a growing membership of over 3,700 voluntary organisations, ranging from large national bodies to community groups, volunteer bureaux and development agencies working at a local level. We work to support the voluntary sector and to create an environment in which voluntary organisations of all kinds can flourish by providing a wide range of information, advice and support services and by representing the views of the sector to government and policy makers.

Our vision
NCVO's vision is of a fair and open society, which encourages and is supported by voluntary action.

Our mission
NCVO aims:
• to give a shared voice to voluntary organisations
• to cultivate an environment that fosters their development
• to help voluntary organisations to achieve the highest standards of practice and effectiveness
• to provide leadership to the voluntary sector in tackling new issues and unmet needs

Published by NCVO Publications
(incorporating Bedford Square Press), imprint of the
National Council for Voluntary Organisations
Regent's Wharf, 8 All Saints Street, London N1 9RL

Published July 2005

© NCVO July 2005

Typeset by JVT Design
Printed and bound by Latimer Trend and Co. Ltd.

British Library Cataloguing in Publication Data
A catalogue record for this book is available from the British Library

ISBN: 0 7199 1656 9

Every effort has been made to trace or contact the copyright holders of original text or illustrations used. The publishers will be pleased to correct any errors or omissions brought to their attention in future editions of this book.

Acknowledgements

Joanna Wootten of NCVO and the author, Wendy Blake Ranken, would like to thank the following people and organisations for their assistance:

This edition of the *Good Employment Guide* would not have been possible if the Big Lottery Fund had not supported NCVO's programme of work promoting good employment practice in the voluntary and community sector.

We would particularly like to thank readers of the previous edition of the *Good Employment Guide*, particularly members of the NCVO Personnel Network, for giving detailed and constructive feedback. We have tried to take your comments into account and make this edition the best ever! Unfortunately, we do not have everyone's names so have decided to thank you all as a group.

We would also like to thank:

Mark Restall of Volunteering England, for his detailed comments on a draft of chapter 15.

Kirstie Axtens of Working Families for her detailed comments on a draft of chapter 8.

Rachael McIlroy of the TUC for reviewing a draft of chapter 12.

Hazel Watkins of Acas read a draft of the entire publication and made detailed comments which were very helpful. We are also grateful to Acas for giving permission to extensively cite its material.

Angeline Hamilton, and Lai-Har Cheung of NCVO for reading earlier drafts of the guide and giving their feedback.

NCVO paid the following specialists to ensure that the law was accurate as at April 2005:

The final draft of the publication (except chapter 11) was reviewed by employment law and human resource specialists: Sherrards, www.harrysherrard.com.

Nick Brion of Complete Health & Safety reviewed chapter 11 to ensure that it was an accurate reflection of the law as at April 2005.

And ... the publication makes extensive reference to other sources of information such as the Royal Society for the Prevention of Accidents, the Health and Safety Executive, and Business Link. We have tried to acknowledge all sources of information whenever possible.

If we have accidentally omitted any acknowledgements or

thanks, we apologise. Please contact the NCVO Publications Team so that we can make the corrections when the publication is reprinted.

Please note that NCVO accepts responsibility for any errors that remain.

A note about the law

Employment law changes very rapidly. This publication's understanding of and statement of employment law was correct, to the best of our knowledge, in April 2005.

If you wish to check the latest legal position, you can do this by following the references in each chapter of the guide.

If you are operating in Scotland or Northern Ireland, please note that legislation may be different in some circumstances. You may wish to check this, for example via Acas.

Contents

Sponsor's Foreword

The Charity People Group are once again proud to sponsor the 2005 edition of the *Good Employment Guide*.

Good Employment practices are the bed rock of a successful not for profit organisation. Key to capacity building and service delivery, good employment practices are also a manifest example of the values and ethos of our sector.

The voluntary sector operates in an environment of rapidly changing employment law, driven by national and European legislation. We have also witnessed a sharp increase in voluntary sector organisations being taken to industrial tribunals by employees and in a recent case a volunteer.

Senior staff and trustees need to keep abreast of developments and ensure they and their organisation are up to date with relevant general and employment law, policies and practices.

As a result the *Good Employment Guide* has become the essential resource for HR professionals in our sector. Whilst useful to protect an organisation in the unfortunate event of conflict, the guide's key aim is to enable you to create the right working environment with focused, motivated staff delivering your mission.

Of course, focused motivated staff is also central to our work at Charity People. As the recruitment centre for the not for profit sector we strive to provide the same excellence in service and employment espoused by the *Good Employment Guide*.

Whether through our traditional permanent, fundraising and temporary staffing services at The Charity People Agency, or at www.charitypeople.com the leading not for profit recruitment web site, through our senior and interim executive recruitment division Prime Executive or indeed through forum3, (www.forum3.co.uk) Europe's biggest and best recruitment and volunteering event which attracts 150 organisations and 20,000 visitors every October to the Business Design Centre, we also aim to provide innovative solutions to creating a successful staffing and volunteer teams deliver services across the UK.

I hope you find this excellent guide as useful as do our 2,500 clients, to whom we dedicate this sponsorship.

Paul Canal
Managing Director
paulc@charitypeople.com

charity**people**   **prime**executive   14th–15th October 2005
The Business Design Centre, Islington, London   **forum**3

I

Introduction

By Joanna Wootten
Workforce Project Manager
NCVO

The voluntary sector as an employer

The voluntary sector is now a major force in the UK economy, with an annual income of £15.6bn and employing 569,000 people – that's one in 50, or 2 per cent, of the UK workforce (source: UK Voluntary Sector Almanac 2004).

However, many voluntary organisations struggle to be good employers. This guide has been written for all voluntary organisations which do not have in-house human resource specialists. The idea behind the guide is to make it as easy and stress free as possible for your organisation to be a good employer.

It is worth noting that it is expensive to be a poor employer. For instance, if you have a high turnover of staff, you are spending a lot of money. The Chartered Institute of Personnel and Development estimated the average impact of turnover was £4,800 for each employee (Recruitment, Retention and Turnover survey 2004). If you have a high level of sickness absence, this will cost your organisation money. Can you afford this? Do your beneficiaries suffer because they receive a poorer service?

It makes sense to recruit, train, develop and reward your employees with care and to retain them for as long as possible. It makes sense to have the best employment practices and procedures that you can. Wendy Blake Ranken, the author, has done a fantastic job of telling you how you can do this in a straightforward way.

I hope that you find this guide relevant, useful and time saving.

Who is this guide for?

Many voluntary organisations get to the stage where they feel the time has come to recruit their first paid worker or workers. However, this can be a daunting process. Even if you are already an employer, there is still a lot to remember and the law is changing all the time.

This guide aims to make the process of employing people easier. The guide is equally relevant to trustees taking on

3

responsibilities as an employer for the first time; and to chief executives and managers of small to medium sized organisations, where there may be no in-house human resources expert.

What the guide covers

The guide 'walks you through' all the main stages of employing staff, hopefully answering some of the main 'how do I?' questions such as:
How do I ...
   find the right person?
   pay them?
   draft their contract of employment?
   appraise them?
   comply with the law?
   deal with performance, attendance or conduct problems?
   deal with requests for maternity, paternity or adoption leave?
   tackle redundancy?
   ensure that all employment practices meet good equal opportunities/diversity practice?

Having read this guide, you should be more confident about the basics of employing people and you should have more knowledge of where you can find out more information.

Making the most of this guide

Chapter summaries
Each chapter starts by telling you what the chapter is about. Read this information first, to help you decide what you want to read in more detail.

Case studies and good practice examples
Throughout the guide, we have included case studies and examples of good practice. Several of these are based around a fictitious voluntary organisation, the Westwich Association. Others are from a variety of voluntary organisations.
   The case studies and good practice examples may be useful to help you relate back to experiences in your own organisation.

Checklists

At the end of each chapter, you will find a checklist of the main points arising from the chapter. You can use the checklists to review what you are doing currently, and what you need to do next.

Further information

In each chapter, there are references to where you can find out more. There are lots of references to websites. The internet is a quick and effective way of gaining information. If you do not have access to the internet, telephone numbers are also provided. You may also wish to note that many public libraries provide free internet access.

Other NCVO Good Guides

This book is the part of series of Good Guides published by NCVO. The other guides include: *the Good Management Guide; the Good Trustee Guide; the Good Financial Management Guide; the Good Campaigns Guide; the Good Investment Guide* and *the Good Membership Guide.* You can go to www.ncvo-vol.org.uk/publications for more information or call NCVO on 0800 2 798 798 or textphone 0800 01 88 111, or to order any of the above call 0845 458 9910.

NCVO Forums

The purpose of NCVO networks is to enable members to network and swap ideas and resources as well as updating on relevant issues via email and meetings and events.

NCVO's **Personnel Network** is free and open to anyone who has responsibility for human resources/personnel within a voluntary organisation.

NCVO's **Charity Trainers' Network** is free and open to anyone who has responsibility for training within a voluntary organisation.

NCVO's **Diversity Forum** is free and open to anyone who is responsible for promoting and enabling diversity within a voluntary organisation.

If you would like further details about the networks, visit NCVO's website at www.ncvo-vol.org.uk, contact NCVO's HelpDesk free on 0800 2 798 798 or textphone 0800 01 88 111.

Tell us what you think

We welcome your comments on this guide, to help us make sure that future editions are as relevant as possible. If you would like to comment, you can fill in the feedback form at the back of this guide and return it to NCVO, or email publications@ncvo-vol.org.uk.

Overview of rights and responsibilities in the employment relationship

What this chapter is about

This chapter gives an overview of the essential things you need to know about employing people. It explains the legal obligations between employer and employee in an employment relationship, and the legal rights of employees.

You might find this chapter of particular use if you are a first time employer. Alternatively, you might find that the chapter is a helpful 'route map' to the rest of this Good Guide.

The chapter includes a practical case study of an employer appointing their first employee and how they ensured they complied with their employment obligations.

General obligations in the employment relationship

Regardless of what is actually written down in an employment contract, employees and employers are expected to abide by certain unwritten obligations.

The employee must:	The employer must:
• render faithful service to the employer and not compete with the employer • obey lawful and reasonable orders (consistent with his or her contract) • exercise reasonable care and skill • provide a personal service • maintain confidentiality	• pay agreed wages • provide work • provide a safe workplace • pay out of pocket expenses • maintain the relationship of trust and confidence by behaving reasonably towards the employee

Regardless of what is actually written down in an employment contract, employees and employers are expected to abide by certain unwritten obligations.

Legal rights of employees

Over the years, the law has provided a number of legal rights for employees.

The following information is adapted from the Acas Advisory Handbook, *Employing People – a handbook for small firms* (downloadable from www.acas.org.uk). Acas is a Government organisation that provides employment advice and support to employers and employees.

All employees have the right ...

- Not to be discriminated against or to suffer a detriment (including the right not to be dismissed) – on grounds of race, sex, marriage, disability, sexual orientation or religion or belief. By December 2006 they will also be protected on the grounds of age. See chapter 2 for further information.
- To equal pay – with members of the opposite sex if it can be shown that they are doing like work or work of equal value.
- Not to be unfairly dismissed – employees have the right to complain to an Employment Tribunal within three months of their dismissal, provided they have at least one year of continuous service. However, there are several circumstances where no continuous service is required; these are known as automatically unfair dismissals. These include where the dismissal was:
  - for participation in trade union activities, for membership or non-membership of a trade union and in respect of trade union recognition or derecognition;
  - for activities as an employee representative, or as a candidate for election, for purposes of statutory consultation over redundancies or business transfers;
  - because the employee asserted or sought to assert a statutory right;
  - for taking (or proposing to take) action on health and safety grounds as a designated or recognised health and safety representative, or as an employee in particular circumstances;
  - for taking part (or proposing to take part) in consultation on health and safety matters, or taking part in elections for representatives of employee safety (representatives elected by groups of employees not covered by trade union safety representatives);
  - because of pregnancy or childbirth;
  - for being a trustee of an occupational pension scheme and performing, or proposing to perform, any of the

trustees' functions;
- because of qualifying for working families' tax credit or disabled persons' tax credit, or seeking to enforce a right to them;
- taking or seeking to take parental leave or time off for dependents.

- To an itemised pay statement.
- To maternity benefits/rights. See chapter 8 for further information.
- To two weeks' paid paternity leave. See chapter 8.
- To adoption leave. See chapter 8.
- To unpaid parental leave – of up to 13 weeks in total (over 5 years) for each child, for employees with one year's qualifying service. See chapter 8.
- To time off for dependants – all employees have the right to take a reasonable period of unpaid time off work to deal with an emergency involving a dependant and not to be dismissed or victimised for doing so. See chapter 8.
- To apply for flexible working – employees who are parents of children under the age of six, or disabled children under the age of 18, have the right to apply to their employer to work flexibly. See chapter 8.
- To notice of termination of employment – most employees are entitled to receive from their employers at least one week's notice after one month's service, two weeks' after two years and an additional week's notice for each complete year of employment up to 12 weeks for 12 years' service.
- Not to have unlawful deductions from pay – employers must not deduct from an employee's pay unless the deduction is required or authorised by statute or by a relevant provision of the employee's contract; or if the worker has previously given written agreement or consent for the deduction to be made.
- To pay when laid off – whether or not an employer is entitled to lay off an employee is determined by what has been agreed in the individual contract of employment. Most employees who can be laid off by their employers are entitled to a minimum payment – a guaranteed payment, for up to five workless days in any period of three months.
- To redundancy pay – employees with at least two years' service are entitled to redundancy payments, the size of which depend on the individual's pay, age and service. See chapter 13 for further information.
- To a safe system of work – when an employer hires someone, the employer becomes legally responsible for their

all employees have the right to take a reasonable period of unpaid time off work to deal with an emergency involving a dependant

health and safety at work. See chapter 11 for further information.

- To statutory sick pay (SSP) – paid by the employer (provided the employee meets the qualifying conditions) for up to 26 weeks. However, where an organisation has an exceptionally high level of sickness in any month, the employer may be able to claim reimbursement of a proportion of SSP paid out. For further information about SSP, including the current rates, see the Business Link website: www.businesslink.gov.uk.
- To time off.
  i) for public duties (civic, magistrate, etc);
  ii) to look for work if declared redundant with at least two years' service;
  iii) for trade union activities, duties and training (including acting as a Union Learning Representative) where a trade union is recognised for collective bargaining;
  iv) for duties as an employee representative, or as a candidate for election, for purposes of statutory consultation over redundancies or business transfers or European Works Councils;
  v) for carrying out functions as a safety representative (trade union or non trade union) or as a candidate for election as a representative of employees not in groups covered by trade union safety representatives;
  vi) for performing the functions of a pension fund trustee or undergoing relevant training;
  vii) to study, if employees aged 16 or 17 have not attained a certain standard of education;
  viii) for medical suspension if continued employment would endanger health (e.g. in the case of pregnancy).
- Trade union membership – employees have the right:
  - to belong or not to belong to a trade union;
  - to time off to take part in trade union activities/duties;
  - not to be excluded or expelled from a trade union other than for a permitted reason;
  - not to be unjustifiably disciplined by a trade union;
  - not to be refused employment because of membership or non-membership of a trade union;
  - not to suffer unauthorised or excessive deductions from trade union subscriptions;
  - not to have political fund deductions made from trade union subscriptions where they object to this or have a certificate of exemption.

See chapter 12 for further information.

- To protected employment rights – employees have the right to be transferred automatically, on the same terms without loss of service-related employment rights, from one employer to another when the business in which the employee is then employed is transferred to a new employer.
- To written reasons for dismissal on request – provided they have at least one year's service (if an individual feels they have been dismissed for reasons related to pregnancy or maternity, however, they have the right to written reasons for dismissal on request, even if they do not have one year's service) no request or service period is required where the dismissal is on maternity grounds).
- To a written statement – of the main terms of the contract. See chapter 4 for further information.
- To minimum pay – under the National Minimum Wage Act 1998, workers are entitled to be paid at least the level of the National Minimum Wage. See chapter 6 for further information.
- To annual leave and working time limits – under the Working Time Regulations 1998, workers are entitled to four weeks paid leave per year, to rest periods and in-work rest breaks and health assessments in certain circumstances. The Regulations also limit the average working week to 48 hours and limit night working to an average of eight hours in any 24 hour period. Special rules apply to young people. See chapter 11 for further information.
- To protection from being required to work on Sundays – shop workers and betting workers have the right to opt out of the requirement to work on Sundays.
- To payment on insolvency of the employer – dismissed employees can receive payments for certain debts, within limits, from the National Insurance Fund on the formal insolvency of their employer.
- To be accompanied at disciplinary and grievance hearings – workers are entitled to be accompanied by a fellow worker or a trade union official of their choice at certain disciplinary and grievance hearings provided that they make a reasonable request to be so accompanied. The right applies when the hearing could result in the administration of a formal disciplinary warning or demotion or dismissal. The right to be accompanied at grievance hearings applies only where the grievance relates to the performance of a legal duty by an employer in relation to a worker. See chapter 9 for further information.

- For part-time workers to be treated no less favourably than comparable full-timers – the Part-time Workers (Prevention of Less Favourable Treatment) Regulations 2000, aim to ensure that part-time workers have the same terms and conditions as comparable full timers. Less favourable treatment must be objectively justified. See chapter 4 for further information.
- For employees on fixed-term contracts to be treated no less favourably than comparable permanent employees – the Fixed-term Employees (Prevention of Less Favourable Treatment) Regulations 2002, aim to ensure that employees on contracts of fixed duration have the same terms and conditions of employment as comparable permanent employees. Less favourable treatment must be objectively justified. The regulations came into force on 1 October 2002. See chapter 4.
- To protection when making disclosures of wrongdoing to the employer – the Public Interest Disclosure Act 1998 protects employees who have a reasonable belief that they are disclosing information relating to criminal offences, miscarriages of justice, danger to health and safety or the environment or breaches of legal obligations to their employer. See chapter 12 for further information.

Legal obligations of employers

As well as the obligations to provide all the above rights to employees, employers must:

Register with the Inland Revenue if they are taking on an employee
The Inland Revenue will then send a new employer's starter pack with all the forms and tables required to run a payroll. You can call the New Employer's Helpline on 0845 60 70 143 to find out more.

Adhere to data protection principles
Some Employee data is considered to be personal data and the Data Protection Act therefore applies to the processing of that data.

The Data Protection Act 1998 covers both computer and manual records and works in two ways:

Employees can ask to see the data you hold on them.

- It gives individuals certain rights, including the right to see information that is held about them and to have it corrected if it is not right. Employees can ask to see the data you hold on them.
- It says anyone who records and uses personal information

(data controllers) must be open about how the information is used and must follow eight principles of good information handling.

The eight principles of good information handling are that data must be:

- fairly and lawfully processed
- processed for limited purposes
- adequate, relevant and not excessive
- accurate
- not kept for longer than is necessary
- processed in line with the data subject's rights
- secure
- not transferred to countries outside the EU without adequate protection.

As an employer, you may need to register under the Data Protection Act. You can find out whether you need to register by calling the Information Commissioner on 01625 545740.

Case study – first time employer

As a first time employer, you may feel that all the information above is a bit daunting! Here is a case study to help you think about what you may actually need to do when you are thinking of employing a first member of staff.

The **Westwich Association** was formed in 1995, in response to local concerns about high unemployment in the area and a lack of facilities for young people.

The Association's first steering committee was elected from local residents, mainly comprising parents.

Money for the Association was raised via jumble sales and community events. A weekly youth club, run by volunteers, was established in a local hall.

By 2001, the Association had obtained charitable status. The Management Committee found that there was more work than could be done by the available volunteers. Several youth groups had been formed, but the youth work was somewhat disjointed and there was a feeling that resources could be used better. It was decided to employ a youth worker, whose job would be to co-ordinate all youth work. Funding was applied for and gained from a local charitable trust to employ a youth worker for two years.

In preparation for employing the youth worker, the Association did the following:

Looked on the Acas website www.acas.org.uk and downloaded a copy of *Employing People: a handbook for small firms*. As they did not have internet access at the Association premises, they made use of free internet access at the local library.

They contacted the Inland Revenue (New Employer's Helpline 0845 60 70 143) to register as an employer and the Inland Revenue sent them a new employer's starter pack, with all the tables, forms and information they would need to operate their payroll.

They also contacted the Information Commissioner to check if they needed to register as a data processor under the Data Protection Act (tel: 01625 545740). They downloaded information from the Business Link website www.businesslink.gov.uk on data protection, so that they knew their responsibilities.

Acas advised them that they could attend a training session on employing people – which at the time was free as they were an employer of less than five employees.

After the training, the Association drafted a written statement ('contract of employment') for the new employee – based on a model written statement downloaded from the Acas website.

The Association also used resources from the Acas website to draft brief disciplinary and grievance procedures.

The Association wanted to be a fair employer and so put together an equality statement of intent, to which all should comply. Having such a statement was also a condition of receiving funding for the youth worker post. They used the Acas handbook *Tackling discrimination and promoting equality – good practice guide for employers to guide them*.

The management committee checked whether they needed to provide a pension. They found that as they had less than five employees, they did not have a legal obligation to provide a pension scheme.

The management committee agreed who would manage the new employee.

They also agreed how the individual's salary would be administered, who would do Inland Revenue returns and who would arrange for the employee to be given an itemised pay statement each month.

The Association considered health and safety matters. Although there is a legal requirement to have a health and safety policy only when an organisation has five employees, they decided to draft a policy, using the free leaflet from the Health and Safety Executive called *Starting Your Business: Guidance on preparing a health and safety policy document* for small firms. They downloaded the leaflet from the internet at www.hse.gov.uk/pubns/indg324.pdf. They already had first aiders amongst their volunteers, procedures for reporting accidents, fire procedures and a fire certificate.

They found information on the Working Time Regulations from the Department of Trade and Industry website www.dti.gov.uk/er and found out what rest breaks they needed to give. As a result, they made sure that if the youth worker worked late one evening, he or she would not be require to work the next day until 11 hours had passed.

They decided that as soon as the new employee was recruited, they would undertake a risk assessment on VDU use. They would also do a risk assessment on any danger to safety that may arise for the employee, due to working with some vulnerable young people.

They were ready to recruit!

Checklist

Make sure you know the basic rights of employees, and the obligations of employers, outlined in this chapter.

Action	See chapter
✓ Draft a health and safety policy, if you do not have one. Undertake any risk assessments that are required.	11
✓ Produce a written statement of terms and conditions of employment. This document forms the basis of the contract of employment. It has to be given to employees within the first two months of employment, but ideally, you should give it when confirming a job offer, to avoid misunderstandings. *continues overleaf*	4

Action	See chapter
✓ Set yourself up as an employer with the Inland Revenue. Make sure you deduct your new employee's tax and National Insurance contributions from his/her salary and pay this money to the Inland Revenue under PAYE.	4
✓ Draft disciplinary and grievance procedures, which comply with statutory minimum requirements, as soon as you are able.	9
✓ Draft an equality and diversity statement of intent or policy, as soon as you are able.	2

Where to find out more

You can get information for free from the following organisations:

1. Acas

Acas has a wealth of information available to new and existing employers. Most publications are free and can be downloaded from its website. www.acas.org.uk, tel: 08457 47 47 47 or textphone: 08456 06 16 00.

2. The Department of Trade and Industry (DTI)

The DTI website, www.dti.gov.uk, has an employment section, with several useful guides for employers on a variety of employment matters.

3. ask NCVO

www.askncvo.org.uk offers a wealth of free, practical, up-to-date advice on all aspects of running a charity or voluntary organisation. Hundreds of pages cover trusteeship, financial management, human resources and more.

4. Business link

Business Link has a useful section on its website about becoming an employer for the first time. This site also has links into the relevant Inland Revenue pages. www.businesslink.gov.uk

5. The Inland Revenue

Try the following link for new employers. www.inlandrevenue.gov.uk /employers/first_steps.htm
Alternatively, tel: 0845 60 70 143.

2 Non-discrimination and good diversity practice

What this chapter is about

The UK population is changing. For example:
- 36% of the workforce will be aged 45 or over by 2005.
- Women make up nearly half the workforce in the UK, double the numbers of 25 years ago.
- It is estimated that over 14 per cent of the adult population of the UK is disabled.
- Minority ethnic communities will account for more than half of the increase to the working age population in the next 10 years.
- By 2010, it is predicted that only 20 per cent of the UK working population will be white, male, able-bodied and under 45.

To be able to recruit the most appropriate people for your jobs, you will need to ensure that your organisation is one that celebrates diversity and is attractive to people from lots of different backgrounds.

There are also other reasons to promote equality and diversity:
- Legislation requires that you do not discriminate against certain groups. If you are actively working towards equality and diversity, you are less likely to discriminate.
- As a voluntary organisation, you may be working to champion the rights of people who may suffer discrimination or be marginalised. If you are to reach the whole community in your work, it makes sense that your workforce and volunteers reflect the make-up of that wider community.
- It is likely that your funders will require you to be able to demonstrate how you promote diversity and equality in your organisation.

Legislation requires that you do not discriminate against certain groups.

In this chapter, you can find out about:
- The main items of equality legislation that exist in the UK.
- Institutional discrimination.
- What we mean by diversity, and how it fits with equal opportunities.
- How to develop a diversity and equality policy.
- Some 'top tips' on how to recruit and retain a diverse workforce.
- How to undertake equality monitoring.

This chapter sits towards the beginning of this Good Guide, because diversity and equality need to underpin all aspects of managing people. The chapter gives an overview of diversity practices. You will find in later chapters, further information on how to implement diversity and equality into all aspects of employing people.

Equality legislation

The law says that you must not discriminate against others on the grounds of:
- Race, ethnic origin or national origins (Race Relations Act 1976 and Race Relations (Amendment) 2000).
- Gender, marital status, transgender status or if pregnant (Sex Discrimination Act 1975 and Equal Pay Act 1970).
- Disability (Disability Discrimination Act 1995 and Disability Discrimination Act 2005). The Disability Discrimination Act now applies to all employers, regardless of their size.
- Part-time status (Part-Time Workers (Prevention of Less Favourable Treatment) Regulations 2000).
- Fixed term status (Fixed Term Employees (Prevention of Less Favourable Treatment) Regulations 2002).
- Sexual orientation (Employment Equality (Sexual Orientation) Regulations 2003).
- Religion or belief (Employment Equality (Religion or Belief) Regulations 2003).
- Taking maternity, paternity, adoption or parental leave (Employment Rights Act 1996).

Discrimination on the grounds of age will also be unlawful after legislation (anticipated for the autumn of 2006) is passed.

Direct and indirect discrimination

The law says that both direct and indirect discrimination is unlawful.

Direct discrimination is when you specifically treat someone less favourably on one of the grounds covered by legislation. The following are examples of direct discrimination:

- Not appointing a woman to a job because she is deemed to be 'of childbearing age'. This would be direct discrimination on the grounds of her gender. After 2006, it is also likely to be direct discrimination on the grounds of age.
- Not appointing someone to a job because of their perceived sexual orientation.
- Giving less favourable benefits to a part-time member of staff, simply because they are part-time.
- Failing to offer employment to a wheelchair user who was the best person for the job, on the grounds that the wheelchair might 'get in the way' in the office.

Indirect discrimination is more subtle and may not be intentional. Whether it is intentional or not, it is unlawful. It involves applying a 'provision, criterion or practice' which considerably fewer people of the relevant group can comply with and which cannot be objectively justified. The following are examples which may constitute indirect discrimination:

- The imposition of a height restriction of 6ft, for example – because fewer women and individuals from certain minority ethnic groups would be able to comply.
- Refusing a request from an employee who wishes to reduce his/her working hours in order to be able to leave early on Friday afternoons in winter – so as to be home before nightfall – a requirement of his/her religion. This would be indirect discrimination unless you could justify the refusal (e.g. some of the employee's work had to be done at that time and no one else could do it).
- Requiring a person whose second language is English to complete an employment application form, when there is no requirement to write in the job.

Reasonable adjustments in the Disability Discrimination Act 1995

Disabled people are defined under the DDA as having a "physical or mental impairment which has a substantial and long term adverse effect on their ability to carry out normal day to day activities". The definition of 'disabled' is quite wide and has recently been expanded (under the Disability Discrimination Act 2005) to include people with HIV, cancer or multiple sclerosis (MS) from the point of diagnosis; and to include people with a mental illness without the requirement that the mental illness is 'clinically well recognised'.

The term "indirect discrimination" is not found in the DDA, but instead there is a requirement for employers to make "reasonable adjustments" to remove unreasonable physical, organisational or communication barriers which a disabled person may encounter.

The Act does not specify what is reasonable and what is not, but the following examples highlight what adjustments could be considered:

- reallocating duties;
- altering hours of work;
- providing a reader or interpreter;
- giving time off for therapy or rehabilitation;
- modifying instructions and reference manuals;
- assigning a disabled worker to a different place of work, e.g. the ground floor;
- making adaptations to the written test used in an interview;
- allowing job applications to be submitted on tape;
- providing a blind or partially sighted person with a reader or adapted computer with large character, Braille display or speech output;
- reallocating some minor duties to another colleague.

The Act says that an employer should pay regard to:

- the extent to which making the adjustment would assist the disabled person;
- the practicability of taking the step;
- the financial and other cost in making the adjustment and the extent to which taking it would disrupt any of the organisation's activities;
- the extent of the employer's resources;
- the availability of financial or other assistance for making the adjustment;
- the nature of the employer's activities and the size of the undertaking.

This means that in some circumstances, an adjustment may not be 'reasonable' for you to make and you may be justified in refusing the adjustment. However, do make sure you have explored all possible options before you refuse.

Victimisation and harassment

Victimisation or harassment of another employee is illegal, on any of the grounds covered by legislation, such as sex, race, disability, sexual orientation or religion.

Victimisation would occur if you treated someone less favourably (for example, by denying them promotion) because they made a complaint of discrimination under one of the discrimination laws.

Harassment is where one individual engages in unwanted conduct that violates the dignity of another person, or creates an intimidating, hostile, degrading, humiliating or offensive environment for that person, on one of the grounds covered by legislation.

Here are some examples of what might constitute harassment:

- An employee making remarks about 'September 11th' and relating this to all Muslims. This is likely to be offensive to Muslim employees.
- The display of calendars and posters displaying nude or semi-nude women could be deemed to be harassment of female staff.
- Making derogatory remarks to colleagues about an employee with a learning disability.

Equal pay

Men and women have the right to an equal wage when the work they do is:

- the same or like work;
- or of equal value;
- or rated as equivalent.

For example, if you have a male and a female employee doing the same job, or a job of equal value, and if one is earning more than the other, you must be able to justify the pay difference if challenged. If you cannot justify it objectively, it could be deemed to be discriminatory on the grounds of gender.

It is normally (but not exclusively) women who make equal pay claims against men.

For more information about equal pay, see chapter 6.

Positive duty to promote equality

There are two items of equality legislation that require certain employers to do more than simply not discriminate, but to positively promote equality. These items of legislation are: the Race Relations (Amendment) Act 2000; and the Disability Discrimination Act 2005.

> It is normally (but not exclusively) women who make equal pay claims against men.

The **Race Relations (Amendment) Act (RRA(A)A)** requires public authorities to:
- eliminate unlawful race discrimination
- promote equality of opportunity
- promote good race relations.

Public authorities are required to develop and publish race equality schemes, outlining how they will achieve the above requirements. Whilst the RR(A)A does not apply directly to voluntary organisations, public sector funding bodies are required to ensure that those with whom the have a contractual relationship adhere to the main requirements of the legislation. It therefore makes sense to put in place positive steps to promote racial equality in your organisation.

The **Disability Discrimination Act 2005** mirrors the requirements of the Race Relations (Amendment) Act 2000. The new duty to positively promote disability equality comes into effect from December 2006. Like the RR(A)A, it applies to public authorities. However, the definition of a public authority is wider as it covers public bodies including those that provide 'functions of a public nature.' This is likely to include many voluntary organisations which undertake service provision on a contract basis for public authorities.

For further information on the requirements of the Race Relations (Amendment) Act 2000, go to the Commission for Racial Equality website at www.cre.gov.uk.

For further information on the requirements of the Disability Discrimination Act 2005, go to the Disability Rights Commission website at www.drc-gb.org.

Forthcoming legislation
Age discrimination legislation is anticipated in October 2006 and will implement the age provisions of the EC Employment Directive.

The Government's main proposals are currently that legislation should:
- State a default retirement age of 65, but give employees a right to request to work beyond 65. The right to request would follow the model of the right to request flexible working (see chapter 8) – in other words, the employer must give a reason for any refusal.
- Allow employers to set a retirement age of under 65 if it can be objectively justified.

The Government proposes to monitor the retirement age to see if it should be changed five years after the legislation comes into force.

The Government's proposals can be seen at:
www.dti.gov.uk/er/equality/age.

The Government has also issued a *Code of Practice on Age Diversity in Employment*, which contains a set of good practice standards to encourage employers not to discriminate on the grounds of age. The Code can be accessed at:
www.agepositive.gov.uk/complogos/AgeDiversityAtWork.pdf.

Statutory bodies for equality

There are currently the following statutory bodies, which promote the relevant discrimination legislation, issue good practice, campaign and support test cases in Employment Tribunals:
- The Equal Opportunities Commission
- The Commission for Racial Equality
- The Disability Rights Commission

See the end of this chapter for contact details for the above Commissions.

There are currently no commissions for sexual orientation or religion/belief and none is planned for age diversity. The intention is that in the future, there will be a single body know as the Commission for Equality and Human Rights. This body will take on responsibility for race, sex, disability, religious, sexual orientation and age discrimination issues and will also fulfil the role of a Human Rights Commission.

Exceptions to discrimination legislation

There are a small number of exceptions to discrimination legislation. These are outlined below.

Genuine occupational qualification/genuine occupational requirement

Discrimination may be lawful in limited circumstances, if being of a particular group is a necessary (and not just desirable) genuine occupational qualification or requirement for a job.

Here are some examples to illustrate this:
- A welfare rights adviser to African-Caribbean people might be sought from the African-Caribbean community, on the grounds that someone from the same ethnic group is most able to provide the necessary services.
- A female care assistant at a women's refuge may be an exception for reasons of decency or privacy.
- A faith-based care home may be able to show that being of a particular faith is a genuine requirement of its carers because they are required to carry out their duties in a

manner that fulfils both the physical and spiritual needs of its patients. However, they may not be able to justify a similar requirement for their maintenance or reception staff whose jobs do not require them to provide spiritual leadership or support to service users.

If you are in doubt about whether it is appropriate to apply a genuine occupational qualification/requirement in a particular circumstance, you are advised to seek advice.

Positive action
It is possible to take certain steps to redress the effects of previous inequality of opportunity. This is called positive action and it is taken to encourage people from particular groups to take advantage of opportunities for work and training. This can be done when under-representation of particular groups has been identified in the previous year.
Examples of positive action are:
- Stating in recruitment advertisements that you particularly encourage disabled people or people from a certain gender, ethnic origin, sexual orientation or religion/belief to apply.
- Providing additional training for these groups.

You should note that there is a difference between 'positive action' and 'positive discrimination'. Positive discrimination could be, for example, selecting someone for employment specifically because they are black, in order to address an imbalance in your organisation. Positive discrimination is unlawful in the UK. Whilst positive action enables you to encourage people from certain groups to apply, you should make clear that selection will be on merit without reference to background.

You should note that there is a difference between 'positive action' and 'positive discrimination'.

Disability charities
Disability charities are allowed to favour, in recruitment, those individuals who have a disability applicable to that charity. So, for example, a learning disability charity may specifically decide to recruit people with a learning disability.

Codes of practice
Codes of practice exist on race, sex and disability discrimination. Whilst they are not part of the legislation, they may be taken into account by an Employment Tribunal as evidence that an employer was or was not following good procedure. The Codes have lots of useful information on how to promote equality and diversity and how to avoid discrimination.

The Codes can be downloaded from the internet as follows:
- *Race Relations Code of Practice*
  www.cre.gov.uk/gdpract/employ_cop.html
- *Sex Discrimination Code of Practice*
  www.eoc.org.uk/cseng/legislation/law_code_of_-
  practice_sex_discrimination.asp
- *Disability Code of Practice for Employment*
  www.drc-gb.org/thelaw/

In addition, Acas has two advisory guides, one on Sexual Orientation and the Workplace and another on Religion or Belief and the Workplace. These contain good practice guidelines and information to help you comply with the law. You can find the guides at www.acas.org.uk/publications/pdf/sexual.pdf and at www.acas.org.uk/publications/pdf/religion.pdf.

You can also find more information about the Employment Equality (Sexual Orientation) Regulations 2003 and the Employment Equality (Religion or Belief) Regulations 2003 at www.dti.gov.uk/er/equality/eeregs.htm.

NCVO has also produced a plain English guide to the regulations. You can download a guide from www.ncvo-vol.org.uk/making it simple.

Institutional discrimination

Sometimes, discrimination can take place in an organisation, not because individuals discriminate, but because different needs are not taken into account. Policies and practices that have previously gone unchallenged may lead to unthinking ways of doing things that put some groups at a disadvantage. When there is a whole framework of practices in an organisation that may marginalise some people, institutional discrimination may be particularly strong.

Here are some examples of practices that may lead to institutional discrimination:
- Recruitment practices which favour younger people, when there is no objective justification for this.
- Long salary scales, which may discriminate against women because they tend to have shorter service due to career breaks.
- Buildings and work arrangements that take into account the needs of able-bodied people, but not disabled people.

By developing an equality and diversity policy and action plan (outlined later in this chapter), you can avoid or work to eliminate institutional discrimination.

By developing an equality and diversity policy and action plan you can avoid or work to eliminate institutional discrimination.

Diversity and equal opportunities

Equal opportunities is concerned with keeping within the law and ensuring that all personnel decisions concerning pay, recruitment and promotion, are based only on an individual's ability to do their job well.

Managing diversity effectively follows on from, and expands on, equal opportunities.

Managing diversity effectively follows on from, and expands on, equal opportunities. It incorporates the principle that all workers should receive equal rights but, rather than ignoring the differences between people in terms of their gender and race, this diversity is recognised and respected. By valuing the varying qualities that different workers bring to their job and organisation, you can create an environment where everyone feels valued for their individual talents, and where skills and competencies are fully utilised. This will, in turn, help your organisation to better achieve its objectives.

When we look at diversity, we are looking at a wider range of differences than those protected by legislation. People's differences include: race; culture; national origin; region; gender; sexual orientation; age; marital status; politics; religion; ethnicity; disability; socio-economic differences; family structure; health; values; education; and so on.

Developing a diversity and equality policy

The importance of a policy

Your starting point in promoting diversity and equality in your organisation is to develop a policy, with an action plan to back it up.

It is important to have a policy and action plan because:

- It will help to clarify the main issues and priorities for your organisation.
- It is a basis for making required changes.
- It sends a clear statement to staff about what is and is not acceptable, and on how they can be expected to be treated.
- It may be required by your funders.
- It helps you comply with the law.

Make sure you consult with your staff when developing your policy and action plan – your staff may have useful insights and they are also more likely to help with implementing change if they have been involved.

Your policy

You could follow the format below for your policy.

Introduction

Make a statement of your organisation's commitment to eliminate discrimination and promote diversity and equality, and its desire to reflect the make-up of the community it serves.

Scope

You could list the main areas where you will ensure that discrimination does not occur. Include at least the areas that are currently or shortly to be covered by legislation, namely sex (including marital status and gender reassignment), race (including ethnic origin, colour, nationality and national origin), disability, age, part-time status, sexual orientation and religion. Consider also including other factors which may lead to unfair discrimination, such as family background, values and educational background.

Expectations

You could list here the expectations of behaviour that you have of all staff.

You could explain, for example, that you expect all staff members to treat each other with respect, regardless of personal differences.

You should also explain what staff can expect from your organisation. This might include:

- A work environment where individuals are judged on the work they do, not on who they are.
- A work environment where harassment and bullying are not tolerated.
- That if staff feel they are being treated unfairly or being harassed, they may use the grievance procedure, and that their complaint will be dealt with swiftly and with due regard to confidentiality.
  Note that some organisations have a specific policy on harassment, but for smaller organisations, it is normally sufficient for employees to be able to raise their concerns via the grievance procedure.

Commitments

You could list your commitments, which might include:

- Developing an annual action plan.
- Communicating the policy and action plan to all employees and volunteers.
- Providing training on equality awareness.
- Regular review of employment policies and procedures, to eliminate any discrimination or unnecessary barriers.
- Monitoring (e.g. the workforce, applicants for employment, volunteers and service users) and taking action as a result of monitoring.
- Procedures for reviewing your equality and diversity policy.

Here is an example equality policy, from the Acas handbook: *Tackling Discrimination and Promoting Equality – Good Practice Guide for Employers.*

(Organisation name) is committed to eliminating discrimination and encouraging diversity amongst our workforce. Our aim is that our workforce will be truly representative of all sections of society and each employee feels respected and able to give of their best.

To that end the purpose of this policy is to provide equality and fairness for all in our employment and not to discriminate on grounds of gender, marital status, race, ethnic origin, colour, nationality, national origin, disability, sexuality, religion or age. We oppose all forms of unlawful and unfair discrimination.

All employees, whether part-time, full-time or temporary, will be treated fairly and with respect. Selection for employment, promotion, training or any other benefit will be on the basis of aptitude and ability. All employees will be helped and encouraged to develop their full potential and the talents and resources of the workforce will be fully utilised to maximise the efficiency of the organisation.

Our commitment:
- To create an environment in which individual differences and the contributions of all our staff are recognised and valued.
- Every employee is entitled to a working environment that promotes dignity and respect to all. No form of intimidation, bullying or harassment will be tolerated.
- Training, development and progression opportunities are available to all staff.
- Equality in the workplace is good management practice and makes sound business sense.
- We will review all our employment practices and procedures to ensure fairness.
- Breaches of our equality policy will be regarded as misconduct and could lead to disciplinary proceedings.
- This policy is fully supported by senior management and has been agreed with trade unions and/or employee representatives. (Insert details if appropriate).
- The policy will be monitored and reviewed annually.
- We will implement the intentions in this policy via an annual action plan.

Your action plan

Your action plan should state each objective, how it will be achieved, by whom and by when.

Equality action plan (excerpt)

target	action	who?	by when?
To encourage people from the local Bengali community to work and volunteer for us	Hold open day	Director to organise	January 2006
	Introduce an equality statement in all our advertisements	agree with trustees; Administrator to ensure the statement is used	By August 2006
	Advertise in places accessed by the whole community e.g. doctor's surgeries	Staff team to agree best places to advertise; administrator to follow up	From now, with ongoing review of effectiveness
Update our recruitment documentation	Revise letters to applicants – offer to make adjustments	Joe to take on as a project	Review with Director end November 05 and end Jan 06 Complete by end Feb 06
	Review our person specifications to ensure that there are no unjustifiable criteria		
	Remove date of birth from application form and enlarge font size		
Etc			

Whilst the above actions are focused on employment matters, you could also build into your plan anything you want to achieve with regard to delivering your services or with regard to attracting and retaining volunteers. For example, you might want to take specific actions to reach a certain part of the local community which does not currently access your services.

Practical steps to being an organisation that promotes diversity

Below are some practical steps that you could consider taking, to become an employer that promotes diversity. In addition to the steps below, you will find that throughout this guide, there are hints and tips on good diversity practice.

Be flexible

For job applicants:
- Offer to produce documentation in alternative formats e.g. large print, online, Braille.
- Offer different ways of contacting you for an application pack e.g. email and fax as well as phone.
- Offer to receive application forms in different media, such as on tape (provided you have the capacity to listen).
- State in your documentation that you are committed to employing disabled people and ask all candidates if there are any adjustments they may require to the selection process.
- Offer flexible times to attend interviews, so that, for example, candidates can avoid times of religious observance or can accommodate child care responsibilities.
- State that if a candidate is offered the job, you will be happy to discuss at that stage, adjustments required, and that this will not form a part of the selection process.
- Make adjustments that are requested.

For existing employees and new recruits:
- Offer flexible working (e.g. flexible start/finish times, compressed week, working from home, job-share or term-time only working), as appropriate to the job.
- Tell staff about your parental leave policies and flexible working policies, so that they know what is available to them.
- Allow flexibility where possible in the way employees approach tasks: concentrate on results being achieved, on time and to standard; be less concerned about where, how and when the work was undertaken. You may need to train and support managers in this.
- If possible, provide to all staff the right to take annual leave on the days of their major religious festivals.

Check your image
- Undertake a review of the images you use in your publications and website. Make changes if needed.
- Consult with your existing staff, volunteers and service-users about the image they consider that your organisation portrays.
- Make sure that the images you portray and the wording you use convey your positive stance to people from a variety of backgrounds, e.g. from black and minority ethnic groups, carers, those with different religions, different ages etc.

Allow flexibility where possible in the way employees approach tasks

- Consider becoming a 'two ticks' positive about disabled people symbol user. For further information, contact your local JobCentre Plus, or see www.jobcentreplus.gov.uk/ cms.asp?Page=/Home/Employers/DisabilityServiceshelpfor Employers/DisabilitySymbol.

Be welcoming
- Train staff (such as receptionists) who 'meet and greet' applicants for employment to treat everyone appropriately and with respect.
- Provide a work environment that is welcoming and accommodates individual lifestyles and needs (e.g. providing a room which is available during part of the day for quiet or prayer, providing a special chair for a back pain sufferer).

> Provide a work environment that is welcoming and accommodates individual lifestyles and needs

Show commitment
- Adopt and implement fair employment practices – use this Good Guide as a start!
- Use an equal opportunities or diversity statement in your advertisements. If you have one already, check to see if it needs to be updated.
- Include in application packs your organisation's equal opportunities or diversity policy. Give brief details of what you have done to implement the policy as it will give the message that it is not just a piece of paper.

Improve your skills in assessing and appraising others
- Make sure you and other managers are trained in interviewing skills – an unskilled interviewer may not be able to draw out the information needed to make a selection decision – and may therefore fall back on his/her assumptions.
- Focus your selection criteria more on the skills that are required and less on where the skills need to have been acquired; it is not only university graduates who are able to think analytically, for example.
- Consider and question stereotypes and 'baggage'. Such 'baggage' might include unconscious perceptions of the 'right' sort of person in a job – a female secretary, for example.
- In appraisals, ensure you focus on the job requirements, not on individual and irrelevant personal characteristics.
- Check that your training and development practices are sufficiently flexible. Are there alternatives to residential courses, for example?

Be willing to experiment and learn

- Advertise your jobs in a variety of media – experiment to see what works.
- Have a look at the job advertisements placed by other organisations – obtain ideas for good practice.
- Listen to the views of others (volunteers, staff, trustees, service-users) and learn from these views – don't always stick to 'this is how we do things around here'.

Influence others

- Even in the smallest charity, you'll need to influence others about what you want to do – you can't recruit and retain a diverse workforce on your own!
- Think about who you need to influence and why, such as managers, staff, volunteers, the board.
- Consider what other people's viewpoints might be – and how you will deal with objections or concerns.
- Use statistics and data to persuade people (use the statistics as the beginning of this chapter, together with monitoring information from your organisation – see below).
- Have diversity as a standing item at meetings.
- Establish a network e.g. an equality and diversity working group with other similar voluntary organisations.

Monitoring

If you want to improve the diversity of your workforce, you'll need to monitor both job applicants and existing employees.

The Commission for Racial Equality has commented that:

'To have an equality policy without monitoring is like aiming for good financial management without keeping financial records'. (from *Ethnic Monitoring – a guide for public authorities*, CRE, downloadable at www.cre.gov.uk/pdfs/duty_ethmon.pdf.)

Monitoring can:

- highlight possible inequalities
- enable an investigation of possible causes
- allow you to remove unfairness or disadvantage.

Monitoring is not a legal requirement in the voluntary sector, but it is good practice and your funders may also expect you to do it.

Workforce monitoring

If yours is a very small organisation, formal monitoring of your workforce won't be necessary. You are likely to know the age, gender, ethnic group and any disability of your staff. However, if your organisation is larger, it can be useful to monitor the percentages of people from different groups. This can help you to assess, for example, whether disabled people or people from a particular minority ethnic group are under-represented in your organisation or not.

You could monitor your workforce as follows:

In employment
- numbers of staff from different ethnic groups
- numbers of disabled staff
- numbers of male and female staff
- age ranges of staff
- sexual orientation and religion/belief (but note that this information is particularly sensitive and staff may not wish to divulge it).

You could analyse this information by salary level and grade.

Recruitment monitoring

It is good practice to monitor applicants for employment, because this will tell you whether you are attracting applicants from all sections of your local community. It will also tell you how applicants from different groups fare during the selection process.

Further information on recruitment monitoring is given in chapter 2.

Starting to monitor

Start monitoring at a level you can cope with – and don't collect more information than you will use. You might decide, for example, to focus on ethnic origin in one year, and disability, gender, age, sexual orientation or religion in other years.

If your organisation is small, you may want to analyse the data less frequently, e.g. every few months, as the data will be more meaningful. It may also be several years before clear patterns emerge.

> Start monitoring at a level you can cope with – and don't collect more information than you will use.

Qualitative monitoring

As well as the statistical monitoring outlined above, you could also consider:
- Surveying staff to gain their views about equality in the organisation (see chapter 12 for an example staff survey).
- Surveying successful and unsuccessful applicants to gain their impressions of how they were treated during the recruitment and selection process.

Benchmarking your monitoring data

In order to assess whether your workforce is representative of the local community, you will need to compare ('benchmark') your data with external data. The main source of information is the 2001 census, which you can download from www.statistics.gov.uk/census.

In addition, you can benchmark your data against internal data from previous years, or from department to department (if you are a larger organisation).

What to do with the results

Differences between groups are not, in themselves, evidence of discrimination. However, you will need to study the results further, find out why there are differences, and tackle any barriers you find.

The Commission for Racial Equality identifies three categories of actions:

- **Removing unfair barriers** – for example, considering whether the qualifications you are asking for are strictly necessary and whether they are barring certain groups in the community from applying for your jobs.
- **Examining decision making** – considering, for example, whether you and your managers are taking fair decisions, or whether there may be a tendency to 'recruit like me'; or 'recruit like the previous post holder.'
- **Outreach and positive action** – considering what you could do to encourage people to work for you. Experiment with advertising in different areas or with putting positive statements on your recruitment advertising. See chapter 3 for further information.

Think carefully about implementing a monitoring system that is easy to maintain and make sure you keep the momentum up with monitoring.

Keep monitoring

Think carefully about implementing a monitoring system that is easy to maintain and make sure you keep the momentum up with monitoring. The Commission for Racial Equality (in its publication *Ethnic Monitoring – A guide for public authorities* comments that: 'Monitoring is part of an ongoing process of analysis, asking questions, investigation and change.'

Case study – monitoring

Below is an example of how one organisation has monitored lesbian, gay, bisexual and transsexual people in its organisation.

Nacro, the crime reduction charity describes its vision as enabling "a safer society where everyone belongs, human rights are respected, and preventing crime means tackling social exclusion and re-integrating those who offend". Nacro has been established since 1966 and has about 1400 staff. It is very proud of being listed number 24 out of 100 employers in Stonewall's Corporate Equality Index 2005.

The organisation has a self-organised lesbian, gay, bisexual and transgender (LGBT) group called Pride in Nacro which is funded by Nacro. Nacro canvasses staff attitudes in an annual equality and diversity audit. Staff asked for the organisation to start monitoring with respect to sexual orientation – this was one of the outcomes of the audit. In 2004 Nacro found that 8.1 per cent of its staff defined themselves as lesbian, gay or bisexual: an increase from 6 per cent the year before. The audit does not tell Nacro if the number of LGBT staff has gone up or if the increase in numbers is more about the confidence of their employees in answering that particular question.

Pride in Nacro, however, does report that the last recruitment drive in Manchester resulted in half of those appointed identifying as LGBT and that those people applied to work for Nacro because they felt comfortable to apply for a post with a company which is obviously an equal opportunities employer and sympathetic to LGBT issues. Nacro also organised a very successful conference on LGBT issues in November 2004 that was attended by 90 staff. The conference generated a lot of interest and received excellent feedback.

The monitoring information is collected anonymously and confidentially by the group's Race Equality Adviser whose position is located within the Chief Executive's Office.

Checklist

- ✓ Make sure you are aware of discrimination legislation and what you need to do to comply.
- ✓ Make reasonable adjustments so that disabled people can work in your organisation.
- ✓ Draft a diversity and equality policy.
- ✓ Develop a diversity and equality action plan. Review progress regularly.
- ✓ Take practical steps to promote diversity – avoid institutional discrimination.
- ✓ Monitor applicants for employment and (unless your organisation is very small) your workforce.
- ✓ Keep checking how you are doing – implementing diversity is an ongoing process and not 'done' once!
- ✓ Investigate fully and promptly any allegations of discrimination, harassment or victimisation.

Where to find out more

1.Acas

The following publications can be downloaded from the Acas website:

An advisory booklet on tackling discrimination and promoting equality www.acas.org.uk/publications/B16.html.

An advisory guide on sexual orientation and the workplace www.acas.org.uk/publications/pdf/sexual.pdf

An advisory guide on religion or belief and the workplace www.acas.org.uk/publications/pdf/religion.pdf.

An advisory leaflet on bullying and harassment at work www.acas.org.uk/publications/al04.html

You can also order the above publications from:
Acas Publications
PO Box 235
Hayes
Middlesex
UB3 1DQ

Tel: 08702 42 90 90
Fax: 020 8867 3225
Email: acas@eclogistics.co.uk

For specific questions, you can contact the Acas helpline tel: 08457 47 47 47 or textphone: 08456 06 16 00.

In addition, the Race and Equality Advisory Service (REAS) is a part of Acas; the service provides strategy and advice so that employers can develop and implement policies and practices for racial equality amongst their workforce. Contact REAS via the Acas helpline above.

2. The Department of Trade and Industry (DTI)

The DTI employment website, www.dti.gov.uk/er has the following guidance:

General equality information at: www.dti.gov.uk/er/equality/index.htm

Proposals on age discrimination legislation at: www.dti.gov.uk/er/equality/age.htm

3. askNCVO

www.askncvo.org.uk offers a wealth of free, practical, up-to-date advice on all aspects of running a charity or voluntary organisation. Hundreds of pages cover trusteeship, financial management, human resources and more.

It may also be worth looking at www.voluntaryskills.org.uk, as this website will link to the new Workforce Development Hub for the voluntary sector.

NCVO has published a number of diversity related publications:

Are You Looking at Me? A practical guide to recruiting a diverse workforce

Making it Happen! A guide for voluntary and community organisations

Making Equality Simple: A plain English guide to the 2003 Employment Equality Regulations (on religion, belief and sexual orientation) for voluntary and community organisations

Find out more at www.ncvo-vol.org.uk/publications. To order call 0845 458 9910, or email: publications@ncvo-vol.org.uk.

4. Business Link

Business Link has a section on equality on its website. Go to www.businesslink.gov.uk and enter 'equality' into the search field.

5. Equality direct

This is an England-wide telephone advice service for business, offering authoritative, confidential and down-to-earth advice about equality issues.

Tel: 0845 600 3444.

6. Commission for Racial Equality (CRE)

The CRE provides extensive advice and guidance on employing black and minority ethnic staff. Its website includes the downloadable Race relations Code of Practice for the elimination of racial discrimination and the promotion of equality of opportunity in employment.

> The Commission for Racial Equality
> St Dunstan's House
> 201-211 Borough High Street
> London SE1 1G2
> Tel: 020 7939 0000
> Fax: 020 7939 0001
> www.cre.gov.uk

7. Equal Opportunities Commission (EOC)

The EOC provides advice and information on all aspects of promoting gender equality, including equal pay. You can download the Code of Practice for the Elimination of Sex Discrimination from the EOC website.

> Equal Opportunities Commission
> Arndale House
> Arndale Centre
> Manchester
> M4 3EQ
>
> Tel: 0845 601 5901
> Fax: 0161 838 1733
> www.eoc.org.uk

8. Disability Rights Commission (DRC)

The DRC has a large amount of information, including a 'top tips' guide on employing disabled people for small businesses. The guide can be downloaded from www.drc-gb.org/uploaded_files/documents/4008_310_TOP%20TIPS.pdf or you can order a copy from the DRC.

> The DRC can be contacted as follows:
> DRC Helpline
> Freepost MID 02164
> Stratford-upon-Avon
> CV37 9HY

Telephone helpline: 08457 622 633
Fax: 08457 778 878
Textphone: 08457 622 644

www.drc-gb.org

9. Jobcentre Plus

Employment Service's Disability Employment Advisers and Disability Service Teams are based in Jobcentres and can offer advice and practical assistance with employing disabled people.

You can view the services of Jobcentre Plus on www.jobcentreplus.gov.uk. Alternatively, you can find your nearest Jobcentre Plus in your local telephone directory.

10. Age Positive

The Age Positive Team is a team working in the Department for Work and Pensions, responsible for strategy and policies to support people making decisions about working and retirement. The Age Positive campaign promotes the benefits of employing a mixed-age workforce that includes older and younger people.

Age Positive Team
Department for Work and Pensions
Room W8d
Moorfoot
Sheffield S1 4PQ

Email: agepositive@dwp.gsi.gov.uk
www.agepositive.gov.uk
You can download the *Code of Practice on Age Diversity in Employment* from the Age Positive website.

3 Recruitment

What this chapter is about

This chapter gives you information about each step in the recruitment process. It covers:
- Defining what you need
- The job description
- The person specification
- Finding applicants for your job
- The application process
- Shortlisting
- Arranging and preparing for interviews
- The interview
- Other selection methods
- Deciding who to appoint
- References
- Asylum and Immigration Act checks
- Criminal Records Bureau checks ('Disclosures')
- Monitoring recruitment
- Genuine occupational qualifications (this is when you need to recruit someone of one gender or the other, or from a particular ethnic group)

Please note that NCVO also has a specific publication on recruitment, called Are you looking at me? *It is available for order from the NCVO website www.ncvo-vol.org.uk/publications, or by calling 0845 458 9910, or by sending an email to publications@ncvo-vol.org.uk.*

Defining what you need

Before spending time and money on recruiting someone, take some time to consider what you actually need. For example:
- Is your need long-term or short-term?
- Is it full-time or part-time?
- Is the need a permanent or temporary one?
- What hours are required and how constant is the work?
- Do you need a permanent employee, an employee for a fixed

term, someone on a zero hours contract, or perhaps a freelance consultant to complete a specific project?

- How will this role interact with the current responsibilities of your trustees and volunteers?
- Who will manage the new employee?

The job description

Once you have decided broadly what you need, you can draft a job description. The job description sets out the position to be filled and the responsibilities involved.

There is no one 'right' way to draft a job description, but try and make it clear using straightforward language. Generally, you should need to specify no more than around eight key responsibilities. It is good practice to include a statement in the job description outlining the employee's equality and diversity responsibilities.

Below is an example job description.

Job Description

> **Job Title:** Personal Assistant
> **Responsible to:** Director
> **Responsible for:** Office Administrator
> **Purpose of role**
> To be responsible for providing administrative support to the Director and for ensuring the smooth running of the office.
>
> **Key Responsibilities**
> 1. To manage the Director's diary, including booking meetings and making travel arrangements.
> 2. To arrange Trustee meetings and take minutes.
> 3. To manage the information services (reference library, filing system, database and address lists).
> 4. To ensure input to (organisation's) database is consistent and accurate.
> 5. To manage the stationery supplies, ensuring that there is always adequate stationery and that costs are controlled.
> 6. To manage the photocopier contract.
> 7. To provide general administrative support to the Director.
> 8. To undertake all duties in a way that values others, does not discriminate and promotes equality.
> 9. To undertake any other duties as may be required from time to time.
>
> **Date drafted/updated: July 2005**

There is no one 'right' way to draft a job description, but try and make it clear using straightforward language.

The person specification

The person specification sets out the knowledge, skills and experience that are required for the job. This is an important document, because you will use it to decide who to shortlist for interview and who to appoint.

Make sure that all the criteria you use in the person specification are justified and necessary for the job, to avoid putting barriers in the way of applicants who may actually be suitable.

Consider the following:

- Specify clearly which criteria are essential (the ones that applicants must have) and which criteria are desirable (these criteria could be acquired after appointment).
- Avoid stating the number of years experience in a job that may be required, because people learn at different rates. It may also constitute discrimination on the grounds of age, when legislation is passed in 2006. Instead, define the specific experience required.
- State that the required experience may have been gained from paid or voluntary work.
- Only ask for qualifications if they are necessary for the job. For example, 'A level standard or above' could be made more specific by explaining what you actually need. Your need might be, for example, an ability 'to analyse information and produce logical conclusions'.
- If you do need a qualification, make sure you say 'or equivalent overseas qualification.'
- Avoid subjective words such as 'intelligent' or 'energetic'. Instead, say what you mean! For example, 'able to manage and organise several tasks at once'.
- Don't put in any age restrictions, such as 'age 18-30'. Not only is it irrelevant to the ability to do the job, it may potentially constitute discrimination when age discrimination legislation comes into force in late 2006.
- If you want 'good interpersonal skills', define what you mean by this. For example, do you mean 'able to deal with a wide range of people in a courteous and helpful manner' or: 'able to present proposals in a logical manner, argue a case and resolve conflict'?
- Avoid requiring applicants to be able to drive, unless absolutely necessary. You might state instead: 'Must be able to travel around the xx area'. This allows for applicants who are unable to drive, for reason of disability or other reason, to propose how they could do the job without driving a car.
- State whatever flexibility you can in terms of working hours – job share or part-time working, for example.

Avoid subjective words such as 'intelligent' or 'energetic'. Instead, say what you mean!

Below is an example person specification.

Person Specification

Job title	Personal Assistant		
Criteria		**E or D*?**	**S or I**?**
KNOWLEDGE Knowledge of Microsoft Word, Excel, PowerPoint, databases and electronic diary management.		E	S/I
A knowledge of office procedures.		E	I
SKILLS Able to prioritise and carry out administrative tasks independently.		E	I
Shows initiative and takes personal responsibility for completing tasks.		E	I
Able to communicate with others courteously on routine matters.		E	I
Adopts a positive attitude – willing to assist others even when busy.		E	I
Able to write clearly, with correct grammar and punctuation.		E	S/I
Able to work under pressure on occasions, to achieve administrative deadlines.		E	I
Able to type quickly (60wpm) and accurately.		E	S/I
Able to pay attention to detail, ensuring that nothing is forgotten.		E	I
EXPERIENCE Previous experience of administration (in paid or unpaid work), including: drafting correspondence independently; diary management; and dealing with a variety of administrative matters simultaneously.		E	S/I
Experience of taking minutes.		D	S/I
Experience of supervising others.		D	S/I
QUALIFICATIONS No specific qualifications required.			
CIRCUMSTANCES This post is based at our Head Office in xxxx. The post is a full-time job, but we will positively consider applications from part-time workers and job sharers. Flexible working hours are available for this post. There is a very occasional requirement for evening/weekend work in this job.			
*E = essential criteria D = desirable criteria **S = shortlisting criteria I = interview criteria			

Finding applicants for your job

There are a number of ways of finding applicants for your job. The way you choose to advertise will depend on:
- how much you are willing and able to pay
- how fast you want to get a response
- how much time you have to administer the response
- the type of job to which you are recruiting.

Jobcentre Plus

The Jobcentre Plus service is similar to that offered by employment agencies, but is free of charge.

Within two hours of receipt Jobcentre Plus will post your vacancy on its website. Your vacancy will also be shown on the touchscreen computer 'jobpoints' which are available in job centres.

Jobcentre Plus offices may also offer extra services, for example:
- use of interview rooms
- help with sifting applications
- job fairs
- government support for employers.

You can find out more about Jobcentre Plus on its website at www.jobcentreplus.gov.uk. Alternatively, you can find your nearest Jobcentre Plus in your local telephone directory.

Website recruitment

Recruitment via the internet can be relatively quick and lower cost than, for example, a newspaper advertisement.

There are several recruitment websites and the one you choose will depend on which job you are filling.

Here are three websites for the voluntary sector:
www.charitypeople.co.uk
www.jobsincharities.co.uk
www.charityjob.co.uk

There are also general websites that include voluntary sector jobs. One of the largest is www.totaljobs.com.

You can place details of your vacancy on the recruitment website you choose, for a fee. Once you have placed the information, applicants can then contact you in one of the following ways:
- By following a weblink to your organisation's website (if you have one) and from there downloading an application pack

> Recruitment via the internet can be relatively quick and lower cost than, for example, a newspaper advertisement.

and application form.
- By contacting you via your phone number, address or email address to request an applicant pack.
- By applying online by sending a CV to you.

Try and give applicants as many ways of contacting you as possible to meet different needs.

Newspaper and magazine advertisements

Newspapers and magazines may help you target more accurately (you could use a fundraising magazine if you are looking for a fundraiser, for example) but may not be as quick or as cheap as using an internet site.

Here are some things that your newspaper or magazine advertisement should include:
- A brief summary of the job – enough information for applicants to decide whether to apply.
- The skills and experience needed (base these on your person specification and beware of adding subjective words such as 'dynamic' or 'energetic').
- The location (as specific as possible) and the pay.
- How the applicant should apply: by sending a CV or requesting an application form. Include a variety of ways of contacting you, such as telephone, email or via your website.
- The closing date for applications.

The more you include in your advertisement, the more it will cost, but if possible, you could also include the following:
- A statement of commitment to equality and diversity.
- A statement of commitment to flexible working including job share.
- A statement offering the advertisement and other recruitment material in an alternative format if required.
- A statement indicating that experience may have been gained from paid or voluntary work.

For ideas on drafting advertisements, have a look at some local and national papers. Alternatively, you could ask a recruitment advertising agency to draft and typeset your advertisement for you. Their artwork is likely to be better than most voluntary organisations could produce in house. This approach may be no more expensive than placing the advertisement yourself, because recruitment advertising agencies often have discounts with local and national newspapers.

Recruitment agencies

Recruitment agencies have a database of job applicants and will search the database to find suitable applicants for your job. They can also place an advertisement and shortlist on your behalf. This can save you time.

If you are recruiting to particular types of job, such as IT staff, you may wish to approach an agency that specialises in this field. Alternatively, you could approach an agency that deals in the not-for-profit sector. You can find a list of recruitment agencies that specialise in the not-for-profit sector on www.voluntarysectorskills.org.uk.

If you decide to use an agency, make sure you have agreed fees, including any advertising costs, and terms before you appoint them.

Internal advertisements

Make sure you always advertise your vacancy amongst your existing workforce. It can be very demoralising for an existing member of staff seeking promotion to learn about a vacancy only when it is filled.

Some organisations only advertise internally in the first instance, in order to give staff career development opportunities and to alert volunteers to vacancies. If no suitable applicant is found, only then is the post advertised externally.

Other organisations always advertise internally and externally at the same time. This will be particularly important if your current workforce is not very diverse, because an internal advert will just perpetuate the profile of your existing workforce. Some funders also require all new posts to be advertised externally.

Other sources of applicants

You could try a number of free ways of advertising, such as local colleges and schools or a notice outside your own premises.

Targeting specific sections of the community

You may find that your workforce is not representative of specific sections of the community. For example, you may find that you have few BME (black and minority ethnic) staff at senior levels, or that you are not attracting older workers.

You can use advertising to target specific sections of the community. You could place your advertisement with Jobcentre Plus and discuss recruiting disabled people with the Jobcentre Plus Disability Employment Adviser. You could try the publications produced by the Ethnic Media Group, in order to attract more BME (black and minority ethnic) applicants at www.ethnicmedia.co.uk or tel: 020 7650 2000. You could simply advertise in the local or national media (which after all will be

You can use advertising to target specific sections of the community.

read by people with diverse backgrounds) but also include a welcoming statement in your advertisement, that you wish to attract people from all sections of the community, or that you are particularly keen for certain groups to apply.

Experiment with different approaches and monitor the result.

Case study

The Westwich Association is looking to recruit an Outreach Worker. Here is the advertisement:

Community Outreach Worker

15 hours per week (flexible working hours possible)
£ 18,000 pro-rata.
One year contract (may be extended subject to funding)
The Westwich Association exists to provide youth services in the local community. We are looking for an Outreach Worker to help us reach the Asian community.
You should have experience of working (on a paid or voluntary basis) in the Asian community. Computer skills, ability to travel round the local area, ability to speak Bengali and to work independently are essential.
For an application pack, telephone 0103 666 345, write to Westwich Association, 12 Holly Hill, Westwich, WA2 6EN, or email vacancies@westwich.org.uk. If you would like to receive the application pack in an alternative format, please let us know.
Closing date: 15 July 2005
Interviews date: 22 August 2005
We strive to be an equal opportunities employer.

The application process

You will need to make clear to applicants how you want them to apply.

You may find that for some types of job, applicants are more likely to apply if they can just send in their CV, rather than having to complete an application form. CVs may also be less work for you initially, because you do not need to send out an application form to prospective applicants. However, the shortlisting process may take you longer, as it can be more difficult to shortlist when applications do not come in a common format.

Application forms are generally considered better from an equal opportunities/diversity point of view, because information on each applicant is presented in a common format and there is therefore less possibility of bias creeping in.

If you want to use an application form, you can draft your own. You could look at examples of application forms from other employers to get ideas. Alternatively, you could use the model form available from the Acas website at www.acas.org.uk/publications/pdf/A%20Employing%20people/A4_application_form.pdf.

You could consider having an application form where the front page containing individuals' names, addresses and other personal details is removed from the rest of the application form before shortlisting, to avoid bias.

Application pack

It is helpful to produce an application pack as well as an application form because it gives applicants additional information and is also your opportunity to sell your organisation. You could send or email your pack to applicants with an application form or make it available on your website if you have one.

Here are some of the things you should consider including in the pack:

> **A covering letter** This should welcome the application and give details of: the closing date for applications; the date for interviews, and a named person whom applicants can call to discuss the job. You could also include a statement of your organisation's willingness to cater for specific requirements, for example on grounds of religion or belief, disability or caring responsibilities. The letter could ask applicants what adjustments they may need to the selection process, such as larger print or an application on tape. You could also include a statement of your organisation's positive attitude towards ex-offenders and that criminal records will only be taken into account if relevant to the job.
> In order to minimise administration, some voluntary organisations include a statement in the covering letter to say that if the applicant has not heard from the organisation by a certain date, the applicant should assume that he or she has not been shortlisted for interview.

Application forms are generally considered better from an equal opportunities/diversity point of view

49

Application form and any guidance about completing the form.

Job description See the earlier section in this chapter.

Person specification See the earlier section in this chapter.

Your equality and diversity policy See chapter 2 for further information.

A summary of the terms and conditions of employment for the job You could produce a one-page document, which would give details of the salary and any salary scale, annual leave, sick pay, pension and any flexible working arrangements. A word of caution here, though – when someone is appointed, they may be able to rely on information given in this summary or elsewhere in the application pack as a contractual term. You therefore need to make sure that any information terms and conditions are correct.

Equal opportunities monitoring form This enables you to monitor the diversity of applicants. The information on this form should not be used in the shortlisting process. The form should make clear why it is important for applicants to complete it. The section on monitoring later in this chapter provides an example form.

Some information about your organisation A brief and positive overview of what your organisation does and about the part the job plays in the organisation can be helpful in encouraging applicants.

Shortlisting

Shortlisting is the process of deciding who you will invite for interview.

After the closing date for applications and before shortlisting, the recruitment monitoring forms should be removed. They should be removed if possible by someone who is not involved in the shortlisting and selection process.

Once removed, the monitoring forms should be set aside until the end of the recruitment process. The section on monitoring recruitment, later in this chapter, explains what to do with the forms.

You can now consider which applicants you wish to invite to interview. You should look to shortlist a manageable number of applicants. About seven or eight applicants is probably about right.

You should compare the knowledge, skills and experience of each applicant against the essential criteria outlined in your person specification. It can be helpful to list the criteria on a sheet of paper, then mark the candidates against these criteria, for example in terms of 'meets criterion', 'partly meets criterion' and 'does not meet criterion.' You could use a shortlisting form for this process. For an example form, see the NCVO recruitment publication *Are you looking at me?* (details at the end of this chapter).

If you still have a large number of applicants, you can then further reduce the number you will shortlist by assessing them against the desirable criteria in the person specification.

You could take a policy decision in your organisation that disabled applicants who meet the essential criteria for the post will be automatically interviewed, even if they do not meet the desirable criteria. This is one of the commitments that 'two ticks' (positive about disabled people) symbol users make. You can make this commitment whether or not you are a 'two ticks' symbol user (if you want to become a 'two ticks' symbol user, contact your local Jobcentre Plus, or see www.jobcentreplus.gov.uk/cms.asp?Page=/Home/Employers/Dis abilityServiceshelpforEmployers/DisabilitySymbol).

Don't unfairly discriminate against applicants, for example on the grounds of sex, race or disability, sexual orientation, religion or belief – see chapter 2 for further information.

Arranging and preparing for interviews

Invite shortlisted applicants to interview by letter or by telephone.

You should tell them:
- When, where and how long the interview will be.
- How to get there – provide a map if necessary – and whether you will pay travel expenses.
- What, if any, documents they should bring.
- Who they should ask for on arrival.
- The names and job titles of the people conducting the interview.
- Details of any test or presentation they may be required to do.
- Your willingness to cater for specific requirements, for

example due to disability or religious belief. You should ask applicants to tell you if they have any such requirements.

You should prepare for the interview in advance. The more preparation you do, the easier it will be for both you and the applicant. You should interview with at least one other person, to avoid bias and gain a 'rounded' view of each applicant.

Use the criteria from the person specification to develop a set of questions.

Use the criteria from the person specification to develop a set of questions. For example, if one of the requirements is to organise one's own workload, you could prepare a question about how applicants have gone about organising their workload in previous employment or voluntary work.

Decide between yourself and other interviewers who will deal with which topics.

Think about what information applicants may want about the job and your organisation.

Make sure that the interview venue is as accessible as possible and that the interview room is properly prepared, with drinks available.

It is best not to hold the interview sitting behind a desk, or use a higher chair than the person being interviewed. Sitting around a round table can be a good idea, to make the applicant feel more comfortable and therefore enable them to give a better performance at the interview.

Make sure you have made any requested adjustments for disabled applicants. A person with a learning disability may wish to bring a supporter, for example, or a hearing impaired person may wish to have a copy of the interview questions.

Avoid holding the interview on the date of a major religious festival. Bear religious requirements in mind.

The timing of the interviews should be flexible to help applicants with family commitments.

Make sure there will be no interruptions and switch off mobile phones.

Brief other members of staff, such as receptionists, to expect the applicant.

Allow enough time for each interview so you don't have to rush. This is particularly important if you need to accommodate an applicant with a disability.

The interview

Start by welcoming the applicant and try and put them at their ease. Introduce yourself and the other interviewers. Explain the structure of the interview.

Avoid making up your mind within a few minutes of meeting an applicant. It is not likely that this will be on the basis of the abilities, but rather on the basis of appearance, or interests, experiences and views which may be shared.

Use the questions you have prepared in advance, based on the criteria in the person specification.

Depending on the answer each applicant gives, you may need to rephrase the question or ask follow up questions which are related to the criteria you are testing. It is quite acceptable for these follow up questions to be different for each applicant, as each applicant is also different.

Make sure your questions are open-ended. These are ones which need more than a 'yes' or 'no' to answer.

Ask additional questions that arise from the application form if relevant. For example, if a criminal conviction is declared, you should ask about the circumstances surrounding the conviction, to assess if it is relevant to the post. If there are gaps in employment, you will need to ask about these.

You should ask all applicants if they have any 'unspent' criminal convictions.

An 'unspent' conviction is one that all applicants should reveal if asked. Convictions which have become 'spent' (i.e. the individual has served a specific rehabilitation period) do not need to be revealed in most circumstances.

However, for posts which involve working with children or vulnerable adults, an Exception Order to the Rehabilitation of Offenders Act 1976 allows you to ask about spent convictions as well as unspent ones.

You can explain to applicants that if they do have a criminal conviction, your organisation takes a positive stance towards ex-offenders and that the conviction will be taken into account only if considered relevant to the job.

Make sure that you don't ask irrelevant, possibly discriminatory questions such as asking how the applicant will cope with childcare.

Keep control of the interview. If you feel the applicant is going off-track turn the conversation back to the information you need.

As the interview progresses, make notes on how well the applicant meets each criterion – based on his or her answers to questions.

At the end of the interview, ask the applicant if he or she has any questions. If you give information about terms and conditions, make sure this is correct – if someone is later appointed, they may rely on this information as part of the

Use the questions you have prepared in advance, based on the criteria in the person specification.

Keep control of the interview. If you feel the applicant is going off-track turn the conversation back to the information you need.

employment contract.

Inform the applicant of the next stage in the recruitment process, e.g. appointment, second interviews, tests and the estimated timescales.

Thank the applicant for coming.

Keep your interview notes. Only record what has been said in the interview and how the selection decision was made. Be aware that applicants who later make a complaint to an Employment Tribunal have the right to ask for copies of any notes made during the interview, and that you may need them for defending any possible discrimination case relating to the process.

Other selection methods

Interviewing on its own is not always the most reliable method of choosing the right person for the job.

As well as interviewing, there are other ways of selecting the best applicant. Studies have indicated that interviewing on its own is not always the most reliable method of choosing the right person for the job, especially if interviewers are relatively inexperienced.

To find out more information about whether applicants possess the criteria you are looking for, you could consider the following:

Practical tests

A practical test might be a case study that the applicant needs to comment on.

Alternatively, you might simulate a typical 'in tray' which the applicant might need to deal with, if appointed.

Such practical tests can show the knowledge and skills the applicant may possess to undertake the job 'for real'.

Psychometric tests

Psychometric tests can be used to assess skills such as: problem solving, decision making and interpersonal skills.

You should bear in mind that these tests:
- are not always a good indicator of future performance
- should not be used unless there is a proven need and a suitably qualified person to administer them
- often require a fee when you use them.

Presentations

You could ask applicants to make a presentation on a specific topic. You would be able to assess from this, the applicant's verbal communication skills or their knowledge of a specific subject.

Role plays
You could ask applicants to role play a specific scenario. This can be helpful to assess how they act and cooperate with others.

Assessment centres
Assessment centres typically run over one or two days and may use all the above selection methods, including an interview. Assessment centres can give a thorough picture of applicants, but they can also be expensive and time consuming.

Deciding on a selection method
If you are considering using any of the above selection methods, consider the following:

- Make sure you know which criteria you are assessing from each test. For example, if you ask an applicant to undertake an in-tray exercise, are you testing their ability to communicate in writing, to plan and organise, their knowledge of their job or all three of these?
- Don't use a test that is irrelevant. For example, if someone will rarely be required to make presentations in the job, then don't ask them to do one as part of the selection process.
- Make sure you make adjustments for disabled people. An applicant with a stammer may require more time for a verbal presentation. You may need to provide documents in a larger text size for a visually impaired applicant.
- Make sure that the subject matter of your tests does not disadvantage some people. If there is no need to have knowledge of the voluntary sector for a particular job, then don't give applicants a case study about a management committee. This might disadvantage very suitable applicants who may not be familiar with the voluntary sector.
- If you want to use tests but are not sure how, you could take advice from a human resources specialist.

Deciding who to appoint

Once you have undertaken all interviews and other selection tests, you and other members of the selection panel should consider the suitability of each applicant against the requirements of the person specification. A good way of deciding which applicant is the most suitable is for members of the selection panel to jointly score the extent to which applicant meets each criterion. For example, 3 would be meets

> A good way of deciding which applicant is the most suitable is for members of the selection panel to jointly score the extent to which applicant meets each criterion.

requirements, 2 would be partly meets requirements and 1 would be does not meet requirements. Evidence should be cited to back up any scores.

Be cautious about simply adding up all the scores given to each applicant and offering the job to the applicant with the highest overall score. You need to consider the matter in more depth than this. If, for example, an applicant has scored extremely well on most criteria, but scored badly on his or her ability to deal effectively with conflict in a non-confrontational manner; you may feel that this one criteria is sufficiently important that the applicant is not suitable, regardless of whether he or she was the highest scoring applicant overall.

Once you have chosen the most appropriate person for your job, you can send them a provisional offer of employment. This can be in the form of a letter, stating the position you are offering, the salary and when you hope the person will start. Make sure that the salary and any terms and conditions you mention are correct – they could be relied on later as part of the employment contract.

The letter should state clearly that the offer is provisional on receipt of references; Asylum and Immigration Act checks; confirmation that the employee has passed a medical examination (where relevant), and CRB clearance (where relevant).

If you can, it is good practice to offer people feedback on their interview performance.

Once the provisional offer of employment has been accepted, you should send a letter to those who were not successful at interview, thanking them for their time. If you can, it is good practice to offer these people feedback on their interview performance.

References

References from previous employers should always be followed up. The present employer should not be contacted until the applicant has accepted your provisional offer of employment and has told their employer.

If there is only one previous employer, or none, academic references should be sought in preference to personal references.

References should be used to support or deny the information gained about an applicant, not to choose between applicants.

A reference request should cover the following areas:
- name of applicant;
- post applied for;
- who the reference is from, who it needs to be returned to and by when;

- a request for confirmation of the role and duties the applicant undertook with the referee, and the dates of employment;
- the reason for leaving (where applicable);
- whether there were any live disciplinary warnings on file;
- a request for comments on the applicant's reliability, trustworthiness, attendance, performance in the job and relationships with others;
- a request that the referee give any other information that he/she feels may be useful.

Someone named as a referee by an applicant is not under any legal obligation to provide a reference. However, a person who does provide a reference is under a legal obligation to ensure that the information given is accurate and truthful.

If a reference does not provide straightforward information in response to the initial request, you might want to follow up with a telephone conversation. Make notes of the telephone conversation for future reference.

Consider references in an impartial manner and be aware that on occasions, an applicant may have experienced prejudice in a previous organisation.

Asylum and Immigration Act checks

The Asylum and Immigration Act 1996 (updated in May 2004) states that it is a criminal offence for an employer to employ someone who does not have permission to live and work in the UK.

The Act puts an onus on employers to check the status of anyone whom they propose to employ. You should make sure you check everyone's status. It is not appropriate, for example, to only check the status of people whom you consider may not be British because of their accent or ethnic origin. Such assumptions are inappropriate and could imply discrimination – remember it is illegal under the Race Relations Act 1976 to discriminate against people on the grounds of colour, race, nationality or ethnic or national origins.

The process you need to go through involves checking a document or combinations of documents which have been specifically listed by the government in order to prevent forged documents being used.

If you follow the steps below, this will provide you with a defence in the event that any employee is found to be working illegally.

> It is a criminal offence for an employer to employ someone who does not have permission to live and work in the UK.

Step 1

Ask the potential employee to provide the original of **one document from list 1** below.

If the potential employee cannot provide a document from list 1, then he or she must provide **two documents from list 2** below.

List 1

- Passport showing the holder as a British citizen or as having the right of abode in the United Kingdom.
- Document showing the holder is a national of an EEA country or Switzerland. This must be a national passport or national identity card.
- A residence permit issued by the United Kingdom to a national from an EEA country or Switzerland.
- A passport or other document issued by the Home Office which has an endorsement stating that the holder has current right of residence in the United Kingdom as the family member of a national from an EEA country or Switzerland.
- A passport or other travel document endorsed to show that the holder can stay indefinitely in the UK or has no other time limit on their stay.
- A passport or other travel document endorsed to show that the holder can stay in the UK and that this endorsement allows the holder to do the type of work you are offering if they do not have a work permit.
- An application registration card issued by the Home Office to an asylum seeker stating that the holder is permitted to take employment.

List 2

It is necessary to have two documents from either the first combination or the second combination. One document from each combination will not provide the statutory defence.

First combination

- A document giving the person's permanent national insurance number and name (P45, P60, national insurance card or letter from a government agency).

Plus one of the following:

- full birth certificate issued in the UK which includes the names of the holder's parents; or
- a birth certificate issued in the Channel Islands, the Isle of Man or Ireland; or
- a certificate of registration or naturalisation stating that the holder is a British citizen; or
- a letter issued by the Home Office which indicates that the person named in it can stay indefinitely in the UK or has no time limit on their stay; or
- an immigration status document issued by the Home Office with an endorsement indicating that the person named in it can stay indefinitely in the UK or has no time limit on their stay; or
- a letter issued by the Home Office which indicates that the person named in it can stay in the UK and this allows them to do the type of work you are offering; or
- an immigration status document issued by the Home Office with an endorsement indicating that the person named in it can stay in the UK and this allows them to do the type of work you are offering.

Second combination

- a work permit or other approval to take employment that has been issued by Work Permits UK.

Plus one of the following:

- a passport or other travel document endorsed to show that the holder is able to stay in the United Kingdom and can take the work permit employment in question; or
- a letter issued by the Home Office confirming that the person named in it is able to stay in the United Kingdom and can take the work permit employment in question.

Step 2

You must take reasonable steps to satisfy yourself that the potential employee is the rightful holder of these documents. The reasonable steps are listed below.

Reasonable steps

- Check any photographs, where available, to ensure that you are satisfied they are consistent with the appearance of your potential employee.
- Check the dates of birth listed so that you are satisfied that these are consistent with the appearance of your potential employee.
- Check that the expiry dates have not been passed.
- Check any UK Government stamps or endorsements to see if your potential employee is able to do the type of work you are offering.
- If your potential employee gives you two documents from List 2 which have different names, you should ask them for a further document to explain the reason for this. The further document could be a marriage certificate, divorce document, deed poll, adoption certificate or statutory declaration.

Step 3

You should make a copy of any such documentation – especially parts containing photographs/signatures and keep it with other documentation that you should put on the individual's file as and when he/she starts work with you.

Please note that if an individual has the right to work in the UK only for a limited period, you should only offer work for that period. You should not offer a contract that extends beyond the time that the individual has the right to work in the UK.

Worker Registration Scheme

There are certain additional procedures that you must follow if you want to employ a foreign national from one of the eight accessions states which joined the EU in 2004. These states are: Czech Republic, Estonia, Hungary, Latvia, Lithuania, Poland, Slovakia and Slovenia.

Nationals from all of the above countries are free to work in the UK. However, they are required to register with the Home Office. Registration is the responsibility of these individuals, not your responsibility. However, you should ensure that the individual is provided with a letter on your organisation's letter head, confirming the date on which they began working. The individual will need this when applying for registration.

You are responsible for ensuring that the worker has a registration certificate within the first month of starting work with you.

You should:
- take and retain a copy of the individual's completed application form as evidence that they have applied for registration within one month of starting work for you;
- receive and retain a copy of a valid registration certificate.

You may be guilty of committing a criminal offence and face a fine if:
- the worker does not apply for a registration certificate to the Home Office within one month of starting work for you;
- and you do not have a copy of a completed application form;
- and you continue to employ them.

The Government Worker Registration Team will send you a copy of the registration certificate once approved or a copy of the refusal letter.

If you do not receive a copy of the worker's registration certificate within one month of employing them, you can contact the Worker Registration Team tel: 0114 259 6262 or fax: 0114 259 5961.

If you want further information, you can go to www.workingintheuk.gov.uk and search under Worker Registration Scheme.

Applying for a work permit

If you know that an applicant does not have the right to live and work in the UK, you can consider applying for a work permit for them. However, it appears that the Home Office is unlikely to provide a work permit unless you can show that the skills required are scarce such that you cannot recruit appropriate individuals in the UK, or in the EC. If you want further information, you can go to the Government website www.workingintheuk.gov.uk.

Criminal Records Bureau checks (Disclosures)

A Disclosure is a document containing information held by the police and government departments.

A Disclosure is a document containing information held by the police and government departments. You can use it to make safer recruitment decisions. Disclosures are provided by the Criminal Records Bureau (CRB), an executive agency of the Home Office. They are available for England and Wales.

If you are recruiting to a post which involves working with children or vulnerable adults, you must obtain a Disclosure which is acceptable to you before confirming an applicant in post. You should only seek a Disclosure on the person to whom you have actually offered the post, not to all applicants.

Disclosures can be obtained for both paid employees and volunteers. There is a charge for obtaining a Disclosure for paid employees, but no charge for volunteers. It is good practice to pay this charge for the prospective employee.

There are two levels of Disclosure, as follows:

Standard Disclosures

Standard Disclosures are primarily for posts that involve working with children or vulnerable adults.

The Standard Disclosure contains details of all convictions held on the Police National Computer including current and 'spent' convictions as well as details of any cautions, reprimands or final warnings.

If a position involves working with children, the Disclosure will indicate whether information is held on certain government department lists, of those who are banned from working with children.

If a position involves working with vulnerable adults, the Disclosure will indicate whether information is held on a government department list of those who are banned from working with vulnerable adults. This is called the POVA (Protection of Vulnerable Adults) list.

Enhanced Disclosure

Enhanced Disclosures are for posts involving a far greater degree of contact with children or vulnerable adults.

In general the type of work will involve regularly caring for, supervising, training or being in sole charge of such people. Examples include a Care Worker/Support Worker, Scout or Guide leader or Sunday school volunteer.

This level of Disclosure involves an additional level of check to those carried out for the Standard Disclosure. An Enhanced Disclosure includes a check on local police records. Where local police records contain additional information that might be relevant to the post the applicant is being considered for, the Chief Officer of Police may release information for inclusion in an Enhanced Disclosure. Exceptionally, and in a very small number of circumstances (typically to protect the integrity of current police investigations), additional information may be sent under separate cover and should not be revealed to the applicant.

Registration

The Disclosure service is only available to organisations that have registered with the CRB. It is also available to organisations that have not registered by using an Umbrella Body to obtain their Disclosure. An Umbrella Body is a Registered Body that acts on behalf of other organisations.

You may prefer to access the Disclosure service via an Umbrella Body for one or more of the following reasons:

- You do not have the necessary additional administrative resource.
- You are a relatively small organisation and therefore paying the annual fee to register with the CRB would be uneconomic.
- You are unable to comply with the storage and handling provisions of the CRB Code of Practice.

Some Councils for Voluntary Services (CVSs) offer Umbrella Body services, or they may know of a local organisation that acts as an Umbrella Body. Alternatively, you can find an Umbrella Body by calling the CRB information line on 0870 90 90 811 or by searching for a relevant Umbrella Body on the Disclosure website: www.disclosure.gov.uk.

Application process

The prospective employee is responsible for making the Disclosure application. The most frequent approach is via telephone application.

You should ask the prospective employee to telephone the Disclosure application line on: 0870 90 90 844, to start the application process. Give them your 11 digit Registered Body number (of your own organisation or of the Umbrella Body which processes Disclosures for your organisation) – they will need this when they call. The prospective employee should be advised to make the phone call as soon as possible, so that their start date with you is not delayed.

The CRB will then send the prospective employee a Disclosure application form to complete. The employee must sign this, and then send it to a registered counter signatory, with the originals of a number of identity documents. The registered counter signatory is a person in the Registered Body who is authorised by the CRB to check and sign Disclosures. The registered counter signatory will check the form and the documents, then sign the form and send it to the CRB.

The completed Disclosure should then be sent to the prospective employee within a few weeks, with a copy to you, or to your Umbrella Body if you are using one.

If the Disclosure indicates that the applicant has a criminal record, you should consider whether it is relevant to the post for which they are applying. If you consider it is, and if you are considering withdrawing your offer of employment, you should meet with the individual to ask them about any convictions and give them the opportunity to explain the circumstances surrounding the conviction(s). You can then take a decision as to whether or not to proceed with appointing the applicant.

The prospective employee can refuse to apply for a Disclosure, but if this is the case, you may withdraw the job offer. Thus it is particularly important that if an offer is made, it states that it is dependent on receiving an acceptable Disclosure from the CRB.

In some cases, if an employee already has a Disclosure from a previous post, you may choose to accept it rather than seek a fresh Disclosure. The Disclosure website www.disclosure.gov.uk/index.asp gives more information on the circumstances where you should and should not reuse Disclosures.

Starting an employee before a Disclosure has been received
If you are recruiting a care worker for vulnerable adults or a childcare worker, **you must make sure you have received a Disclosure, before allowing the individual to start work**. This is because it is a legal offence to knowingly employ someone in these positions, if they may be on the lists of people barred from working with children or vulnerable adults.

In other circumstances, you may allow the applicant to start work, provided that you ensure that the employee is fully supervised in his or her work, whilst you are waiting for the Disclosure to come through.

For vulnerable adults only, there is a service which is available in England only called the POVAFirst check. This allows you to check an individual against the list of people barred from working with vulnerable adults (the POVA list) within a few days, with the full Disclosure following later. It means that you can start the employee (under supervision) once an acceptable POVAFirst check has been received, even if you are still awaiting the full Disclosure. You can use this service if you have a very urgent need to fill a vacancy.

POVAFirst checks are intended to be for exceptional circumstances only. If you want to get a POVAFirst check, you should contact the CRB, either directly, if your organisation is a Registered Body, or via your umbrella body.

> If the Disclosure indicates that the applicant has a criminal record, you should consider whether it is relevant to the post for which they are applying.

Confidentiality

Disclosure information must be treated with the utmost confidentiality. Under Section 124 of the Police Act 1997, it is an offence to pass Disclosure information to persons not authorised to receive it. Those authorised to receive Disclosure information are those who have a need to know, i.e. those responsible for the recruitment decision or for advising on it. Records must be kept securely and destroyed after use.

If your organisation is a Registered Body, you will need to comply fully with the CRB Code of Practice regarding the correct handling, use, storage, retention and disposal of Disclosure information. The Code is available from the CRB website www.crb.gov.uk.

If you are using an umbrella body, it will be able to advise you further on the process and any matters that may arise.

Monitoring recruitment

It is good practice to monitor each recruitment exercise, in order to assess whether you are attracting applicants from a range of backgrounds, and how different applicants fare in the selection process. Your funders may also expect this of you.

You should consider monitoring recruitment by gender, ethnic group, age and disability. You may also wish to monitor by sexual orientation and religion, although some applicants may be less keen to tell you about these.

Below is an example monitoring form. The ethnic origin categories used are those used in the 2001 Census. The Commission for Racial Equality advises that organisations should use these categories. This enables organisations to make comparisons with census output data.

WESTWICH ASSOCIATION Equality monitoring form

The Westwich Association wishes to be representative of the community it serves. To do this, we monitor applicants for employment, so that we can check we are attracting and recruiting a diverse group of people.

Please complete this form. It will be separated from your application form on receipt and will not be taken into account when we shortlist applicants or choose who we appoint to the job.

Post applied for:

I would describe myself as:

☐ White British   ☐ Black British   ☐ Asian British   ☐ Other

WHITE
☐ Irish
Other white background, please state:

BLACK
☐ African-Caribbean
☐ African
Other black background, please state:

MIXED
☐ White and Black Caribbean
☐ White and Black African
☐ White and Asian
Other mixed background, please state:

CHINESE OR OTHER ETHNIC GROUP
☐ Chinese

ANY OTHER ETHNIC GROUP,
PLEASE STATE:_____

ASIAN
☐ Indian
☐ Pakistani
☐ Bangladeshi
Other Asian background, please state:
_____

YOUR DATE OF BIRTH:_____

YOUR GENDER
☐ Female
☐ Male

If you wish, you may tell us about your religion and sexual orientation below.

How would you describe your religion or other belief?
My faith is_____

☐ I do not have a faith

How would you describe your sexual orientation?
☐ Towards persons of the same sex
☐ Towards persons of the opposite sex
☐ Towards persons of the same and the opposite sex

☐ I consider myself to have a disability
☐ I do not consider myself to have a disability

Where did you see this job advertised?_____.

For office use only.
Applicant reference number_____

You should monitor at the following stages:
- applications received and source of applications
- shortlisted
- offered post
- accepted post.

You can use this information to consider any action needed if the profile of applicants does not reflect the population profile within your organisation's area of remit.

For further information about how to monitor, and how to use the results, see the Acas good practice guide: *Tackling Discrimination and Promoting Equality*, which you can download from the Acas website at the following link www.acas.org.uk/publications/B16.html#9, or order from the Acas publications order line: 08702 42 90 90.

There is also additional information about monitoring in chapter 2 of this guide.

Genuine occupational qualification/requirement

A 'genuine occupational qualification/requirement' is an exception in law. In most circumstances, it is unlawful to say, for example, that you want to recruit a woman or a man, a person from a particular ethnic group or a person from a particular religion.

However, if the job requires a particular type of person for reasons of decency, privacy, or authenticity in dramatic performances, then the advertisement may be selective on the grounds that the job requires a 'genuine occupational qualification or requirement'. An example might be where the job requires a woman rather than a man to be a care assistant at a women's refuge.

For further information about Genuine Occupational Qualifications/Requirements, see chapter 2.

Checklist

- ✓ Establish exactly what tasks need to be done and whether there is a budget to recruit someone to do the tasks.
- ✓ Write a job description and person specification.
- ✓ Draft your advertisement. Always advertise internally. When choosing the best place to advertise externally, think about where your potential recruits might look for jobs.
- ✓ Produce an application form.
- ✓ Include an equal opportunities monitoring form with the application form.
- ✓ Establish a panel of interviewers.

✓ After the closing date, select applicants for interview based on the person specification.

✓ Interview applicants based on the person specification.

✓ Design other selection tests as required.

✓ Focus only on the requirements of the job when selecting – remember that discrimination on grounds of race, sex, marital status, disability, sexual orientation and religion/belief is unlawful.

✓ Select the most suitable applicant taking account of interview scores and offer him or her the position.

✓ Inform unsuccessful applicants once the position has been provisionally accepted.

✓ Seek and review references on the successful applicant. Check the applicant's right to work in United Kingdom. Seek a Disclosure (if required for the post) via the Criminal Records Bureau.

✓ Maintain records for at least six months, so that you can explain why you chose one applicant over another. Remember that applicants can now request to see any interview notes.

✓ Ensure all papers relating to the successful applicant are transferred to their personnel file.

✓ Go through the Equal Opportunities monitoring forms to see if your organisation is attracting and selecting a cross-section of applicants. If it is not, consider reviewing your advertising and recruitment processes.

Where to find out more

1. Acas
Acas has an advisory booklet on recruitment and induction. You can download a copy for free from its website, at: www.acas.org.uk/publications/B05.html. See page 36 for more details of how to order Acas publications.

2. Equality Direct
If you want advice on recruiting a diverse workforce, try calling the Acas Equality Direct helpline telephone/textphone: 0845 600 3444.

3. NCVO
www.askncvo.org.uk offers a wealth of free, practical, up-to-date advice on all aspects of running a charity or voluntary organisation. Hundreds of pages cover trusteeship, financial management, human resources and more.

4. Business Link

The Business Link website: www.businesslink.gov.uk has a very useful section on recruitment.

5. Jobcentre Plus

You can view the services of Jobcentre Plus on www.jobcentreplus.gov.uk. Alternatively, you can find your nearest Jobcentre Plus in your local telephone directory.

6. Criminal Records Bureau (CRB)

If you would like more information about Disclosure or the CRB, you can look at the Disclosure website at www.disclosure.gov.uk/index.asp or the CRB website at www.crb.gov.uk.

PO Box 110
Liverpool
L69 3EF

Tel: 0870 90 90 811
Minicom: 0870 90 90 344

6. Asylum and Immigration Act

For further information on your obligations to check employees' right to work in the UK, see the government Immigration and Nationality Directorate website: www.workingintheuk.gov.uk

Email: indpublicenquiries@ind.homeoffice.gsi.gov.uk.

Immigration & Nationality Directorate
Lunar House
40 Wellesley Road
Croydon
CR9 2BY

Tel: 0870 606 7766
Minicom: 0800 38 98 289

4   Types of contract

What this chapter is about

This chapter gives information about the contractual relationship between employer and employee, and explains what documentation has to be provided. It covers the following areas:

- An explanation of the 'written statement of terms and conditions of employment'
- The minimum clauses that must be included in a written statement
- Other clauses that can be useful to include in the written statement
- Different types of employment contracts, such as permanent or fixed term, part-time or full-time
- Transfers of Undertakings and the implications on the contract of employment
- Differences between an employment contract, a contract for a worker and a consultancy contract

What is the written statement?

The 'written statement of terms and conditions of employment' is the principal document that gives evidence of the contractual agreement between an employer and an employee.

Whilst the written statement is the main evidence of the contract of employment, contractual agreements can be entered into in other ways. A verbal promise of a pay rise in six months' time could be considered to be part of an employee's contract, even if that promise were given by a manager or trustee unauthorised to give it. That employee could then apply to an Employment Tribunal claiming breach of contract, if the pay rise did not materialise. You are therefore advised to always put in writing any discussions with employees which might be deemed to be of a contractual nature.

The Employment Rights Act 1996 Section one says that a written statement must be given to all employees who will be employed for more than one month. The written statement must

> Whilst the written statement is the main evidence of the contract of employment, contractual agreements can be entered into in other ways.

be given within two months of the employee joining the organisation. In practice, it makes sense to provide the statement when offering the job, or at the latest, on the person's first day at work. This helps avoid confusion and misunderstanding.

The minimum clauses that the law says must be included in a written statement

The Employment Rights Act 1996 (ERA) says that the written statement must contain certain clauses. These clauses are listed in the model written statement below.

In addition, the ERA says that some particulars may be given by reference in the written statement to some other document. For example, you must make a reference in the written statement to your disciplinary procedure, but you do not need to include the whole procedure in your written statement. Where the law allows you to make a reference, this is indicated in the model written statement below by a *.

Using the model written statement

The model written statement below can be adopted for different types of contractual arrangements, such as full-time, part-time, permanent, temporary or fixed-term.

Please note that the model written statement is for your guidance. You can use it as a basis for producing a written statement for your organisation. However, since the written statement is such a key employment document, and since employment law may change after this guide is published, you are advised to seek human resources or legal advice before finalising your written statement.

MODEL WRITTEN STATEMENT
This written statement replaces any previous agreements and arrangements, whether verbal or written, relating to your employment with (employer).

1. Name of employer and employee
Name of employer_____
(state full name of organisation and address)
Name of employee _____
(state full name)

2. Date the employment and continuous employment began
Your employment with (employer) begins/began on (date).

No employment with a previous employer counts towards your service with (employer)

OR your employment with (previous employer, state name) counts towards your service with (employer). Your continuous employment started on (date).

Note: in most cases, the date of employment and date of continuous employment will be the same. In a minority of cases, for example in the case of a merger, the date of continuous employment may be an earlier date.

3. Remuneration and the intervals at which it is to be paid
Your salary will be £xx,xxx per year. You will be paid monthly by direct debit into your bank account.

Salaries are normally reviewed, and may be increased, each April.

Note: you must pay at least the minimum wage. For further information, see chapter 6.

4. Working hours
EITHER
You are employed on a full-time basis, that is xx hours per week. Your normal working hours will be (for example) 9.30am to 5.00pm Monday to Friday. Overtime is paid at a rate of xxx/is not paid. Time off in lieu is/is not given. *You should also state here any flexibility in working hours, such as evening or weekend work, that may be required.*
OR
You are employed on a part-time basis, for xx hours per week. Your normal working hours will be (state hours). You should also state here any flexibility in working hours, such as evening or weekend work, that may be required.

Note: the Working Time Regulations 1998 limit, for health and safety reasons, the maximum working hours for most employees. For further information see chapter 11.

5. Holiday entitlement
Your annual holiday entitlement is xx days per year (this is pro-rata for part-time staff). The dates of your leave must be agreed with your line manager.

In addition, you are entitled to paid leave for the eight normal bank and public holidays *(NB there are 10 bank/public holidays in Northern Ireland each year)*. This entitlement is pro-rata for part-time staff. If you need to work on these days, you will be entitled to equivalent time off in lieu at a time to be agreed with your line manager.

Note: the Working Time Regulations state that a minimum of 4 weeks' leave (i.e. 20 working days for a full-time employee) must be given each year. These 4 weeks' leave can include bank and public holidays. Most employers give more leave than the statutory minimum).

On leaving, any accrued leave not taken will be calculated to the nearest day and given to you as pay in lieu of holiday. If you have taken more leave than you have accrued, the excess leave will be deducted from your final salary.

6. Place of work

Your normal place of work is (state place and address). However, if needed by (employer), you may be required to change your work location.

Note: the above clause gives flexibility, but must be implemented reasonably, taking into account: the distance of the move; the ease/difficulty of travel; and the employee's personal circumstances.

7. Job description or job title

You are employed as a xx.

Your manager will give you a copy of your job description. Your job description does not form a part of your contract of employment and may change from time to time.

Note: it is preferable only to give the job title, rather than the full job description, in the written statement. This makes the written statement more manageable.

8. Collective agreements that affect employment

EITHER:

There are the following collective agreements that affect your employment:...

OR:

There are no collective agreements in force that affect your employment.

Note: a collective agreement is an agreement entered into between an employer and a trade union. Its effect is that the terms and conditions of individual employees can be changed via agreements between the employer and the union. If you are a new or small employer, it is unlikely that you will have entered into a collective agreement with a union, but you still need to indicate in the written statement whether or not there is such an agreement.

*9. Entitlement to sick leave and pay

If you are not able to come into work, you must inform your manager by (time) on your first date of absence. You must state the reason for your absence and its likely duration.

EITHER

If you are off sick, and adhere to notification and certification procedures, you will normally be entitled to statutory sick pay for up to 28 weeks, subject to the scheme rules.

OR

If you are off sick, and adhere to notification and certification procedures, you will be entitled to full pay for a short period, followed by half pay for a further period. Your exact entitlement depends on your length of service.

Note: there is no requirement on an employer to provide anything more than statutory sick pay for absent employees.

For further information, please see the sickness absence procedure, available from.... This procedure does not form a part of your contract of employment and may be changed from time to time.

*10. Pension scheme and pensions contracting-out certificate

(Employer) offers a stakeholder pension scheme. You may contribute up to x% of your salary to the scheme each month.

OPTION

(Employer) will also contribute x% of your salary to the scheme.

A pensions contracting-out certificate is/is not in force in respect of this scheme.

For further information on the pension scheme, please contact

(Employer's) contribution levels and the scheme administrator may change in the future.

Note: if you have five or more employees, you must provide access to a stakeholder pension scheme. For further information, see chapter 6.

*11. The entitlement of employer and employee to notice and termination

EITHER

For information about the notice you are required to give and entitled to receive, please see (document).

OR
You are required to give the following notice if you leave
(employer):
During the probationary period: one week.
After the probationary period: two months.

(Employer) will give you the following notice:
During the probationary period: one week.
After the probationary period: two months or the
statutory minimum, whichever is higher.
*Note: the above notice periods are examples only. You can
determine different notice periods if you wish. However,
the law says that as a minimum, one week's notice of
termination of employment must be given by the employer
after the employee has completed one month's service.
This notice increases to two weeks after two years' service
and then by a further week for each year served up to a
maximum of 12 weeks' notice after 12 years' service.*

*12. Duration of employment
EITHER
Your employment is intended to be permanent, although is
subject to funding.
*Include the reference to the employment being subject to
funding if you wish, and if relevant.*
OR
Your employment is temporary and will terminate at the
end of your temporary assignment, with notice in
accordance with clause 11 above.
OR
Your employment is for a fixed term. The fixed term will
end on (date), and no notice will be given. However, if
either (employer) or you wish to terminate the
employment prior to the end of the fixed term, notice will
be given in accordance with clause 11 above.
Any termination of employment will take place in
accordance with the statutory minimum dismissal procedure.

*13. Disciplinary procedure and rules
(Employer's) disciplinary procedure and rules are attached
to this written statement/are available from xxx.
The disciplinary procedure does not form a part of your
contract of employment and may be changed from
time to time.

*14. Disciplinary appeal
If you are unhappy with any disciplinary decision relating to you, you should apply in writing to (name, e.g. the director or the chair of the trustees), within the timescales indicated in the disciplinary procedure.

*15. Grievances
If you have a grievance relating to your employment, you can apply in writing to (name, e.g. the director or the chair of the trustees).
The grievance procedure is attached to this written statement/is available from...
The grievance procedure does not form a part of your contract of employment and may be changed from time to time.

Other useful clauses that you may wish to include in the written statement

Whilst there is no legal obligation to include the following clauses, they can be useful to include in the written statement:

16. Probationary period
You will be on probation for the first xx months (e.g. six months) of your employment with (employer). Your probationary period may be extended if more time is needed to assess your suitability for the job.
If your performance or conduct is not considered to be satisfactory either during or at the end of the probationary period or during any period of extension, your employment may be terminated with one week's notice, in accordance with the statutory minimum dismissal procedure.

17. Retirement age
The normal retirement age of (employer) is (state age).
Note: under Government proposals for age discrimination legislation (due to come into force in 2006), retirement ages below 65 will only be allowed if they are deemed to be 'appropriate and necessary.' In addition, it is proposed that employees will have the right to request to work beyond 65 and employers will have a duty to consider that request.
If you want to include a retirement age in your written statements, you are advised to set it at age 65.

18. Health and Safety

(Employer) sets great importance by health and safety. You are required to adhere to (employer's) Health and Safety Policy, which is displayed on xxxx. Failure to do so will render you subject to (employer's) disciplinary procedures.

19. Employer's property

You must take good care of (employer's) property at all times. On leaving (employer), you must return all (employer's) property in your possession to (employer) in the same condition as it was provided to you, subject to normal wear and tear. Failure to do so will render you subject to (employer's) disciplinary procedures.

20. Other work

You must not engage in any paid or voluntary work with another employer/organisation without first seeking written permission from (name). Permission will not be unreasonably withheld.

21. Copyright and inventions

You will promptly disclose to (employer) all copyright works, inventions, discoveries or designs originated, conceived, written or made by you alone or with others (except only those conceived, written or made by you outside your normal working hours and wholly unconnected with your employment) to enable (employer) to determine whether it is an (employer) invention and will until such rights are fully and absolutely vested in (employer) hold them in trust for (employer).

You will at the request and expense of (employer) do all things necessary or desirable to enable (employer) or its nominee to obtain the benefit of the (employer) invention and to secure patent or other appropriate forms of protection for it throughout the world.

Decisions as to the patenting and exploitation of any (employer) invention will be in the sole discretion of (employer).

You assign to (employer) by way of future assignment all copyright design right and other proprietary rights, if any, throughout the world in respect of all (employer) inventions during the period of your employment.

22. Confidential information

You must not disclose any confidential information about

the work of (employer), its service users, staff or volunteers, without prior authorisation. If you are unsure about whether something is confidential, you must check with your manager.

23. Criminal records checks

If you may be working directly with children or vulnerable adults, you must have a criminal records check (via the Criminal Records Bureau) which must be satisfactory to (employer), before joining (employer). It is a condition of your employment that you consent to periodic criminal records checks during the course of your employment.

24. Parental rights

EITHER

Maternity, paternity, adoption and parental leave are provided in accordance with legal requirements. For further information, please refer to/see ...

OR

We offer some enhancements to maternity, paternity, adoption and parental leave. For further information, please refer to/see ...

Note: There is no legal requirement to include information on parental rights in the written statement. If you are simply offering parental rights at statutory levels (see chapter 7), then there is really no need to mention them here. Keeping things brief means that you don't need to update written statements every time the law changes.

25. Equal opportunities

(Employer) is an equal opportunities employer and will not treat any job applicant or employee less favourably on grounds of their sex, sexual orientation, age, disability, marital status, creed, colour, race, religion or philosophical beliefs or ethnic origins, nor will any job applicant or employee be disadvantaged by conditions or requirements which cannot be shown to be justifiable. It is the duty of all employees to ensure that this policy is observed at all times. (Employer) will seek to ensure that individuals are selected and promoted on the basis of their aptitude, skills and ability.

26. Expenses

Reasonable expenses, incurred solely as a result of your work with (employer), will be reimbursed. You must provide receipts or other proof of expenditure and you must not make an expense claim if you have claimed or intend to claim the expense from elsewhere.

Please check with your manager before incurring expenses, so that you know what is considered to be a reasonable expense.

27. Deductions from salary

If at any time you owe (employer) money, you hereby authorise (employer) to deduct money from your salary. This includes, but is not limited, to overpayment of wages and any loan provided to you by (employer).

28. Ability to alter the written statement

(Employer) may change the terms and conditions of this written statement in certain circumstances. Minor changes will be made and notified to you in writing. You will be formally consulted in respect of more significant changes. *Note: you cannot unilaterally change significant terms (such as someone's working hours), unless they agree to this. You must therefore consult with them. The length of the consultation will depend on the number of employees that will be affected by the variation. If they disagree to any change and there is a strong business reason why you must implement the change, one option (not to be taken lightly!) is to terminate the existing contract of employment and offer a new contract on revised terms. If you are considering such a step, you are strongly advised to take advice from an employment lawyer or human resources specialist. This may potentially constitute a fair dismissal but requires that a fair process is also followed.*

29. Data protection

You accept and understand that (employer) will keep personnel records during your employment here and for a period of time after you leave which will be dependent on business needs taking into account professional guidelines and statutory requirements. You understand that the information contained in these records may be used for monitoring the effectiveness of (employer's) equal opportunities programmes, for personnel administrative tasks and for business management purposes. Information known as 'sensitive personal data' will also be processed as part of your personnel records which includes details of any medical condition, and you agree to the (employer) processing such data. You understand that where this is the case, processing will take place in accordance with the provisions of the Data Protection Act 1998. (You further understand that data may be sent to [country]). By signing this document you acknowledge that you will be providing (employer) with your consent to these uses.

30. Lay-offs and short-time working

(Employer) reserves the right to lay you off without pay, or to reduce your pay and hours of work, for a period of up to two weeks, should there be a case of extreme financial difficulty and/or where no work is available. Such a step would not be taken without consultation with staff and would be a measure to avoid or minimise the need for redundancies.

Note: Employees can be laid off without pay only where there is a specific term in their contract allowing the employer to do so.

When employees are laid off, they may be entitled to a statutory guarantee payment from the employer.

On days on which a guarantee payment is not payable, employees may be able to claim Jobseekers Allowance and should contact their local Jobcentre about eligibility.

31. Third party liability

If you shall become entitled to receive any payments from a third party (including your own insurance company) in respect of damages for absence from employment due to incapacity, then you hereby warrant that you will pursue payment of such entitlement. If you receive any such payments from a third party, any sums paid by (employer) to you in excess of its obligations under Statutory Sick Pay regulations and in respect of the same period of absence shall be recoverable by (employer) out of such damages as money due to (employer).

32. Acknowledgement (signature)

This document is agreed to cover the terms and conditions of employment for (name).

Signed _____
(for the employer)
Job title _____
Signed _____
(employee)

Different types of employment contracts

The 'traditional' employment relationship has historically been permanent and full-time. However, this is changing, with an increasing number of staff working a on a variety of part-time contracts (such as job-sharing and term-time working) as well as contracts which are fixed term or temporary.

This section identifies a number of different employment contracts, and highlights some points of note about each.

Fixed-term contracts

No less favourable treatment
The Fixed-term Employees (Prevention of Less Favourable Treatment) Regulations 2002 state that workers on fixed-term contracts should be treated no less favourably than workers on comparable permanent contracts. So, for example, if you have two project workers, one on a permanent contract and one on a fixed-term contract, their terms and conditions should be equally favourable overall.

You should tell employees on fixed-term contracts about permanent vacancies that may be available and you should give them access to training.

After a fixed-term contract has run for four years, it automatically becomes permanent. This became the law from 10 July 2002. Service on a fixed-term contract prior to 10 July 2002 does not count towards the four years.

Waiver (removal of rights) clauses
A few years ago, fixed-term contracts were used quite extensively in the voluntary sector. They were popular for the following reasons:

- Funding was frequently for a fixed period, so a permanent contract could not be guaranteed.
- The law allowed clauses to be inserted into the contract, which meant that the employee 'waived' their rights to a redundancy payment and to any claim for unfair dismissal on termination of their contract at the end of the fixed term.

Whilst funding is frequently still for a fixed period, the clauses preventing an employee on a fixed-term contract from claiming a redundancy payment or unfair dismissal are no longer permitted. The exception is where a waiver clause was agreed before 1 October 2002. In this case, any waiver clause will continue to be valid for the duration of the fixed-term contract. However, if the contract is renewed or extended, the clause will cease to be valid.

The current legal position means that:

- If an employee has two years' service or more at the date of termination of the contract, he or she will be entitled to a redundancy payment (at the minimum statutory rate of £280 per week [as at 1 February 2005], for each year of service).
- If the employee has one year's service or more at the date of termination of the contract, he or she has the right to claim that he or she was unfairly dismissed.
- Even where a fixed-term contract is due to expire, there must still be a fair reason for dismissal. Fair reasons for dismissal in law include capability, conduct and redundancy.
- A fair procedure for the dismissal must also be followed. This is outlined below.

Minimum procedures for terminating a contract

The Employment Act 2002 brought into force new minimum procedures for the termination of employment. These procedures came into force on 1 October 2004. If the minimum procedures are not followed, a dismissal will be found to be automatically unfair by an employment tribunal. These minimum procedures should be used for terminating all contracts and are also outlined in the chapters in this Good Guide on probation, discipline and redundancy.

Below, the minimum procedures are outlined in respect of termination of a fixed term contract.

- You must set down in writing the reasons why you are contemplating terminating the contract (this will normally be the non-existence of work or that funding has stopped). This statement must be sent or given to the employee.
- You must arrange a meeting in order to discuss the basis for the proposed termination of employment. This meeting should be held at a reasonable time and place. The employee should take reasonable steps to attend and may be accompanied by a colleague or trade union representative.
- After the meeting you should inform the employee in writing of the decision and offer him/her the right of appeal.
- The employee must inform you if he/she wishes to appeal (we would advise that you ask them to do this in writing). You should then invite the employee to a hearing which should be chaired, where possible, by a more senior manager or by a trustee. Afterwards, the outcome of the hearing should be communicated in writing to the employee. The employee is entitled to be accompanied by a colleague or trade union representative at the meeting.

> **Even where a fixed-term contract is due to expire, there must still be a fair reason for dismissal.**

- If the appeal confirms that the employment should be terminated prior to the end of the agreed fixed term, the employee will be entitled to the notice outlined in his/her written statement of terms and conditions of employment or the statutory notice (if longer). If the termination is as a result of the natural end of the original fixed term, there may be no entitlement to notice.

Case study – terminating a fixed-term contract

The following case study illustrates how a worker on a fixed-term contract should (or should not!) be treated.

Joe is a caretaker at Westwich Association (WA).
At the time Joe was taken on, it was felt that WA would move to new premises within the next three years and that after the move, a caretaker would not be needed.
Joe was therefore given a fixed-term contract of two and a half years.
In actual fact, by the time Joe's contract was due to end, it was clear that WA would not be moving premises.
However, WA general manager is not keen to keep Joe on, because his work performance is poor and his time-keeping erratic.
The general manager has never addressed these problems, because she has only been in post for a year and knew that Joe's fixed-term contract was due to expire.
After consultation with the management committee, the general manager therefore informs Joe that it has been decided that his fixed-term contract will not be renewed when it expires at the end of next month.
Joe is totally surprised – he thought that as the Westwich Association were not moving to new premises, his employment was safe.
Joe has been to the Citizens Advice Bureau to check his rights. He has now asked for written reasons for his dismissal.

Some points to consider
Joe is entitled to have written reasons for his dismissal. WA must provide them.
In order to prove that Joe's dismissal is fair, the WA must first show that the dismissal was for one of the reasons which are potentially fair under the law. The three main ones are conduct, capability and redundancy.

If the dismissal was for conduct, then WA will have problems proving that it was reasonable – Joe was never warned that his conduct was below standard and was not given the chance to improve. Nor was a disciplinary procedure followed.

If the dismissal was for capability (poor performance), then WA will have similar problems – Joe was never warned nor given the chance to improve, and no capability procedure was followed.

WA could say that the dismissal was for redundancy. But to prove this, they must show that the requirement for Joe's work has ceased or diminished, and as far as we know, this is not the case. In addition, WA has not consulted Joe about redundancy or tried to redeploy him. WA would also need to give him redundancy pay.

If WA had followed the statutory minimum procedures when contemplating dismissal, it could have discussed Joe's concerns and the general manager's concerns at an earlier stage, and hopefully come to a more considered decision about Joe's employment. As it is, the termination of Joe's employment may be found by an Employment Tribunal to be automatically unfair, because the statutory minimum procedures were not followed. Regardless of the statutory procedures, it is likely to be found to be an unfair dismissal because of the unreasonable procedure that was followed.

Part-time contracts

The Part-Time Workers (Prevention of Less Favourable Treatment) Regulations 2000 state that part-time employees should enjoy terms and conditions pro-rata to full-time employees. Two examples of part-time contracts are job-sharing and term-time only contracts.

Job sharing contracts

Job sharing contracts are a type of part-time contract. Job sharing is where one job is shared between two people. It is different from two part-time jobs, because the two parties should work together to ensure that the job runs smoothly and that there is continuity throughout the week.

You are still employing two individuals and each should receive their own written statement. If one resigns or is dismissed, the other still has the right to remain employed. You could then seek a job sharer for the other half of the job.

If you are employing a job sharer, you may wish to include the following clauses in the written statement:

'You are employed on a job share basis. You are expected to work with your job-share partner to ensure that the work of the full job is covered during the working week. You are expected to agree matters of planning and completing work with your job share partner and in discussion with your manager.'

'You are employed for your own skills and abilities and your performance will be assessed using (employer's) normal procedures. Should your job share partner leave, any decision about appointing a new job share partner will be taken by (employer) in line with its normal recruitment procedures.'

More information is given about job sharing in chapter 8.

Term-time only contracts

A term-time only contract is a further type of part-time contract.

Under a term-time only contract, an employee works only during school term times.

If an employee on a term-time only contract leaves an organisation, a reckoning needs to be made as to the salary paid compared with the hours worked up to the date of leaving. This may mean that additional salary needs to be paid, or that some salary needs to be deducted.

You could include the following clauses in your written statement for term-time only working:

'You are required to work during term time only. You will not be required to work during the following times: for two weeks over the Christmas/New Year period; for two weeks over the Easter period; for six weeks from late July and during August; and for one week during each of the three school half terms. You are therefore required to work during 39 weeks of the year and not to work during 13 weeks of the year. You must agree your non-working weeks with your manager each January, for the following 13 months.

Your annual leave will be calculated pro-rata according to your working time. You will also receive paid leave, pro rata, for bank and public holidays.

'Your salary will be spread evenly over the year. If you leave (employer) having been paid for more hours than you have worked, the amount of excess pay will be deducted from your final salary, or if this is not possible, you will be required to pay the amount back to (employer).'

Zero hours contracts

Some contracts state that the individual is employed on 'zero hours.' These contracts might be used when work is required on a casual basis, for example, to cover for unexpected sickness in work where continuity is required at the work place (such as a care home). If such contracts are used, it should be clear that there is no mutual obligation on either side – either for the employer to offer work or for the employee to accept any work that is offered. It is not appropriate for an employee to be 'reserved' for work for a certain number of hours, without any guarantee of those hours.

You could use the following clause in your written statement:

'You have no guaranteed minimum contracted hours of work. Your hours of work will vary according to the needs of (employer). Your actual hours of work will be determined by your manager, who will, wherever possible, give you at least 24 hours notice of a commitment to work. There is no obligation on the part of (employer) to provide work or for you to accept any work offered. Once work has been accepted you are committed to undertake that work.'

Annual hours contracts

An annual hours contract states the number of hours that must be worked over the year, rather than over a week. It can be a full-time or a part-time contract. It can give flexibility for employers where work is seasonal, or can offer flexibility to employees who wish to work more at certain times of the year and less at other times of the year.

Generally, the salary for an annual hours contract is paid evenly throughout the year.

It is important to have an effective system of recording hours, so that employer and employee can keep track over the year.

As with termtime only contracts, if an employee on an annual hours contract leaves an organisation, a reckoning needs to be made as to the salary paid compared with the hours worked up to the date of leaving. This may mean that additional salary needs to be paid, or that some salary needs to be deducted.

You could use the following clauses in your written statement:

'You are employed on an annual hours contract, that is on the basis of 1924 hours per year, over a period from 1 January to 31 December each year. This is an average of 37 hours per week, but you may be required to work more hours in some weeks and less in others, depending on the requirements of (employer). You may also request to work fewer or more hours in a particular week. Your request will be met where possible and taking into account the hours you have already worked in the year.

'If you leave (employer) having been paid for more hours than you have worked, the amount of excess pay will be deducted from your final salary, or if this is not possible, you will be required to pay the amount back to (employer).'

Transfers of undertakings – the implications on contracts of employment

The Transfer of Undertakings (Protection of Employment) Regulations 1981 (TUPE) states that an employer is not permitted to change contract terms if the changes are connected with a transfer of an undertaking. This means that if you accept employees from another organisation, they retain their original terms and conditions of employment, including salary level. You cannot change these terms, unless the employee agrees. Likewise, if any of your employees transfer to another organisation, their original contract terms will move with them to the new organisation.

If you are involved in a TUPE transfer, you are advised to get human resources or legal advice.

Differences between an employment contract, a contract for a worker and a consultancy contract?

Sometimes, you may have a specific and short-term job that needs doing, such as the setting up of a new computer network or specific advice on an employment matter.

For such cases, you will probably need a self-employed person rather than an employee.

Below is an example agreement for engaging a self-employed consultant.

CONSULTANT'S AGREEMENT

1. Introduction and definitions
This Agreement is between _____
(organisation's name and address) (herein after called
_____) and (_____) (herein after
called 'the Consultant').
The Agreement will be in accordance with the following
Terms and Conditions unless and until an alternative is
specifically agreed between the Parties.

2. Purpose of the Agreement
The purpose of the Agreement is:
Further details of the Agreement are set out in the attached
Schedule.

3. Commencement date and duration of the Agreement
This Agreement will commence on (_____)
and is to be carried out in accordance with the following
conditions:

It may be terminated by either party giving one month's notice in writing.

_____ may terminate the agreement immediately in the event that the Consultant commits any material breach of the terms of this Agreement, or is guilty of gross misconduct.

4. Fees and expenses

Fees for the Agreement will be as follows:

Where necessary, VAT will be added at the appropriate rate. Where appropriate, travel, subsistence and other expenses will be paid at cost and in accordance with arrangements specifically agreed, in advance, with the Consultant.

5. Invoices and payment

Unless specifically agreed otherwise, invoices will be submitted monthly by the Consultant and payment made within 30 days.

6. Taxation

The Consultant is a self-employed person responsible for taxation and National Insurance or similar liabilities or contributions in respect of the fees and the Consultant will indemnify [organisation] against all liability for the same and any costs, claims or expenses including interest and penalties.

7. Confidentiality

The Consultant will not divulge to third parties matters confidential to (_____) (whether or not covered by this Agreement) without (_____) explicit permission. Except where specifically agreed otherwise, all material, data, information etc. collected during the course of the Agreement will remain in the possession of (_____) and not used without their permission.

8. Publication of material

Where the Agreement provides for the publication of material, the following specific conditions shall apply:

(a) _____ will retain the right to edit the final draft prior to publication subject, in the case of joint publications, to amendments proposed being agreed with the author(s).

(b) prior to publication, the Consultant and/or others associated with the publication shall not disclose any material obtained or produced for the purposes of the project to any other party unless _____ have given prior approval in writing.

(c) the Consultant will provide to _____ copies of all material, data etc collected specifically for the project and indicate the source of other material used.

(d) _____ will, except where specifically agreed otherwise, hold copyright to the publication.

Other matters relating to the use of the material shall be covered as an Appendix to this Agreement. Where other uses are agreed, all material and publications based on the project shall acknowledge _____ .

9. Restrictions

The Consultant shall not whilst this Agreement is in force, be engaged or concerned directly or indirectly in the provision of services to any other party in the same or similar field of business or activity to _____ without the prior written consent of _____ .

10. Other conditions

Any other conditions, including variations to the terms set out above, shall be included as an Appendix to this Agreement.

For _____(Organisation)
Signed: _____
Date: _____
Name: _____
Designation: _____

For the Consultant
Signed: _____
Date: _____
Name: _____
Designation: _____
Name: _____
Designation: _____

Don't be tempted to take someone on as a 'consultant', when really they are doing the job of an employee for you.

It is important that you are clear when you may need a consultancy agreement/contract for services and when you may need a contract of employment. Don't be tempted to take someone on as a 'consultant', when really they are doing the job of an employee for you. There are the following possible danger areas:

- Someone you thought was not an employee, claims employment rights (e.g. claims you have dismissed them unfairly, claims a redundancy payment or claims holiday pay).

- The Inland Revenue declares that someone you thought was self-employed should have been paid on the payroll, with tax and National Insurance deducted. In this case, you may be liable to pay the employee's tax as well as employer's and employee's National Insurance.

There is no single test of employed/self-employed status and indeed an Employment Tribunal and the Inland Revenue could come to a different conclusion about the same case. However, in general terms, an individual is likely to be an employee if they meet all or most of the following criteria.

- They work standard hours for you under your control.
- They are part and parcel of your organisation (they are integrated into the organisation).
- There is a mutuality of obligation – you are expected to offer ongoing work and they are expected to do it.
- They are not in business on their own account, i.e. they do not bear the financial risks of failure to perform and they use your equipment rather than their own.

An individual is likely to be self-employed if they meet all or most of the following criteria:

- They have a lot of control over their work (e.g. over hours and place of work).
- They are separate from your organisation.
- They do not expect ongoing work and are not under an obligation to perform it.
- They provide the main items of equipment needed to do their job.
- They are free to hire other people to do the work they have taken on.
- They are responsible for correcting unsatisfactory work in their own time and at their own expense.

Case study

Zoe was initially taken on as a gardener for Westwich Association (WA) grounds. When unable to come (either because of illness or because she was doing something else), Zoe would ask a friend to do the work instead. WA did not have any gardening tools; Zoe would supply these.

The WA assumed Zoe to be self-employed, although nothing was in writing. She was paid £16 in cash each week and worked until the job was done – generally for 1.5-2 hours per week. She had several other jobs and would carry her equipment from job to job.

After a while, WA found difficulties with the arrangement. Firstly, Zoe would come at different times in the week. Sometimes the children from the toddler group were in the garden when Zoe was working. There were concerns about the safety of having gardening tools in the garden at the same time as the children. Secondly, the general manager felt that the standard of gardening of Zoe's friend was low. Thirdly, Zoe's lawnmower was becoming unreliable.

By this stage, Zoe was spending more time caring for her elderly father and had stopped all other gardening jobs apart from WA. She was therefore reluctant to purchase a new lawnmower. The general manager agreed that WA would purchase a lawnmower for its grounds. It was also agreed that Zoe would come regularly on Monday morning between 10am and 12pm and that should would no longer ask anyone else to do the work.

The general manager realised that Zoe's employment status had changed. She came at regular times, used WA's equipment, did not have lots of other jobs and could no longer send a substitute. Taken as a whole, Zoe's status was more that of employee than self-employed person.

Having talked the situation through with Zoe, an agreement was reached and Zoe became an employee of WA. Although her hourly rate was lower than her self-employed hourly rate, she felt that generally she was better off, as she could receive paid annual leave, sick pay and could join WA's pension scheme.

Workers

There is one further category of contract that you may wish to use.

In some cases, you may require someone to work on a flexible and casual basis. In this circumstance, you could employ someone as a 'worker'.

'Workers' adopt a middle ground between employees and the self-employed. The Department of Trade and Industry describes workers as follows:

"essentially individuals who do not have a contract of employment, but who have some other contract to perform personally any work or services to another person although they are not genuinely in business on their own account.

"In other words, those who fall between the status of 'employee' and self-employed (in business on their own account)."

If you wish to use workers, the most likely use is for casual work. Casual workers:

- generally supply a short-term or specific need;
- typically, will have periods of work with breaks in-between where no work is performed;
- are offered and accept work 'as and when required';
- are not under an obligation to accept the work;
- have no agreement on the particular number of hours of work.

Such an arrangement may suit individuals who want the flexibility to take work as and when it suits them. The arrangement may suit employers, to fill short term needs, such as to cover shifts in a care home or to deal with occasional peaks in administrative workload.

Workers have some rights under employment law, but not as many as those who are also employees. For example, they do not have the right to claim unfair dismissal, notice pay or redundancy pay.

Workers do, however, have the following 'core' employment rights:

- to receive the national minimum wage
- not to suffer unlawful deductions from wages
- to receive paid holiday at Working Time Regulations levels of four weeks per year.

As workers are not considered to be genuinely self-employed, in most cases, they should be paid via the payroll. You still need to take references on them, check their right to live and work in the UK (under the Asylum and Immigration Act) and, if they work with children or vulnerable adults, you will need to see a Disclosure (criminal record check) on them from the Criminal Records Bureau. You can find out more about all these checks in chapter 3.

You do not need to make a contractual written agreement with a casual worker, but it is good practice and avoids misunderstandings if you do.

You could include clauses such as:

- The intention that they are a worker not an employee.
- The hourly rate of pay.
- The fact that there is no obligation on either side to accept or to offer work.

You do not need to make a contractual written agreement with a casual worker, but it is good practice and avoids misunderstandings if you do.

- That if work is accepted, they must do the work.
- Their entitlement to annual leave and how it will be paid.
- That they may join your stakeholder pension scheme if they wish.

Checklist

✓ Make sure all your employees, whether permanent or temporary, full-time or part-time, have a written statement of terms and conditions of employment.

✓ Remember that the written statement is the fundamental basis of the employment relationship. It is important to get it right.
Use the information in this chapter to create a written statement appropriate to your organisation, but you are advised to seek advice before finalising it.

✓ Do not provide less favourable terms and conditions to part-time employees or employees on fixed term contracts – it could be illegal.

✓ If you are engaging a self-employed person, use the information in this chapter to check that they really do count as self-employed from the perspective of employment law and the Inland Revenue.

✓ If you need casual work to be undertaken, you may need a 'worker'. Whilst there is no legal requirement to do so, it is good practice to enter into a contractual written agreement with the worker.

Where to find out more

1.Acas

The following documents can be downloaded from the Acas website:

A self-help guide on producing a written statement
www.acas.org.uk/publications/G01.html

An example of a written statement
www.acas.org.uk/publications/pdf/A%20Employing%20people/
A5_written_statement.PDF

An elearning self-help guide to producing a written statement
www.acas.org.uk/elearning/.

See page 36 for more details on how to order Acas publications.

For specific questions, you can contact the Acas helpline tel: 08457 47 47 47 or textphone: 08456 06 16 00.

2. Business Link

The Business Link website also has information on written statements. It has an online tool that you can complete and which helps you create a written statement for employees. Go to www.businesslink.org.uk and search under 'written statements.'

Alternatively, you can call Business Link: 0845 600 9 006.

3. Ask NCVO

www.askncvo.org.uk offers a wealth of free, practical, up-to-date advice on all aspects of running a charity or voluntary organisation. Hundreds of pages cover trusteeship, financial management, human resources and more.

5 Induction and probation

What this chapter is about

Good induction and probation programmes can lead to more settled employees, better work performance, lower labour turnover and improved employee relations.

Induction is the process of familiarising the employee with the organisation over the first few days and weeks of employment.

Probation is a period of time during which the employee and employer can assess whether the job and the employee are suitable. Typically, probation lasts for around six months. The employee is normally confirmed in post at the end of the probationary period, although if the employee and job are not suited to each other, termination of employment may occur during or at the end of the probationary period.

This chapter gives you some good practice guidance on what to do during the employee's induction and probation period.

It covers the following areas:
• Employees who may need special attention
• Induction period
• Probationary period
• Terminating employment during or at the end of the probationary period.

Employees who may need special attention

New employees who have done the same sort of work before, have been in the workplace for several years and are of similar background to existing employees may have very different needs during their induction and probationary period, compared; with new employees who, for example:
• have just left school or college;
• have been out of the workplace for some time;
• will be in a minority in the workplace;
• or are disabled.

Induction and probation processes should be flexible to meet individual needs. New employees should gain the impression that

Induction and probation processes should be flexible to meet individual needs.

yours is an organisation which celebrates differences in people, not an organisation that finds such differences a 'problem'.

School and college leavers

The Acas advice on inducting school and college leavers is reproduced below.

For school or college leavers, who may be nervous but excited at their first job, it is particularly important for the employer to encourage a positive attitude to work, and to allay any fears the new recruit may have. They need to be sure of their position in the company, and of the opportunities they will have to train and develop their skills.

Health and safety is a particularly important area to stress. Young people often have no feel for workplace hazards, and may be vulnerable to accidents. A group of young people together may get high-spirited and, without proper guidance on safety, be unaware of the potential dangers. Young workers are seen as being particularly at risk, and employers are required to:

- Assess risks to young people under 18, before they start work.
- Take into account their inexperience, lack of awareness of existing or potential risks, and immaturity.
- Address specific factors in the risk assessment. Employers are required to make a suitable and sufficient assessment of the risks to the health and safety of employees and identify groups of workers who might be particularly at risk.

People who have been out of the workplace for some time

Acas advises the following:

Men or women returning to work after some years caring for children or other relatives may feel apprehensive about the new job – even when they may have worked for the company in the past. They may feel out of touch with developments, and in need of re-establishing themselves. Their induction programme needs to take this into account, offering training and extra help to settle in and become valuable members of the organisation.

This is also true of those who might have been living/working abroad, or who are changing their career focus.

Minorities

Studies have shown that people who are in minorities in organisations (for example, due to disability, gender, racial origin or sexual orientation) tend to take longer to be inducted and socialised. They may be less aware of the expectations of them and what to do to progress in the organisation.

Further research has indicated that managers may not be used to dealing with particular minority groups or be aware of the issues that might affect them. They may have stereotypical views of the capabilities of certain groups.

People who are a minority in an organisation should have the same induction programme as any other new starter, but make sure you pay attention to any specific requirements. Be aware of cultural and religious customs. For example, a Jewish person may feel uncomfortable being invited to socialise with other staff after sunset on a Friday, and a Muslim may feel embarrassed at being offered alcohol. However, individuals will vary in the extent to which they adhere to their religion, so be wary of making assumptions. Try and create an environment where staff know that they can ask for religious or cultural commitments to be accommodated and do not feel embarrassed to do so. The same applies to individuals with caring commitments – ask them what they need and try and accommodate them if needed. Most people will be grateful and will not abuse any flexibility you give them. If you can, find a 'buddy' (see below) who can support the individual to settle into the work environment. You could also consider diversity/equal opportunities awareness training for your employees, so that they have a better awareness of differences.

> Try and create an environment where staff know that they can ask for religious or cultural commitments to be accommodated.

Disabled employees

If an employee is disabled, you must, under the Disability Discrimination Act 1995 consult with the employee about making 'reasonable adjustments' to the work or working environment. Where appropriate, you might also arrange awareness training for existing staff.

Acas has the following advice about disabled employees:

> Careful pre-planning can reduce the problems which may arise for disabled employees, whether in terms of access, equipment or dealing with colleagues. Specialist advice is available from the Disability Employment Adviser and the Disability Service Teams of the Department for Work and Pensions. The Department for Work and Pensions also operates the Access to Work Scheme, whereby assistance may be available in meeting the cost of any aids and adaptations required. These services can be contacted via the JobCentre network.

Induction period

A good induction programme should make new employees feel welcome and ready/able to contribute fully.

When they have completed their induction, each employee should have an understanding of:

- what your organisation does and the jobs people do
- their role – how they will undertake the duties outlined in their job description
- how what they do fits in with the wider aims of the organisation.

Preparing for the new employee

Provide the following information for the new employee before his or her first day:

- start time
- who to report to and where
- brief details of what will happen on the first day
- the employee's written statement of terms and conditions
- your staff handbook (if you have one)
- your health and safety procedure
- your equal opportunities/diversity policy or statement of intent.

Information about the new employee can also be provided to other staff in advance – their name, their start date and what they will be doing. The information could be accompanied by a request for support to help the new person settle in.

The first few days

It may seem obvious, but make sure the employee's line manager is available on the first day!

It may seem obvious, but make sure the employee's line manager is available on the first day! There will be documentation to complete, introductions to be made and essential information such as where to get a cup of tea or coffee. It is also good to give the new employee some (but not too much) work on the first day, so that they feel that they have 'started' in the organisation.

You will find that during the first few days, your new employee will be able to take in only so much information and should not be overloaded.

Managers' responsibilities

Managers should be clear on their responsibilities to ensure that the employees they manage are fully inducted into the organisation.

Managers should ensure that:

- New employees are given time to absorb new information. Information is best given in small 'digestible' chunks.
- Sufficient time is set aside to meet induction needs.
- The induction needs of internal promotees are not overlooked.
- The needs of existing employees still need to be met during induction, i.e. that the 'novelty factor' does not override ongoing work.

Buddying system

Some organisations have a 'buddy' system, whereby a member of staff who is not the line manager is assigned to the new employee, to help him or her settle and to answer any questions, especially those questions that the employee may not want to bother the manager with (such as the best place to buy a sandwich). Such a system can help the new employee to feel settled more quickly.

Induction checklist

Acas suggest that induction should follow a systematic plan, and be written down so that nothing is overlooked. Each stage should be 'ticked off' as it is completed. Not only does this give some structure to the induction but it also ensures that both the new starter and the manager know what has or has not been covered at any given time. Both manager and employee should have a copy of the list. It should be their joint responsibility to ensure that everything is covered.

Induction should follow a systematic plan, and be written down so that nothing is overlooked.

The following checklist is adapted for the voluntary sector, from the Acas checklist which is contained in their *Good Practice Guide to Recruitment and Induction*, available at www.acas.org.uk/publications/B05.html.

Name_____ Date of starting_____

	Carried out by	Date	Comments
Reception			
Received by			
Personnel documentation and checks completed – P45			
Security/identity card issued (where relevant)			
Introduction to the organisation			
Who's who			
History			
Activities and services			
Future plans and developments			

	Carried out by	Date	Comments
Terms and conditions of employment			
Signed written statement of terms and conditions received			
Written statement of terms and conditions reviewed			
Hours, breaks, method of payment			
Holidays			
Flexitime			
Probationary period and procedure			
Notice period			
Sickness provisions			
Pension provisions			
Parental leave provisions			
Equal opportunities policy and employee development			
Equal opportunities policy			
Measures to prevent bullying/harassment			
Training needs and objectives			
Training provision			
Further education/training policies			
Performance appraisal			
Promotion avenues			
Employee/employer relations			
Trade union membership			
Other employee representation			
Employee communications and consultation			
Grievance and disciplinary procedure			
Appeals procedure			
Organisation rules			
Smoking policy			
General behaviour/dress code			
Telephone calls			
Canteen/break facilities			
Cloakroom/toilets			
Health and safety			
Risk assessment			
Preventative and protective measures			
Pregnant women and new mothers			
Emergency procedures			
Awareness of hazards – any particular to type of work			
Safety rules			
Clear gangways/exits			
Location of exits			
Dangerous substances or processes			
Reporting of accidents			
First aid			
Employee benefits			

	Carried out by	Date	Comments
Parking facilities/arrangements			
Discounts available to the organisation			
The job			
Discussions with manager/supervisor			
Requirements of new job			
Standards expected			
Co-workers			
Supervision arrangements			

Reviewing your induction procedures

You could gain feedback from each new employee, after around six months, on what they felt about the induction process – the good points and areas to improve. Make changes to your induction procedures if needed.

Case study

The Westwich Association (WA) has been successful in recruiting a Bengali speaking outreach worker, Rakin. Rakin is a Muslim and there are no other Muslim members of staff at WA.

Rakin started five weeks ago now and the general manager is concerned. Rakin does not seem to be settling into the job quickly and does not seem very enthusiastic about the role. The general manager has been on leave for a couple of weeks and on her return, the WA administrator says that Rakin seems withdrawn, does not mix with other employees, doesn't eat lunch with them and doesn't join in tea or coffee breaks. Indeed, he appears not to be eating anything during the working day at all.

The general manager realises that it is currently Ramadan, during which Muslims fast between dawn and sunset. She realises that she has not discussed this with Rakin or the other employees. She is also conscious that by his gender, race and religion, Rakin is in a minority in the organisation.

As an immediate first step, the general manager finds out more about Rakin's religion. She downloads the Acas guide *Religion or Belief and the Workplace* from www.acas.org.uk/publications/pdf/religion.pdf.
This tells her the following:

Islam (Muslims)

Observant Muslims are required to pray five times a day. Each prayer time takes about 15 minutes and can take

place anywhere clean and quiet. Prayer times are:
- At dawn (Fajr)
- At mid-day (Zuhr) in winter sometime between 1200-1300hrs and in summer
- between 1300-1600hrs.
- Late afternoon (Asr) in Winter 1430-1530hrs
- After sunset (Maghrib)
- Late evening (Isha)

Friday mid-day prayers are particularly important to Muslims and may take a little longer than other prayer times. Friday prayers must be said in congregation and may require Muslims to travel to the nearest mosque or prayer gathering.

Before prayers, observant Muslims undertake a ritual act of purification. This involves the use of running water to wash hands, face, mouth, nose, arms up to the elbows and feet up to the ankles; although often the washing of the feet will be performed symbolically.

Ramadan, which takes place in the ninth month of the Muslim lunar calendar, is a particularly significant time for Muslims. Fasting is required between dawn and sunset. Most Muslims will attend work in the normal way but in the winter they may wish to break fast with other Muslims at sunset. This could be seen as a delayed lunch break. For those working evening or night shifts, the opportunity to heat food at sunset and/or sunrise will be appreciated.

Food

Muslims are forbidden to eat any food which is derived from the pig, this includes lard which may be present in bread or even ice-cream. In addition they are forbidden to eat any food which is derived from a carnivorous animal. Meat that may be consumed must be slaughtered by the Halal method. Islam also forbids the consumption of alcohol, which includes its presence in dishes such as risotto or fruit salad.

Other

Observant Muslims are required to wash following use of the toilet and will therefore appreciate access to water in the toilet cubicle. Often Muslims will carry a small container of water into the cubicle for this purpose. By agreement with other staff and cleaners, these containers could be kept in the cubicle.

Physical contact between the sexes is discouraged and some Muslims may politely refuse to shake hands with the opposite sex. This should not be viewed negatively.

The general manager now feels that she has more information about Rakin's religion and culture, which she wishes she had known before he started. She arranges to meet with Rakin, not to make assumptions about how he practices his religion, but to discuss how he is getting on and what accommodation he may require. She asks about any specific requirements he may have and expresses her willingness to accommodate him.

Mindful that the majority of employees at WA are female, the general manager assigns to Rakin, with his agreement, a male colleague as a 'buddy', with whom he can discuss any issues he wants to.

The general manager arranges to meet with Rakin again in a week's time to discuss work progress and any further specific requirements.

Probationary period

When an employee starts work, their manager must ensure that the employee is clear on how their performance and progress will be reviewed and assessed during the probationary period.

Probation terms

Check the terms on probation, set out in the written statement of terms and conditions, issued to the employee on joining. For example, a term might read: 'you will be on probation for the first six months of your employment with (employer). Your probationary period may be extended if more time is needed to assess your suitability for the job.'

This means that you must have a system in place to ensure that the new employee's performance is assessed regularly during the first six months. You should meet regularly to discuss progress, but you should also have formal review meetings:

- when the employee has been in post for three months
- when the employee has been in post for just under six months.

At the six month stage, you should confirm the employee in post, extend his/her probationary period or terminate his/her employment.

The probationary period does not, however, have to run for the full period in all circumstances. On some occasions, if you are certain that the employee is performing at an appropriate standard, you may wish to confirm the employee in post prior to the end of the probationary period.

On other occasions, you may feel that the employee will never reach the required standard and you may wish to terminate employment prior to the end of the probationary period. If you want to take this step, though, follow the statutory dismissal procedures outlined in this chapter and also make sure that you have been totally fair to the employee and given him or her sufficient time to demonstrate that he or she could do the job.

Formal review meetings

A formal review meeting is an opportunity for the employee and the manager to jointly discuss the employee's performance and identify any needs for training or guidance.

The three month review meeting should cover a review of the employee's performance against the job description and against any specific targets that have been set.

If the employee is performing satisfactorily, say so. Arrange a date for the further formal review meeting just prior to the end of the six months probation. Don't ignore the employee for the next three months, though – keep a track on their work and meet to discuss it as required.

If you have concerns about the employee's performance, you should say so. Be specific and tell the employee what good performance 'looks like'. It is important that the employee understands clearly what he or she should do to improve; and also that he or she understands that if improvement does not occur, the probationary period may be extended or their contract may be terminated.

It is important that the employee understands clearly what he or she should do to improve;

Ask the employee if there are specific barriers preventing him or her from achieving his/her best. If there are, work with the employee to remove these barriers. Provide additional training or coaching if needed.

Give the employee a clear note confirming your discussions. Arrange to meet regularly with the employee to help him or her improve his or her performance and to review progress. How regularly you meet will depend on the specific circumstance, but a brief meeting each week to keep the employee on track is often better than a longer meeting each month.

A further formal review meeting should be held shortly before the employee has completed six months' service.

If at this stage, you feel that the employee's performance and progress are satisfactory, you can confirm the employee in post.

If you feel that the employee's performance is still unsatisfactory, but could reach a satisfactory standard given a bit more time, you could extend the probationary period, say by a further three months. You should make it clear to the employee that if improvement does not occur during the period of extension, termination of the employee's contract may occur. Details of the decision should be recorded in writing and a copy given to the employee.

If you feel that the employee will not reach the required standard and you are contemplating terminating the employee's contract, you must set out your concerns in writing in advance of the meeting, in order to comply with the law on dismissal. The statutory procedure that you must follow is set out below.

Terminating employment during or at the end of the probationary period

If your disciplinary procedure is a part of the employee's contract of employment, you should follow this procedure if you are looking to terminate an employee's contract. Otherwise, as a minimum, you should do the following:

Step one – written statement
You should set out in writing the concerns (conduct, capability or other circumstances) which may result in dismissal or disciplinary action.

You should: give or send this statement to the employee; give the employee the opportunity to consider his/her response; and invite the employee to a meeting at a reasonable time and place to discuss the matter.

Step two – meeting
The employee must take all reasonable steps to attend the meeting. Both you and the employee should have the opportunity to give your points of view. You should fully consider what the employee has to say about his or her work performance. Keep an open mind and don't take a final decision on whether to terminate the employee's contract until you have heard everything that has been said and until you have had a chance to consider it. After the meeting, adjourn and consider what has been said. You should inform the employee about your decision, which could be to dismiss the employee, extend his or her probationary period or to confirm him or her in post. You should offer the employee the right of appeal.

Step three – appeal

If the employee wants to appeal, he or she must inform you in writing. You should give the employee a timescale by which to appeal. Acas advises a timescale of five working days.

You should then invite the employee to a further meeting, which should be arranged without unreasonable delay and should be at a reasonable time and place. The employee must take all reasonable steps to attend. You should arrange for a more senior manager to chair the meeting, where possible. If this is not possible, a trustee may chair the meeting.

After the meeting, you should communicate the final decision to the employee.

You should give the employee the notice period outlined in his or her written statement of terms and conditions of employment, except if the employee is summarily dismissed for gross misconduct.

Please note that at both the stage two meeting and the stage three meeting, the employee has the right to be accompanied by a colleague or trade union representative. If you wish, you may allow the employee to be accompanied by a friend or family member instead. You should inform the employee of his or her right to be accompanied prior to the meeting, so that the employee has the time to make arrangements.

> You should inform the employee of his or her right to be accompanied prior to the meeting.

Checklist

- ✓ Make sure you tailor your induction and probation procedures to employees' specific needs.
- ✓ Think carefully about how you will structure the new employee's first day – and make sure you are available!
- ✓ Use an induction checklist, to ensure you don't forget anything.
- ✓ Monitor the employee's progress and performance carefully during probation and meet regularly.
- ✓ If there are areas where performance is below standard, be honest and say so. Support the employee by being specific about what good performance 'looks like' and by providing additional coaching/training if needed.
- ✓ Confirm the employee in post at the end of the probationary period, if appropriate.
- ✓ In exceptional cases and if the employee's performance is not satisfactory, either extend the probationary period or terminate employment.
- ✓ If you terminate employment, remember to follow the three step statutory dismissal procedures.

Where to find out more

1.Acas
Acas has an advisory booklet on recruitment and induction. You can download a copy for free from their website, at:
   www.acas.org.uk/publications/B05.html. For more details of how to order Acas publications see page 36.

2. askNCVO
www.askncvo.org.uk offers a wealth of free, practical, up-to-date advice on all aspects of running a charity or voluntary organisation. Hundreds of pages cover trusteeship, financial management, human resources and more.

3. Business link
The Business Link website, www.businesslink.gov.uk has a very useful section on induction: www.businesslink.gov.uk.

References

1. Gordon et al (1991) and (Cox 1991)
2. Bauer and Green (1994)

6 Pay and benefits

What this chapter is about

Whilst organisations in the voluntary sector may not be able to pay the highest salaries, you still need to make sure you adhere to the law and that your pay system is fair – and is seen to be fair by your employees. Staff should understand how their pay is determined and where possible should be paid reasonably, relative to similar jobs in other organisations.

Staff should understand how their pay is determined and where possible should be paid reasonably, relative to similar jobs in other organisations.

This chapter tells you about the following areas:
- The Minimum Wage
- Equal pay/fair pay
- Setting and reviewing salary levels in smaller organisations
- Job evaluation
- Determining pay levels against the outcome of job evaluation
- Salary progression
- Developing a salary policy
- Pensions
- Other benefits
- Administering pay

The Minimum Wage

The National Minimum Wage Act 1998 says that you must pay at least the national minimum wage. This is an hourly rate set by the Government. It is reviewed each October. There are three rates of the National Minimum Wage:
- A rate for employees aged 22 and over.
- A development rate applicable to 18- to 21-year-olds (and to workers aged 22 and over during the first six months in new employment, who are receiving accredited training).
- A young workers' rate for 16- to 17-year-olds.

You can find out the current rates by calling the National Minimum Wage helpline on 0845 6000 678.

The Minimum Wage covers almost all workers in the UK. Not

all the money you pay a worker counts as pay for the purposes of the Minimum Wage. For example, allowances, such as London or regional allowances or shift allowances do not count, unless they are consolidated into an employee's basic pay.

The only benefit in kind which can be counted towards the Minimum Wage is accommodation. There are special rules for calculating the value of the accommodation provided which count towards the Minimum Wage.

Making sure you are paying the National Minimum Wage

There are different ways of calculating the hours that count towards the National Minimum Wage, depending on the type of work. This means that if the salaries you pay are relatively low, you may need to undertake some calculations to make sure you are paying the National Minimum Wage.

You can find out how to make the calculations by reviewing the Detailed Guide to the National Minimum Wage, available for download from the Department of Trade and Industry website www.dti.gov.uk/er/nmw/gtmw.pdf. Alternatively, you can call the minimum wage information line on 0845 8450 360 and ask them to send you a copy.

The National Minimum Wage helpline 0845 6000 678 can also provide general advice and assistance.

Equal pay/fair pay

The Equal Pay Act 1970 (amended by the Equal Pay Regulations 1983) says that men and women are entitled to equal pay for work of equal value. Equal pay includes basic pay as well as other contractual conditions of employment, such as hours of work, bonuses and pension contributions.

The Act requires that employers must pay men and women an equal wage when the work they do is:
- the same or like work
- of equal value
- or rated as equivalent via a job evaluation scheme.

Claims for equal pay are applicable only when comparing rates of pay with workers of the opposite gender.

Employees have the right to issue a questionnaire to their employer, asking for information to help them work out whether they have received equal pay, and if not, why.

Employees who believe they haven't received equal pay may take the case to an Employment Tribunal, which may use the information in the questionnaire.

An employer may be able to justify differences in pay, if there is a 'genuine material factor' or reason for the difference. Location may be such a genuine material factor.

For instance, a female employee based in London could be doing identical work to a male employee based elsewhere, but might receive a higher wage as a result of a London allowance.

An employer may also be able to justify differences in pay, if the difference came about because of a TUPE transfer (see chapter 4).

If an Employment Tribunal decides an employer is at fault, the employer may have to pay compensation and the rate of pay claimed may be backdated for up to six years (and in certain circumstances, further than this).

If you carry out regular reviews of your pay system, you can build and maintain a robust, fair pay system which stands up to scrutiny and is less susceptible to claims for equal pay. It is also more likely to be fair not only in terms of gender, but also in terms of matters such as race, disability and age. If you do not review your pay system regularly, you may find that anomalies have crept in over the years and that some differences in pay are no longer justifiable.

The Equal Opportunities Commission (EOC) publishes an equal pay toolkit called *A small business guide to effective pay practices* specifically for small businesses, on their website: www.eoc.org.uk/cseng/advice/equalpaygb.pdf. Alternatively, you can ask the EOC to send you the toolkit on CD ROM, by calling 0845 601 5901 or email info@eoc.org.uk.

> An employer may be able to justify differences in pay, if there is a 'genuine material factor' or reason for the difference.
>
> If you carry out regular reviews of your pay system, you can build and maintain a robust, fair pay system which stands up to scrutiny and is less susceptible to claims for equal pay.

Setting and reviewing salary levels in smaller organisations

The level of formality in your salary system is likely to depend on the size of your organisation.

If you are a small voluntary organisation, with, say, under 10 employees, you may be able to set salary levels in the following way:

- Determine a reasonable rate you can afford and that allows you to attract external recruits. You can determine this rate by looking at local advertisements for similar jobs and by checking with local contacts.
- Keep job descriptions up to date and review them regularly, so that you can make sure that they reflect the actual jobs done and responsibilities held.
- Review salary levels each year, to ensure they continue to reflect responsibility levels and external market rates.

Job evaluation

Once your organisation grows, you may start to need more formal systems, because it may become more difficult to determine relative levels of responsibility of jobs in an objective way. At this stage, you may wish to implement some form of job evaluation.

Job evaluation is the method by which jobs are assessed to determine their level of responsibility relative to each other. The principle is that those jobs which are more responsible will be rated higher in the job evaluation. Job evaluation does not determine pay and it does not assess the ability of the job holder, but it produces a hierarchy of jobs against which to set pay levels.

Job evaluation schemes fall into two types: analytical and non-analytical.

Analytical job evaluation

Analytical schemes are based on the analysis and scoring of elements ('factors') within jobs, as follows:

- A number of factors are selected and defined, such as technical knowledge and skills, freedom to act, interpersonal skills or decision making.
- Each of these factors is described at different levels. These levels are called 'factor definitions' (see below for an example).
- Each of the levels has a points score assigned to it.
- Each job is analysed against each factor and assigned to a level and points score.
- From the above analysis, a total points score for the job is produced.
- All jobs are ranked in terms of their total points score.
- Jobs are then graded according to their ranking.
- Rates of pay are allocated to the grade.

Example factor definitions – interpersonal skills

Level one of a five level factor definition on 'interpersonal skills' might be: 'the job requires the ability to deal courteously with others on the phone and in person, responding to their requests.'

The level five definition would require greater interpersonal skills and might be described as 'the job requires the ability to deal with complex negotiations with influential external bodies on behalf of the organisation; and to reconcile often differing priorities, resolving situations of conflict'.

Analytical job evaluation is a robust approach which should enable employers to defend an equal pay claim. However, it can be more time-consuming that non-analytical job evaluation and may be more appropriate to organisations which feel that they are of a size that needs a more rigorous approach to evaluating jobs.

If you wish to implement an analytical job evaluation scheme, you are advised to seek assistance from an external consultant.

Non-analytical job evaluation

Non-analytical schemes compare 'whole jobs' with one another — there is no attempt to distinguish between the factors within the jobs which may differentiate them. Non-analytical job evaluation is more suited to smaller organisations. Examples of non-analytical schemes are job ranking, paired comparison and job classification.

Under job ranking, all jobs are placed in rank order, based on a review of the responsibilities of each job. It is considered the simplest method since there is no attempt to break down or analyse the whole job in any way. It is therefore easy to understand and implement, particularly with a small number of jobs.

Example

A female office manager and a male supervisor in production may both be involved in allocating and checking work, providing technical advice and assistance, motivating staff, and making sure standards, such as timekeeping and attendance, are met. Even though they work in different areas, an analysis from a job ranking exercise may reveal that their jobs require similar levels of effort, skills, knowledge and responsibility.
(example from the Equal Opportunities Commission *Small Business Guide to Effective Pay Practices*.)

Here is an approach to a job ranking exercise:

Step 1
Planning
- Include all jobs in your organisation in the review, both full-time and part-time.
- Talk to your employees – tell them that you are undertaking the review. They may have comments on how pay arrangements actually operate, that you may not be aware of.

- Decide a good time to start and decide who will do the work – some time will need to be set aside.

Step 2
Analysing jobs
- Update all existing job descriptions.
- Produce job descriptions in a common format.
- Update the person specifications to go with each job description.
- Produce the person specifications in a common format, so that for each, the level of effort, skills, knowledge and responsibility are clearly defined.
- Agree the job descriptions and person specifications with your staff and their immediate managers.
- Assess all jobs. Come up with a rank order.

If you wish, you could undertake **'paired comparisons'**. This is a statistical technique used to compare each job with others. It is based on the premise that it is easier to compare one job with one other, rather than one job with several. Using a ranking form, points are allocated to the job:
- two points if it is considered to be of higher value
- one point if it is regarded as equal worth
- no points if it is less important.

A very simple ranking form might be as follows:

Job ref	A	B	C	D	E	F	Total score	ranking
A	-	0	0	0	I	0	I	=5
B	2	-	2	2	2	0	8	2
C	2	0	-	2	2	0	6	3
D	2	0	0	-	2	0	4	4
E	I	0	0	0	-	0	I	=5
F	2	2	2	2	2	-	10	I

Paired comparisons gives greater consistency, but takes longer than job ranking as each job is considered separately. It is therefore more appropriate for smaller numbers of jobs. Acas advises a maximum of 30 jobs – if you tried 50, it would require 1,225 comparisons!

Job classification is also a 'whole job' evaluation technique. With job classification, the number of grades is decided first and detailed grade definitions are then produced. Jobs are then slotted into the grades, by matching the job descriptions against the grade definitions. The grade definitions should be suited to and drafted for the jobs in your organisation. You can seek external support in achieving this, if you need to.

Job classification is relatively easy to understand but it can be difficult to classify very different jobs (e.g. a fundraising job compared with a project worker job) and some jobs may straddle grade definitions.

Here is an example classification system, reproduced from the Equal Opportunities Commission *Small Business Guide to Effective Pay Practices*.

Levels	Definitions
Foundation skill and knowledge (equivalent to NVQ/SVQ Level 1)	The job involves a range of routine and predictable tasks, carried out under supervision.
Intermediate skill and knowledge (equivalent to NVQ/SVQ Level 2)	The job involves a range of tasks, carried out with limited supervision in a variety of contexts. Some tasks are complex or non-routine and there is some personal responsibility or autonomy. Working in a group or team may often be a requirement.
Advanced skill and knowledge (equivalent to NVQ/SVQ Level 3)	The job involves a defined occupation or a range of jobs where there is a broad range of varied tasks carried out in a wide variety of contexts. Most tasks are complex and non-routine, and there is considerable personal responsibility and autonomy. Supervision or guidance of others is often required.
High skill and knowledge (equivalent to NVQ/SVQ Level 4)	The job involves a broad range of complex, technical, or professional work tasks, carried out in a variety of contexts. There is a substantial degree of personal responsibility and autonomy. Responsibility for the work of others and the allocation of resources is often required.
Very high skill and knowledge (equivalent to NVQ/SVQ Level 5)	The job involves work at a professional level or equivalent, requiring the mastery of a range of relevant knowledge and the ability to apply it at this level. There is very substantial personal autonomy. Significant responsibility for the work of others and for the allocation of substantial resources is often required, as are personal accountabilities for analysis and diagnosis, design, planning, execution and evaluation.

Determining pay levels against the outcome of job evaluation

Once you have evaluated your jobs and put them in a rank order, you will need to determine pay levels.

You will need to review existing annual salaries. You can plot annual salaries onto a spreadsheet if this assists you. The Equal Opportunities Commission advises that you should put down on the spreadsheet whether the employee is male or female. This helps you to assess for equal pay. You can plot on the spreadsheet current pay and then compare this with job evaluation rankings.

Assessing the reason for any differences

If there are any differences in pay levels compared with job evaluation ranking, you will need to consider the reason for the differences. It is possible that the differences may have come about for reasons which are no longer valid.

If you find any unfairness, for example that part-time workers are paid less for a job that requires a similar level of effort, skills, knowledge and responsibility, or that staff with shorter service (who may be predominantly women) are paid less, then you should look to address the anomalies as soon as you can.

Setting new salaries

You can set new salaries that reflect the outcome of your job evaluation.

When setting salaries, you should also take into account market rates of pay, because if you are paying well below market rates, it may be difficult to recruit and retain staff.

Sometimes, you may find that you need to pay a particular job more than others, on account of market rates, even though job evaluation indicates that it is not such a responsible job as those other jobs.

If this is the case, one approach is to pay a basic salary, plus a separate 'market supplement.' This sends a clear message as to why additional pay is being made and will remind you to review the payment against the market at a later date.

Take into account market rates of pay, because if you are paying well below market rates, it may be difficult to recruit and retain staff.

Salary surveys

In order to be able to assess market rates, you can use salary surveys.

You can **undertake your own salary survey.** Here are the steps you would need to take:

- Draft clear job descriptions for your jobs.
- Decide which organisations you wish to approach to exchange salary data. These organisations will be those which have similar jobs to yours.
- Approach the organisations, to see if they would be willing to participate in a salary survey.
- If they would, send them, on a confidential basis, details of your job descriptions, salaries and benefits.
- Gain information from the participant organisations on the salaries and benefits payable for similar jobs in their organisations.
- Summarise the data and give participant organisations a copy.

It is important to gain appropriate job matches and take into account factors such as the date salaries were last reviewed, any allowances and benefits. Salary data is also sensitive. For these reasons, organisations may prefer to ask an external consultant to conduct the salary survey on their behalf. A consultant will collect the salary data and will summarise the results, so that confidentiality of individual salaries is maintained.

As an alternative to conducting your own salary survey, you could **participate in an existing commercial survey**. Two significant salary surveys in the voluntary sector are those run by Croner Reward and Remuneration Economics. Contact details for these two organisations are at the end of this chapter.

If you participate in a survey, you will normally be given a copy of the survey results at reduced or no cost. If you do not participate, you may be able to purchase the survey (if it is not a 'members only' survey), but normally at a higher cost.

'The market rate'
There is a temptation to believe that there is a 'market rate' for each job. In fact, this is not the case. There will be a variety of pay rates and benefits in the external market for any one job. As a result of this, salary surveys do not always give consistent data. Where possible, you should use more than one survey and consider the information from each.

Setting salaries based on the market rate
Some organisations choose to set salaries based entirely on market rate information, rather than any form of job evaluation. However, it is advisable to pay attention both to market rates and to internal relativities. As mentioned above, market rates are not always consistent. In addition, salary survey data may simply

replicate any pay discrimination that exists in the wider employment market.

Salary progression

Once you have set broad pay rates, you will need to decide whether you wish to allow for salary progression and if so, in what form (e.g. based on length of service or performance). Consider all options and choose the most appropriate for your organisation.

If you are thinking of making a change to the way staff salaries may progress, make sure you consult with staff first, and involve them in the development of any new system. You should also check your employees' written statements of terms and conditions (their employment contracts) to check the contractual flexibility you may have to change terms. If, for example, your written statements give your employees the right to automatic incremental progression according to length of service, you will only be able to change this in respect of each individual employee, if you have that employee's agreement to do so.

Incremental salary scales

Some voluntary organisations link salaries to local authority salary scales. They may not link pay rates to specific local authority jobs, but simply place their salaries on the NJC (National Joint Council) pay spine. They may do this on the basis of a 'spot rate' (i.e. no increments are guaranteed), on the basis of automatic annual incremental progression (with a progression range, of, say 3-4 points), or on the basis of progression based on individual contribution/performance.

The advantages of using NJC scales are:
- The NJC scales are familiar to many staff, so they can understand their spinal point and compare it with other jobs externally.
- The NJC scales are familiar to funders, so it may be easier to obtain funding increases if pay rates are linked to NJC.

The disadvantages of using NJC scales may be:
- NJC scales increase by a certain percentage cost of living amount each year. If voluntary organisations follow these scales, then flexibility to pay what the organisation itself can afford may be limited.
- For example, an agreement made in September 2004 confirmed that there would be an increase on all scale points of 2.75 per cent backdated to 1 April 2004, 2.95 per cent from 1 April 2005, and 2.95 per cent (or the RPI [retail

> If you are thinking of making a change to the way staff salaries may progress, make sure you consult with staff first, and involve them in the development of any new system.

price index] at October 2005, whichever is the higher) from 1 April 2006. This means that if voluntary organisations follow the NJC scales, they must be able to afford these increases until April 2007.

- If voluntary organisations do not link their cost of living awards to NJC scales in any one year, but still maintain a pay structure 'based' on NJC rates, then it may give the impression to staff that they have 'missed out' on a pay increase.

If you decide to use the NJC scales, it is recommended that it be made clear to staff that incremental salary progression each year is not guaranteed, but dependent on affordability and is at trustee discretion.

If you decide to use the NJC scales, it is recommended that it be made clear to staff that incremental salary progression each year is not guaranteed.

Graded structure – not using NJC scales

As an alternative, you could develop a pay spine specific to your organisation. You can do this relatively simply on a spreadsheet, with increments of an agreed percentage e.g. 2 per cent or 3 per cent. Grades of, for example, three or five increments could simply be plotted onto the spreadsheet.

Example

EXAMPLE PAY SPINES WITH 3% AND 2% INCREMENTS		
SPINE POINT	3% INCREMENTS	2% INCREMENTS
1	£10,900	£10,900
2	£11,227	£11,118
3	£11,564	£11,340
4	£11,911	£11,567
5	£12,268	£11,799
6	£12,636	£12,034
7	£13,015	£12,275
8	£13,406	£12,521
9	£13,808	£12,771
10	£14,222	£13,027
11	£14,649	£13,287
12	£15,088	£13,553
13	£15,541	£13,824
14	£16,007	£14,100
15	£16,487	£14,382
16	£16,982	£14,670
17	£17,491	£14,963
18	£18,016	£15,263
19	£18,557	£15,568
20	£19,113	£15,879
21	£19,687	£16,197
22	£20,277	£16,521
23	£20,886	£16,851
24	£21,512	£17,188
25	£22,157	£17,532
26	£22,822	£17,883
27	£23,507	£18,240
28	£24,212	£18,605
29	£24,938	£18,977
30	£25,687	£19,357
31	£26,457	£19,744
32	£27,251	£20,139
33	£28,068	£20,541
34	£28,910	£20,952
35	£29,778	£21,371
36	£30,671	£21,799
37	£31,591	£22,235
38	£32,539	£22,679

One matter to consider, if you want to introduce an incremental salary structure, is that long salary scales based on length of service could be seen as discriminatory against women, who tend to have more career breaks and job changes. It is best to keep the number of increments relatively short to avoid this.

Spot rate structure

Some voluntary organisations have a 'spot rate' structure, rather than salary scales.

A 'spot rate' structure can be cheaper than an incremental structure, as there is no expectation that an annual increment will be paid as well as a cost of living award.

The disadvantage of a spot rate structure is that it can be relatively inflexible.

An individual may be recruited on a different spot rate (for example, due to experience) compared with those already in the same type of post. This can cause the spot rate structure to erode. Over time, the rationale for the pay difference may be forgotten or may be no longer relevant.

Sometimes organisations combine a spot rate system with a system of bonuses paid on the basis of individual performance. However, be aware that in a small voluntary organisation, the payment of bonuses to some staff and not others could be divisive.

Linking pay to performance/competence

Some organisations link salary increases directly to performance or competencies, as assessed in the performance appraisal. In these cases, the employee will be awarded higher pay when he or she has met pre-agreed targets.

Such targets may include concrete achievements – such as achieving certain fundraising targets – or may involve demonstrating competence in a new area, such as the use of information technology or the display of specific behaviours such as good team working, communication skills or planning/organising.

Whilst there may be an attraction in the inherent logic of paying for individual performance ('if an individual is performing better, they should be paid more'), the reality of linking pay to individual performance or contribution can be difficult. Paying employees differently according to performance can be divisive and demotivate those who are 'solid performers' but who get no additional pay award. Managers can be reluctant to implement such systems. The annual appraisal system would need to be sufficiently robust in design and implementation to enable

The reality of linking pay to individual performance or contribution can be difficult.

121

judgements to be made about performance awards.

You should also note that linking pay and performance is likely to change the focus of the appraisal meeting, because a member of staff will be conscious that the outcome of the appraisal will determine his or her pay.

Acas makes the following points in its publication about appraisal-related pay (ARP), which can be downloaded from the Acas website at www.acas.org.uk/publications/B10.html.

- There must be commitment to ARP from senior managers.
- The role of managers is critical.
- Adequate resources and suitable training should be provided.
- Employers should consult with managers, employees and their representatives before ARP is introduced.
- All employees involved must receive full and clear information about how the scheme will operate.
- ARP should be fair and open and based on a formal system of performance assessment.
- The scheme should be carefully designed, simple to operate and should encourage consistency and objectivity.
- There should be an appeals procedure and the scheme should be regularly evaluated.

You should also remember that factors other than pay can motivate workers.

You should also remember that factors other than pay can motivate workers. These factors might include feedback, supervision, training and consultation, work-life balance and they sometimes lead to better retention rates.

Linking pay to qualifications

Some organisations link pay increase to qualifications. This can be less subjective than linking pay to performance (as you either have a qualification or you have not). Consider, though, which qualifications you wish your employees to attain in order to progress their salaries. Think also about whether you can link pay increases to qualifications for all employees, or whether the system may in fact only be relevant to some.

As an alternative to linking pay increases to qualifications, you could consider making a small lump sum bonus payment, when an individual achieves a qualification.

Developing a salary policy

You should consider developing a salary policy, so that all staff and managers are clear about how pay is reviewed.

Your salary policy could include the following:

- A statement of intent, explaining the organisation's

commitment to an open and fair pay system, paying within its resources.
- The normal pay review date.
- How jobs are evaluated.
- What salary progression, if any, exists.
- The criteria for pay increases.
- The process that staff can follow if they feel that their pay is unfair.

Case study

The following case study shows how one organisation aimed to have a fair and open pay system and developed a salary policy. What suits one organisation will not necessarily suit the next, so make sure what you do fits the requirements of your organisation.

When the Westwich Association (WA) recruited its first employee (see chapter 1), it set pay by reviewing salaries of similar jobs in the local area, and considering what it could afford.

As it took on more employees over the years, these employees were recruited on a similar basis, but also taking into account the salaries of employees already in post.

By the time WA employed its tenth employee, the trustees decided to review pay. Some jobs had grown in scope, whilst others had stayed the same or grown smaller. Salaries had not changed with these changes in job size. The salaries of new recruits were not always consistent with the salaries of existing staff.

As a first step, WA decided to implement a salary policy. The development of the salary policy helped the trustees to agree between themselves how salaries should be reviewed, when they should be reviewed, who should be responsible for reviewing them, what criteria should be taken into account if increasing pay and what employees should do if they were unhappy about their pay.

The trustees consulted with employees about the policy, made some amendments as a result and then produced the final version.

> With the involvement of employees, job descriptions were reviewed and jobs assessed on a 'whole job' basis, taking into account the level of effort, skills, knowledge and responsibility required for each job.
>
> As a result of the review, it was clear that there was a need to review some salaries that had fallen behind, compared with the level of responsibility of the jobs.
>
> The trustees used the annual pay increase budget to give each employee a small cost of living award, with the remainder of the budget being used to deal with the salary adjustments.

Pensions

From the point at which you employ your fifth employee, you must, within three months, provide your employees with access to a stakeholder pension scheme.

You may be exempt from the above requirement if you:

- offer all employees aged 18 or over a personal pension scheme through which you contribute an amount equal to at least three per cent of the employees' basic pay;
- or offer an occupational pension scheme that all your staff can join within a year of starting to work for you.

If you have an occupational scheme or an arrangement with a personal pension provider (often called a group personal pension scheme), you should check with the provider of the scheme to find out if it meets the conditions for being exempt.

Even if you are exempt you can still give your employees access to a stakeholder pension scheme if you want to.

Stakeholder pension schemes must satisfy certain criteria:

- Currently the pension scheme provider cannot charge more than one per cent a year of the individual's fund.
- Members must be able to transfer into and out of a stakeholder pension scheme, or stop paying into one, without facing additional charges.
- All stakeholder schemes must accept minimum contributions of as little as £20, which can be paid each week, each month or at less regular intervals. Some offer an even lower limit.
- The schemes must be run in the interest of members. They are either run by trustees or by the scheme manager.

Even if you are exempt you can still give your employees access to a stakeholder pension scheme if you want to.

Your obligations include:
- Consulting the employees or their representatives as to the choice of scheme.
- Supplying all employees with information about the scheme.
- Affording representatives of the scheme reasonable access to employees to provide information about the scheme.
- Agreeing, on request, to collect employees' contributions from their pay and remit them to the scheme.

You do not have to make contributions to your employees' stakeholder pension. They are not obliged to make contributions either.

There is no charge for employees changing their contribution amounts. They cannot change the amount more than once every six months, unless you as the employer agree to it.

Employee access

You do not have to provide access to a stakeholder pension for any employee:
- who has worked for you for less than three months in a row;
- who is a member of your occupational pension scheme;
- who cannot join your occupational scheme because they are under 18 or they are within five years of the scheme's normal pension age;
- who decided not to join your occupational pension scheme;
- whose earnings have fallen below the National Insurance lower earnings limit for one or more weeks within the last three months;
- who cannot join a stakeholder pension scheme because of Inland Revenue restrictions (for example, the employee does not normally live in the UK).

Selecting and implementing your stakeholder pension

You can choose a stakeholder pension scheme from the list of providers registered with the Pensions Regulator. You can see the Pensions Regulator's register of approved stakeholder pension schemes at www.thepensionsregulator.gov.uk/stakeholderPensions/theRegister/index.aspx or you can write to request a copy. Full contact details are in the 'further information' section at the end of this chapter.

Once you have compared some different stakeholder pension schemes and you have made your choice, you then need to do the following:
- discuss your choice of scheme with your eligible employees;
- designate (formally choose) your stakeholder pension

> You do not have to make contributions to your employees' stakeholder pension. They are not obliged to make contributions either.

scheme;

- give your employees the name and address of the stakeholder pension scheme;
- tell your employees about your payroll deduction arrangements;
- make the payroll deductions if an employee wants you to;
- send your employee contributions (and any employer contributions) to the stakeholder pension scheme provider within the given time limits; and
- record the payments you make to the stakeholder pension scheme provider.

For further information about stakeholder pensions, you can go to the Government website www.thepensionservice.gov.uk/employer/stakeholder-introduction.asp.

Other benefits

Annual leave

The legal entitlement to annual leave is four weeks, inclusive of bank and public holidays. However, most organisations offer at least four weeks plus bank and public holidays and some may offer five or even six weeks.

Whilst voluntary organisations cannot pay the highest salaries, annual leave is an area where it may be possible to be more generous.

Consider what annual leave provision you can afford and consider also what similar voluntary organisations are offering.

Sick pay

You have an obligation to provide employees who fall ill and cannot work with a minimum level of sick pay. This is known as Statutory Sick Pay (SSP).

Employees are normally entitled to SSP if they are unable to work for four or more consecutive days. SSP can be paid for an upper time limit of 28 weeks for a single period of illness.

SSP is liable to tax and National Insurance Contributions (NIC). You can find out about keeping records for SSP and about the current rate, from the Inland Revenue website www.inlandrevenue.gov.uk/cbr-ssp/index.htm.

You may be able to reclaim a proportion of any SSP you pay. For this to happen, the total SSP payments in any tax month must exceed 13 per cent of the overall gross Class 1 NICs for the entire business. You can then recover the difference between the two. In other words, the recoverable SSP is the amount above 13 per cent of the total NIC liability. Contact the Inland Revenue for more information.

You are free to have a contractual sick pay agreement with your employees above the minimum payment. The contractual sick pay should include SSP payments. In setting contractual sick pay, consider what other similar employers pay and also consider what you could afford to pay, should someone be on long-term sick leave.

Flexitime
Many voluntary sector employers offer flexibility in working times and arrangements. For more information about flexitime, see chapter 8.

Parental benefits
For more information on parental benefits, see chapter 8.

Counselling
You could consider offering access to employee counselling, where needed.

Low cost or no cost benefits
There are lots of benefits you could offer your employees, at low cost or no cost. Some examples are listed below:

Childcare vouchers
As of 5 April 2005 employers can provide childcare vouchers up to a value of £50 per week free from tax and National Insurance Contributions.

To take advantage of this tax beneficial offer the employee makes a contractual agreement to give up part of their salary in exchange for the vouchers. This is known as salary sacrifice. Their employer also needs to have negotiated and implemented a voucher scheme with an appropriate provider. You must make sure that an employee does not take a salary sacrifice such that their new salary falls below the National Minimum Wage.

An employee can save up to £850 per year by not paying 11 per cent NIC and standard rate tax on the vouchers. Employees paying higher rate tax could save over £1,000 per year.

There is no cost to the employer apart from the administration costs and the management fee to the voucher company. However, the savings a company makes in terms of reduced NICs usually exceeds the management fee charged by the voucher company.

Any scheme that is implemented needs to be open to all

employees not just to specific groups of staff. Both parents who are working can claim the benefit on the same child.

For more information on providing childcare vouchers, including information on voucher providers, see the Daycare Trust website at www.daycaretrust.org.uk. Full contact details for the Daycare Trust are at the end of this chapter.

Staff discounts

There are several discounts you may be able to negotiate locally. For example, you might be able to negotiate a staff discount at your local gym. You could also alert your staff to the website www.thankq.org which provides a wide range of discounts for workers in the voluntary sector. Any worker in the voluntary sector can register for free on the website.

Buying and selling annual leave

Some staff may wish for more annual leave than the standard provision in your organisation. You could allow staff to take, say, an additional five days unpaid leave per year ('buying leave'). Some staff may prefer less annual leave and to be paid for the days they do not take, again up to a maximum of five days ('selling leave'). Make sure, though, that employees still take the minimum statutory leave of 20 days (inclusive of bank and public holidays).

Interest free travel loans

You could offer interest free travel loans, for staff to purchase season tickets.

Workplace facilities

You could offer a variety of workplace facilities at low cost, such as:

- access to the internet for personal use in lunchtimes and before/after work;
- online ordering of groceries and delivery to workplace;
- prayer room to accommodate all religious requirements (or a meeting room/office set aside at certain times of the day);
- access to local independent financial consultation 'on site';
- microwave, grill and fridge facilities;
- free tea and coffee.

Administering pay

Most frequently, pay is made weekly or monthly by cheque or credit transfer. Under the Wages Act 1986 an employee can no longer insist on being paid in cash.

Issuing pay statements

As an employer you are legally obliged to give each employee a written itemised pay statement, usually known as a payslip or wage slip. You must issue it at, or before, the time you pay your employee. You do not need to give such a pay statement to people you pay who are non-employees, such as consultants and contractors.

The itemised pay statement must show:
- the gross amount of the wages or salary before deductions;
- the amounts of – and reasons for – any fixed deductions that you make every pay period and any variable deductions that are not the same every pay period;
- the net amount of wages or salary payable after deductions;
- a breakdown of each part-payment – such as part by cheque, part in cash.

The pay statement does not have to include the amount and purpose of every separate fixed deduction every time, but if you don't issue a payslip that does this, you must give the employee a standing statement of fixed deductions at least every 12 months.

If there is any change to an employee's fixed deductions, you must give them either:
- notification in writing of the details of the change;
- an amended standing statement of fixed deductions, which is then valid for up to 12 months.

Making deductions from pay

Ensure that any deductions you make from a worker's pay are allowed for in their contract. Otherwise, you could be in breach of their contract.

A deduction is unlawful unless:
- It is legally authorised, e.g. PAYE income tax and National Insurance Contributions.
- It is allowed by the worker's contract. If this is the case, the worker must have been shown the term or notified in writing of its effect before the deduction is made.
- Workers have agreed in writing before you deduct pay for other reasons, e.g. as loan repayments or pension contributions.

> Ensure that any deductions you make from a worker's pay are allowed for in their contract.

Payments on leaving

When an employee leaves your organisation, you will need to give them:
- Any outstanding pay to the date of leaving.
- Holiday pay.
- Pay in lieu of notice, if you dismissed them (apart from

for gross misconduct) and did not give them their full notice period.

- Any bonus payments, if earned.
- Statutory Sick Pay, if entitled.
- Statutory Maternity Pay, if entitled.

You will need to deduct:

- Tax and National Insurance as normal.
- Any money for outstanding loans, such as a season ticket loan.

Your payroll system

As an employer, you are under an obligation to set up a payroll system, to ensure you deduct the correct tax and National Insurance from your employees' pay and submit the deductions to the Inland Revenue.

When you become an employer for the first time, the Inland Revenue will send you a new employer's starter pack, with all the tables, forms and information you will need to operate your payroll. Chapter 1 gives some information about this.

For further information on your tax and National Insurance responsibilities, you can contact the Inland Revenue Established Employers Helpline on 08457 143 143 or the Payroll Support Unit Helpline on 0845 915 7690.

Outsourcing your payroll function

Calculating tax and National Insurance can be time-consuming and complicated. You may also need to deal with tax credits, maternity pay and pensions.

Many small organisations choose to outsource their payroll functions, so that they can concentrate on their main business.

If you are considering outsourcing your payroll, you could do this either via an accountant's services, or via a specialist payroll service company.

When assessing a possible supplier, consider the following:

- Whether they are experienced with your type and size of organisation.
- Whether they can supply monthly payslips, and provide monthly and annual returns.
- The charge for setting up the payroll system.
- The charge for administering the system.
- Whether the fees include making all the types of deductions.
- Whether they charge any additional fees.
- What software they use, whether it is Inland Revenue accredited, and if it is compatible with your own.

Checklist

✓ Consider the principles of your pay system. Embrace the principles of fairness, openness and responsibility.

✓ Make sure you pay the national minimum wage. Make calculations if you are not sure.

✓ Audit your pay system regularly to ensure you are paying equal pay for work of equal value and that your pay system is fair.

✓ Decide on a systematic way of setting and reviewing salary level, commensurate with the size of your organisation.

✓ Consider forms of salary progression – but be wary of giving guaranteed annual increments unless you are sure you will be able to afford them in the future.

✓ Consider developing a salary policy, so that all staff know how pay is set and reviewed.

✓ Provide a stakeholder pension for your employees, from the point at which you employ your fifth employee (unless you are exempt).

✓ Provide other benefits such as paid annual leave and sick pay, which comply with the law and are as competitive and generous as you can afford.

✓ Investigate low cost/no cost benefits and implement any suitable for your organisation.

Where to find out more

You can get free information from the following organisations:

1. Acas

There are three Acas advisory booklets that may be of assistance. The names of the booklets and where they can be accessed on the Acas website are indicated below:

The Advisory Booklet – Job Evaluation
www.acas.org.uk/publications/B01.html
The Advisory Booklet – Pay Systems
www.acas.org.uk/publications/B02.html
The Advisory Booklet – Appraisal Related Pay
www.acas.org.uk/publications/B10.html

For more details of how to order Acas publications see page 36.

2. The Department of Trade and Industry (DTI)

You can access the Detailed guide to the National Minimum Wage, from the Department of Trade and Industry website www.dti.gov.uk/er/nmw/gtmw.pdf.

3. Equal Opportunities Commission

The Equal Opportunities Commission publishes an equal pay toolkit *A small business guide to effective pay practices specifically for small businesses*, on their website: www.eoc.org.uk/cseng/advice/equalpaygb.pdf. Alternatively, you can ask the EOC to send you the toolkit on CD ROM, by calling 0845 601 5901 or email info@eoc.org.uk.

4. Ask NCVO

www.askncvo.org.uk offers a wealth of free, practical, up-to-date advice on all aspects of running a charity or voluntary organisation. Hundreds of pages cover trusteeship, financial management, human resources and more.

5. Business Link

The Business Link website contains information on all aspects of pay and benefits, including the Minimum Wage, equal pay and pensions. Go to www.businesslink.gov.uk and in the search field, enter the topic you want to look at.

6. Croner Reward

Croner Reward produces an annual survey of salaries and benefits in the not-for-profit sector.

Contact details are as follows:
Tel: 01785 813566
Fax: 01785 817007
Email: enquiries@croner-reward.co.uk
Website: www.croner-reward.co.uk

7. Remuneration Economics

Remuneration Economics produces an annual voluntary sector salary survey, in association with NCVO.
CELRE
Survey House
51 Portland Road
Kingston upon Thames
Surrey
KT1 2SH

Tel: 020 8549 8726
Fax: 020 8541 5705
Email: info@celre.co.uk
Website: www.celre.co.uk

8. The Pensions Regulator

The Pensions Regulator has information about stakeholder pension schemes, as well as a register of approved stakeholder pension schemes. You can access both on the website www.thepensionsregulator.gov.uk.

Alternatively, you can write to the Pensions Regulator for information.

The Pensions Regulator
Napier House
Trafalgar Place
Brighton
BN1 4DW

Tel: 0870 6063636
9am to 5pm, Monday to Friday
Fax: 0870 2411144
Email: customersupport@thepensionsregulator.gov.uk

9. The Daycare Trust

The Daycare Trust has some useful information about childcare voucher schemes.

Daycare Trust
21 St George's Road
London SE1 6ES

Tel: 020 7840 3350
Fax: 020 7840 3355
Email info@daycaretrust.org.uk
Website: www.daycaretrust.org.uk

7 Supervising and developing your staff

What this chapter is about

This chapter contains information about how to supervise and develop your staff. It covers the following areas:
- The legal position
- Producing a learning and development policy
- Developing an annual learning and development plan
- Evaluating learning and development
- Staff supervision and annual appraisal
- Structuring your supervision and appraisal meetings
- Supervision and appraisal forms
- Dealing with performance problems
- Avoiding bias in appraising your staff
- Developing yourself as a manager
- Investors in People

The legal position

There are the following legal rights and obligations concerning employee development:

The Health and Safety at Work Act 1974 states that an employer must provide adequate health and safety training for its employees.

The Offices, Shops and Railway Premises Act 1963 requires an employer to provide training to employees on escape routes and the fire drill.

Young persons aged 16 or 17 who are not qualified to NVQ level 2 and in full-time work are entitled to a reasonable amount of paid time off for study or training.

Employers must allow reasonable time off for representatives of independent trade unions for training, where the union is represented for collective bargaining purposes.

Further, employers must give reasonable time off for training to Union Learning Representatives and to carry out their duties.

Producing a learning and development policy

It can be useful to produce a learning and development policy, for the following reasons:

- it makes clear to your staff your stance on employee development;
- the process of drafting the policy will help you to clarify what staff development you want to do and why;
- you will be able to refer to it in the future as a 'prompt' as to what you should be doing.

Here is an example policy statement, which you could use as a basis for drafting your own statement:

Example policy statement on learning and development

> (Organisation) recognises that its most important resource is its employees. We are committed to employee learning and development, in line with available resources.
> Appropriately trained and skilled employees will be able to assist (organisation) to achieve our objective of providing specialised, high quality care and rehabilitation to vulnerable people.
> Individual learning and development needs will be identified mainly through the staff supervision and appraisal process. Once identified, these needs will form a part of (organisation's) annual learning and development plan.
> The learning and development needs identified will be met through a variety of activities. These activities may include:
> - shadowing another member of staff
> - planned reading
> - working through a computer based package
> - off the job training
> - a qualification or an NVQ
> - mentoring
> - coaching.
>
> All internal training provided will be of no cost to the employee. External courses and professional qualifications may be fully or partly funded, depending on the following criteria:
> - the relevance to the job;
> - the funds available;
> - whether the learning need can be met in another way.
>
> Employees are asked to provide feedback on the value and effectiveness of the learning and development activity they undertake, so that it can be further improved for the future. This policy applies to all employees.

Developing an annual learning and development plan

Whilst some learning and development activities will occur on an 'ad hoc' basis, it can be helpful to plan ahead and develop an annual plan, for the following reasons:

- It helps you to take a strategic approach to learning and development. You can think about what your organisation is planning to achieve and consider whether the skills your staff have are sufficient and relevant to meet the needs of your organisation.
- You can budget for planned activities – it is more difficult to budget for unplanned ones!
- If you collate learning and development needs across the organisation, you can see which staff members have the same need, and plan a learning activity for all of them.

Below is a possible format for your annual learning and development plan:

Learning need identified from annual appraisal	Link with organisational strategy	Staff who need the learning and development	Suggested activity	Likely cost	Proposed date
e.g. making bids for funds	We will need to raise £30,000 from external bids over the next financial year	John, Rima	Frances is already experienced at this – she will work through a bid with them.	Staff time only	By April 2006 at the latest
Etc					

Evaluating learning and development

It is important to evaluate the effectiveness of learning and development activities, so that you can plan for future activities and follow up on any learning needs that have not been met.

Prior to any planned learning, such as a training course or computer based learning, clarify with the employee the objectives of the learning.

After the planned learning, discuss with the employee the extent to which the objectives were met. You could also ask the employee to complete a brief evaluation form immediately after the event.

At the annual appraisal, you could look back at the planned learning and assess the extent to which the learning has been applied in the workplace.

It is important to evaluate the effectiveness of learning and development activities, so that you can plan for future activities.

Supervision and appraisal

Staff supervision

Staff supervision is the process of regular one to one meetings with your employees to discuss:

- progress in achieving work plans
- any problems
- the next steps.

Regular staff supervision meetings can help employees to feel that their work is noticed and valued and can help them keep on track for future work.

Supervision meetings can be held at a frequency which suits your organisation and the experience of the job holders. For example, you may wish to meet fortnightly with a new employee and monthly or even quarterly with more experienced employees. Pick a frequency that suits best.

Appraisal

The annual appraisal is a yearly review of the individual's work progress and performance. It should be a round up of what has been achieved. If you have been holding regular supervision meetings and discussions with your employee, the annual appraisal should hold no surprises.

It can be useful to gain feedback from a variety of sources when undertaking an individual's appraisal. You could ask for comments (where relevant) from service users, volunteers, colleagues and staff managed. This process is called '360 degree feedback' and can give a broad view of the individual's performance. However, if you intend to seek feedback in this way, discuss it with your staff first and gain their agreement. Be clear exactly how it will operate and think about how you will preserve anonymity with sensitive or difficult feedback. Because of the sensitivity of 360 degree feedback, some organisations use an external organisation to collate feedback confidentially.

It is worth training all supervisors and managers in supervision and appraisal. This could cover matters such as the importance of the scheme, giving feedback, setting objectives and dealing with poor performance. It is particularly important that all managers are committed to supervision and appraisal. If they are not, the system will soon fall into disuse and become discredited. You could consider including in managers' own appraisals an assessment of how well they supervise and appraise their staff.

Structuring your appraisal and supervision meetings

The annual appraisal meeting will probably be a longer meeting than your regular supervision meetings. You may not need to cover all the areas outlined below at each supervision meeting. However, the principles and format for each are similar.

Preparation
Have available prior to the meeting:
- a copy of the notes of the employee's last supervision or appraisal meeting
- their job description.

Hold the meeting in a room where you will not have interruptions and set aside sufficient time for the meeting.

Consider the key points you want to raise and make a note of them.

Give the employee at least a few days' notice of the meeting so that he or she has the time to prepare too. Ask the employee to look at his or her previous supervision or appraisal forms and to consider work undertaken since the last review.

Format for the meeting
A useful format is the WASP format:

Welcome
Ask
Supply
Plan and part

Welcome the employee. Try and put him or her at ease if needed. Offer a drink and explain the format of the meeting. Try and create an unhurried atmosphere, so that the employee does not feel that you are trying to rush things in order to get to something more important.

Ask the employee to give his or her views on work progress since the last appraisal or supervision meeting – what they are proud of as well as anything they feel could have gone better. You could ask them to consider what they think their main contribution has been to the work of the organisation.

If you are concerned about any aspect of the employee's performance, it may well be that the employee is too! It is easier for the employee to accept feedback and easier for you to give it, if the employee is able to state the concerns first.

Use phrases that encourage the employee to talk about their work, such as:

- Tell me a bit more about that.
- I can see there is a problem, but what do you think might help?
- What support do you think you need to become more familiar with ... ?

Avoid phrases which may discourage the employee from talking:

- It's really quite easy when you get the hang of it, it won't take long.
- If I were you ...
- You'll be OK, don't worry.
- Everything's going fine, I expect?

If the employee has had specific objectives/targets to achieve over the past year, ask the employee his/her views on the extent to which these were achieved, to standard and to deadline.

Once you have given the employee full opportunity to talk, supply your comments.

Confirm anything you think went particularly well. Explain what you think the employee did that made things go well. This can help reinforce good performance for the future.

Discuss with the employee the areas he or she has identified that could have gone better. If you feel that there are work performance problems that the employee has not mentioned, raise these with the employee now. Give specific examples of your concerns. Jointly consider the possible reasons for problems and consider how the situation could be improved in the future. Make clear how you want their performance to change – what good performance looks like.

Explore reasons beyond the employee's control why things may have gone less well than planned. However, ensure that neither of you uses this as a means of avoiding a discussion on any work performance problems that the employee may have.

You might, particularly in the annual appraisal, also discuss the following areas with your employee:

- Whether they are clear about all the responsibilities of their role – you could use the job description as a basis for these discussions.
- If they feel that any aspects of their role should be changed.
- Whether they feel that there is adequate opportunity to discuss the work they are doing with you.
- What they feel that you as a manager could do to further assist them in their role.

- The training and development activities they have undertaken since the last appraisal or supervision meeting.
- The benefits from the activities.
- Any further need for training and development.
- Whether the employee has particular skills and knowledge that your organisation could perhaps use and is not currently using.

The next stage of the meeting is to **plan** for what next. Jointly agree what follow-up actions should be taken, by whom and by when. If you are holding a supervision meeting, you can discuss what work tasks the employee needs to achieve by the next meeting. If you are holding an annual appraisal, discuss the targets for the forthcoming year. It is a good idea to make the targets SMART, that is:

Specific
Measurable
Achievable
Relevant
Time-bound

Before you close the meeting, check with the employee if they have any other comments or matters they wish to raise. Thank the employee for their time. Inform them of the next steps:

- That you will write up the key points from the discussion.
- That you will give them a copy to sign and keep; and that a copy will be put on their personal file.
- When they can expect to receive the written document.

Dealing with performance problems in an appraisal or supervision meeting

The most difficult appraisal and supervision meetings tend to be those where you feel that an employee is not performing satisfactorily in his or her job. Below are some ideas on how you might handle these meetings.

Preparation
You'll need to do your normal preparation, but in addition, it may help to:

- List the main areas of concern and prioritise them.
- Think of examples of when the employee's performance has caused concern and why.
- Think about some positive aspects of the employee's performance – it is easier to receive criticism if it is balanced by some positive feedback.

Welcome

Try something like: 'I think this has been quite a difficult period with a number of challenges. The purpose of the meeting today is to look at what has gone well, what not so well and how we can deal with any difficulties.'

Try and keep the meeting supportive and not adversarial – you are trying to look for ways to improve the employee's performance and you will achieve this best if the discussion remains constructive.

Ask

You should ask the employee to give feedback (self-appraise) on their own performance. However, sometimes when an employee is not performing well, he or she may be defensive and unwilling to give a view on his or her performance. Give the employee the opportunity to self-appraise, but be prepared to be more directive in giving feedback if needed.

You should also give the employee the opportunity to explain any reasons for difficulties in doing their job – there may be personal circumstances of which you are not aware, for example.

Give the employee the opportunity to explain any reasons for difficulties in doing their job.

Supply

Give specific instances of concern and concentrate on the employee's performance, not personality. For example: 'You take a slapdash approach to your work', is not only likely to invoke a defensive response of 'No I don't!', but is also unspecific.

It is much better to give examples, such as: 'I am concerned that on (date), you didn't send out all the documentation to the conference delegates. As a result, they had less than a week to register for the conference. We spoke about this at the time and I want to discuss how things have gone since then.' This then gives you the opportunity either to confirm that improvements have occurred, or that the same behaviour is being displayed. Either way, you should continue to give specific examples for discussion.

Think about what the employee can cope with – if your point has been accepted, it may be appropriate not to give every example of poor performance, but the main ones.

Targets for the future

Be specific about what you want the employee to do next. Sometimes, it is particular behaviours that are causing the poor performance. You might therefore want to include some objectives about behaviour ('competencies'), as well as about specific tasks to be achieved. For example, if communication is a problem, you might have targets of: 'Show respect and courtesy to others at all times and listen attentively', or: 'Keep manager informed on a weekly basis about progress with updating the contacts database.'

Writing up the notes of the meeting

You need to be very careful about writing the supervision notes or appraisal. It needs to be specific as to the concerns, what will be done by each of you to address them, the timescale for improvement and when you will meet again.

If the situation later reaches the stage where you have to pursue the disciplinary procedure on the grounds of continued poor performance, it is not helpful if supervision and performance appraisal notes give a glowing picture of the employee when this is not in fact the case.

Case study – dealing with a performance problem

The general manager of the Westwich Association (WA) has received some complaints regarding a member of staff who has been working at the Association for some time.

The complaints concern the employee's behaviour towards others. According to the complainants, the individual has adopted a manner which can be rude, abrupt and critical. This is upsetting for anyone dealing with this person. This behaviour is, as far as the general manager knows, relatively new; there were no complaints up until relatively recently.

The general manager plans to raise the matter at the employee's supervision meeting the following week. She is anxious about raising the matter, because she has found the employee to be 'touchy' about feedback in the past. However, she reminds herself that this is a 'difficult', not 'impossible' employee.

She plans to undertake the supervision meeting as follows:

She will start by asking the employee about how her work is progressing, her achievements and any problems. The general manager intends to listen, to give the employee the chance to talk. She wants to try and keep the meeting positive, whilst also making her concerns clear.

If the employee raises any concerns about working relationships, the general manager will use this opportunity to raise the matter with her. She intends to start with praise (commenting on how efficient the employee is), but then ask the employee about how she deals with others.

She will then give specific instances of when the employee appears to have been impatient with others. She will ask the employee for her views. She intends to concentrate on behaviour, not on personality. The general manager intends to use some examples of the inappropriate behaviour that she herself has witnessed, so that she does not need to mention the individuals who have complained.

The general manager intends to encourage self-appraisal –asking the employee if there is anything she might approach in a different manner in future.

The general manager will also ask the employee if there is anything worrying her that is causing her to behave differently. If the employee says there is, the general manager will treat this confidentially, provide support where appropriate, whilst still explaining that the behaviour is not appropriate.

Finally, the general manager intends to end by asking the employee to summarise the areas of her performance that are going well and what can be done to ensure the employee's whole performance is at this standard.

The general manager knows that she will need to be flexible in the meeting and that it may go a little differently from her plan. However, by planning in advance, she feels more confident about what she wants to achieve and how she will do it.

Supervision and appraisal forms

The forms you use can be less important than the actual discussion itself. However, it is very useful to capture the main points of your discussions.

You could draft a simple form which covers the main areas for discussion.

A supervision form could cover the following headings:
- progress with work since last meeting
- particular achievements
- any difficulties discussed and measures to overcome them
- progress with learning and development
- tasks for the period until next supervision meeting
- any other matters arising
- a section for the employee to add his or her views.

An appraisal form might follow a similar format but is likely to be more detailed. It could cover the following areas:

- review of objectives from over the past year
- review of job description
- learning and development completed over the past year
- objectives for the forthcoming year
- amendments to job description if needed
- learning and development plans of the forthcoming year
- a section for the employee to add his or her views.

Some appraisal forms include 'competencies' – the behaviours and capabilities that indicate good performance in the job. The idea is that discussion is held between the manager and the employee, using specific examples, as to the extent to which the employee meets the competencies, and where further development is needed.

Acas has the following examples of competencies in its *Advisory Booklet on Employee Appraisal*, available at www.acas.org.uk/publications/B07.html.

- **Dependability** – The degree to which this person can be counted upon to do what is required in carrying out assigned tasks and to meet deadlines. This could include comments on attendance and punctuality.
- **Innovation** – The degree to which methods and policies are continuously examined and suggestions made for new and better ones.
- **Staff development** – Consideration for subordinates shown; their performance planned, monitored, appraised and developed.
- **Communication** – Ability to convey verbal and/or written information.
- **Teamwork** – Work relationships established with fellow employees within and outside immediate work group.

Below is an example appraisal form taken from the Acas *Advisory Booklet on Employee Appraisal*, available at www.acas.org.uk/publications/B07.html.

Example appraisal form

Name _____

Job title _____

Department _____

_____

Length of time in post _____ Date of appraisal _____

1 Job description (To be agreed with the employee)

_____

_____

_____

_____

2 Objectives for review period

Include any special tasks, personal training and development

_____

_____

_____

_____

3 Progress towards achievement of objectives and factors influencing results

_____

_____

_____

_____

4 Other achievements

_____

_____

_____

_____

5 Were there any obstacles to the achievement of agreed objectives?

_____

_____

_____

_____

6 What steps can be taken to overcome these obstacles?

_____

_____

_____

_____

7 Training, development, education undertaken during review period

_____

_____

_____

_____

Planned for period to next review

_____
_____
_____
_____

8 Summary of objectives for next annual review period

_____
_____
_____
_____

Overall performance rating*

_____
_____
_____
_____

*Achievements outstanding
*Achievements exceeded the requirements of the job
*Some aspects of achievement below requirements
*Performance unacceptable at this level

Comments of reviewer

_____
_____
_____
_____

Signature _____ Date_____

Comments of countersigning manager**

_____
_____
_____
_____

Signature _____ Date_____

Comments of employee

_____
_____
_____
_____

Signature _____ Date_____

*You will see that this example gives an overall performance rating. You don't need to give an overall performance rating, but you can do if you wish.
**Some organisations ask the manager's manager (or it could be a trustee) to add their comments.

For both the appraisal and the supervision forms, it is good practice for both you and the employee to sign them, once completed. Give the employee the opportunity to make comments if he or she feels that you have misrepresented anything in your write-up, or if there is anything else he or she wants to record in writing.

If the employee strongly objects to your perception of his or her performance and refuses to sign the appraisal form, you should try and resolve the matter with him or her. If he or she remains dissatisfied, it is open to him or her to use your grievance procedure (see chapter 9). However, if ultimately there is no agreement, you have the right to expect that the employee will adhere to any reasonable management expectation of him or her.

Avoiding bias in appraisals

Sometimes, appraisers may allow one aspect of an individual to influence their opinion of the individual's whole performance.

Ensure you are not influenced by matters that may irritate you or affect your thinking, but may have no bearing on job performance.

Ensure you are not influenced by matters that may irritate you or affect your thinking, but may have no bearing on job performance. If they DO have a bearing on job performance, keep them in context and avoid letting them cloud your whole view of the individual's performance.

As well as matters covered by law, such as gender, disability, race, sexual orientation and religion, make sure you keep in context matters such as:
- A particular significant event or characteristic, good or bad
- Scruffy appearance or alternatively very formal dress
- Laid-back manner
- Body piercing

You should also beware of belittling the work to yourself and hence to the employee. Just because you may feel their work is dull, it does not follow that they can't really enjoy it and be fully committed.

Developing yourself as a manager

It may be easy to forget the need to develop your own skills.

In the business of running a voluntary organisation, it may be easy to forget the need to develop your own skills.

Think about what you might need. If you are a chief executive of a voluntary organisation, discuss with your chair of trustees your learning and development needs.

One publication that you might find useful is *Leading Managers – a Guide to Management Development in the Voluntary Sector* from the Voluntary Sector National Training Organisation.

The guide includes a checklist of essential management skills/competencies, covering areas such as:

- Personal and communication skills – the way you relate to people from different communities and backgrounds and how you address conflict
- Managing paid staff and teams – the way you supervise and appraise your staff and work with your volunteers
- Resources management – the way you plan your annual budget and monitor financial expenditure.

The guide is available for download from www.voluntarysectorskills.org.uk

Also available from NCVO the *Good Management Guide for the voluntary sector*. Go to www.ncvo-vol.org.uk/publications for more information.

Investors in People

The Investors in People (IiP) Standard is a government quality award given to organisations that can demonstrate to an assessor that they invest in the development of all their employees.

IiP sets out best practice for the training and development of staff to achieve business goals. Employers who hold the IiP standard are able to send a positive message about their investment in employees to the outside world.

The aim of IiP is to help organisations to improve their performance by careful planning of the skills required to achieve their organisational objectives.

If you want to work towards the Investors in People standard, you can contact an accredited IiP assessor. He or she will visit your workplace, assess what processes you have in place already and help you to plan towards the IiP standard.

The IiP framework involves:

- Plan – developing strategies to improve the performance of the organisation.
- Do – taking action to improve the performance of the organisation.
- Review – evaluating the impact on the performance of the organisation.

To achieve the IIP Standard, you must:

- show a thorough understanding of the Standard and its principles
- review your business practices against the Standard
- commit to meeting the Standard and take any action this requires

- provide evidence so that your business can be assessed against the Standard.

For more information, you can go to the IiP website at www.investorsinpeople.co.uk or call their helpline on 020 7467 1946.

Checklist

✓ Produce a learning and development policy and an annual learning and development plan.
✓ Evaluate any learning and development completed, so that you can make changes in the future if needed.
✓ Undertake regular supervision sessions with your staff. How often will depend on the individual and the job, but should be frequent enough that the employee is clear about their progress and work priorities.
✓ Undertake an annual appraisal with all your staff.
✓ Deal with performance problems as they arise – don't wait for the annual appraisal
✓ Be aware of possible personal bias in assessing your staff. Question yourself to avoid unfair judgements.
✓ Don't forget your own learning needs – have a personal learning and development plan!
✓ Consider whether your organisation should work towards the Investors in People Standard.

Where to find out more

1. Acas
The following Acas advisory booklets may be of assistance.
Advisory Booklet on Employee Appraisal
www.acas.org.uk/publications/B07.html. for more details of how to order Acas publications see page 36.

2. askNCVO
www.askncvo.org.uk offers a wealth of free, practical, up-to-date advice on all aspects of running a charity or voluntary organisation. Hundreds of pages cover trusteeship, financial management, human resources and more.

3. Business link
The Business Link website contains lots of information about training. It covers:
- training evaluation
- fitting training to your needs
- turning underperformance into high performance
- developing your management team
- setting up in-house training
- how to find a training provider/course
- learning through networking with others
- skills and training for directors and owners.

Go to www.businesslink.gov.uk and in the search field, enter 'training.'

4. Charity Skills
This is an internet resource for the voluntary sector. Charity Skills run a number of training courses for the voluntary sector.
Website: www.charityskills.org.

5. Voluntary Sector National Training Organisation
The Voluntary Sector National Training Organisation (VSNTO) works to represent the interests of the voluntary sector in the areas of staff, volunteer and trustee training and development.

The website has details of training providers and training courses, including accredited training. It also has publications covering key issues affecting workplace training and development.
Website: www.voluntarysectorskills.org.uk

6. Directory of Social Change
The Directory of Social Change is a well known provider of training courses for the voluntary sector.
Tel: 08450 77 77 07
Fax: 020 7391 4808
Website: www.dsc.org.uk

7. Your local Council for Voluntary Service

Your local Council for Voluntary Service may run training sessions for voluntary and community organisations in the area. See the Yellow Pages to find out the contact details of your nearest CVS, or contact the National Association of Councils for Voluntary Service (NACVS) at www.nacvs.org.uk or using the following contact details:

177 Arundel Street
Sheffield S1 2NU
Tel: 0114 278 6636
Fax: 0114 278 7004
Textphone: 0114 278 7025

8. Investors in People UK

You can contact Investors in People as follows:

Investors in People UK
7-10 Chandos Street
London
W1G 9DQ

Tel: 020 7467 1900
Fax: 020 7636 2386
Email: information@iipuk.co.uk
Website: www.investorsinpeople.co.uk

8 Parental rights and flexible working practices

What this chapter is about

The charity Working Families estimates that currently one in six working women look after children under 16. It estimates that one in six of all workers care for elderly relatives and that this proportion is likely to increase as the population as a whole ages. In addition, with increasing numbers of women entering the workforce, many households have nobody at home to address care issues full-time. It makes sense to ensure that as an employer, you provide flexibility in working arrangements, when carers need it.

In this chapter, you can find out about the rights of your employees to:

- Maternity, paternity and adoption leave
- Unpaid parental leave
- Emergency leave to deal with a dependant
- Make a flexible working request

The above rights are all legal rights and are part of the Government's agenda to make the work place more 'family friendly'.

In this chapter, we also consider how you can provide a flexible and supportive work environment for all your employees. There may be reasons other than care responsibilities why employees may want flexibility at work, such as to pursue a specific interest or sport.

The following areas are covered:

- Flexitime
- Working from home
- Job-sharing
- Career breaks
- Voluntary reduced time
- Term-time only working
- Support with childcare including childcare vouchers.

153

Maternity

Maternity leave

All pregnant women have the right to paid time off for ante-natal care, the right to 26 weeks maternity leave (**ordinary maternity leave**) and the right not to be dismissed because of pregnancy or childbirth. These rights are regardless of whether the employee has worked for you for several years, or joined you in the last few weeks.

In addition, pregnant women who have 26 weeks service with you at the beginning of the 14th week before the week in which their baby is expected can take a *further* 26 weeks maternity leave. This is called **additional maternity leave**.

Maternity pay and benefits

Women who have 26 weeks service with you at the beginning of the 14th week before the week in which their baby is expected will normally be entitled to 9/10 of their average basic earnings for the first six weeks of their **ordinary maternity leave,** then a rate of pay determined yearly by the Government (currently £106 per week from April 2005) for a further 20 weeks. Women will qualify for this pay, provided that they have earnings which are at or above the lower earnings limit for National Insurance Contributions.

Benefits also accrue during ordinary maternity leave. During the 26 weeks **ordinary maternity leave**, the employee is entitled to all rights and benefits, including annual leave and bank holiday leave accrual, except for her salary. If you provide your employee with a car or a mobile phone as part of her employment package, for example, she may retain these during ordinary maternity leave.

There is no legal entitlement to maternity pay for the period of **additional maternity leave**, although some employers give additional contractual rights.

The only benefit that accrues during additional maternity leave is annual leave. This accrues at statutory levels (four weeks per year including public and bank holidays, pro-rated to the length of maternity leave taken by the employee, up to a maximum of 26 weeks).

Health and safety

When a woman is pregnant and during the six months after childbirth, you must take steps to protect her health and safety. She has a right to request a risk assessment during pregnancy – but it is advisable for you to undertake one, whether requested or not. If you cannot adequately protect her health and safety or that of her unborn child and cannot redeploy her to an alternative post on equivalent terms and conditions, you may need to suspend her on full pay.

Further information

The information above is a summary of the statutory maternity provisions. The law surrounding maternity leave and pay is complex. For more detailed information, try the following:

- A very useful fact sheet on maternity, available from the voluntary sector section of the Working Families website, www.workingfamilies.org.uk, or call Working Families on 020 7253 7243.
- If you require more detailed information, you can download a guide on maternity from the Department of Trade and Industry (DTI), at www.dti.gov.uk/er/maternity.htm. The information on the DTI website includes a model letter for you to use to acknowledge the request for maternity leave.
- The Health and Safety Executive has produced a *Guide for New and Expectant Mothers Who Work*, at www.hse.gov.uk/pubns/indg373.pdf, or call 08701 545500.

Likely future changes to maternity leave

The Government has announced proposals to increase the length of paid maternity leave from six to nine months to take effect from 2007. The goal is to increase this to 12 months' paid leave by 2010. In addition, the Government proposes that fathers will have the right to take more than the current two weeks of paid leave (see below) by using some of their partner's paid maternity leave entitlement.

Paternity leave

Two weeks' paid paternity leave is available to the person who has or expects to have responsibility for the upbringing of the child with the mother. This could be the child's biological father or the mother's partner (male or female).

To qualify for paternity leave and pay, the employee must have at least 26 weeks' continuous service with their employer by the 15th week before the week in which the baby is expected. The employee can take one week or two consecutive weeks, but cannot take two separate weeks.

Paternity leave can start on any day of the week as long as appropriate notice has been given. The leave must be taken:

- Within 56 days of the actual birth of the child.
- If the child is born earlier than expected, then the paternity leave must be taken between the date of birth and 56 days

from the first day of the expected week of birth.
- If the child is adopted, within 56 days of the child's placement.

Paternity pay is at a rate set by yearly the Government (currently £106 per week from April 2005). An employee will qualify provided that he/she has earnings which are at or above the lower earnings limit for National Insurance Contributions.

An employee should complete and sign a model self-certificate SC3 in order to be entitled to Statutory Paternity Pay (SPP). This is available from the Department for Trade and Industry website www.dti.gov.uk/er/paternity.htm.

Further information
There is a detailed fact sheet on paternity leave on the Working Families website, at the following link:
-
  www.workingfamilies.org.uk/asp/employer_zone/factsheets , or call Working Families on 020 7253 7243.
- You can find further information on the DTI website at www.dti.gov.uk/er/paternity.htm.

Adoption leave

The law provides for 26 weeks' paid leave ('ordinary adoption leave') and a further 26 weeks' unpaid leave ('additional adoption leave') when an employee is newly matched with a child for adoption from an approved adoption agency.

To be entitled to adoption leave, the employee must have 26 weeks' continuous service with their employer leading into the week of being notified of the match. Adoption leave is available to one member of the couple only; the couple can choose who takes the leave. The other member of the couple may be entitled to two weeks' paid paternity leave if they meet the eligibility requirements for paternity leave.

The paid part of adoption leave is at a rate set annually by the government – currently £106 per week from April 2005. The employee should be entitled provided that she or he has earnings above the Lower Earnings Limit for National Insurance Contributions.

You can ask employees to complete the model self-certificate form for adoption. This is available on the DTI website at www.dti.gov.uk/er/adoption.htm.

Further information

- There is a very clear guide to adoption leave available on the working families website: www.workingfamilies.org.uk or call Working Families on 020 7253 7243.
- Several pieces of information, including a model letter for you to use to acknowledge the request for adoption leave, are available from the DTI website: www.dti.gov.uk/er/adoption.htm.

Recovery of statutory maternity, paternity or adoption payments

If you qualify for Small Employers Relief (SER), you can get back 100 per cent of the Statutory Maternity, Paternity or Adoption Pay you've paid plus 4.5 per cent compensation. Whether or not you qualify for SER depends on the amount of Class 1 National Insurance Contributions (NICs) you were liable to pay to your Inland Revenue Accounts Office in the qualifying tax year.

If you don't qualify for SER, you can get back 92 per cent of the Statutory Maternity, Paternity or Adoption Pay you've paid.

You take the Statutory Maternity, Paternity or Adoption Pay out of your NICs and tax due to be paid in that tax month or quarter. If that's not enough you can take it from next month until the end of the tax year. If you can't wait for the money or if you need it in advance you can write to your Inland Revenue Accounts Office.

For further information on recovery of maternity, paternity or adoption pay, contact your local tax office or see the Inland Revenue website: www.inlandrevenue.gov.uk.

Offering more generous terms for maternity, paternity and adoption leave

Whilst you must provide the minimum terms required by law, you can provide more generous terms if you wish.

Enhancements that some voluntary organisations may make are as follows:

Pay enhancements

- Paying a higher rate of maternity and adoption pay, such as the first two months at full pay.
- Providing the two weeks' paternity leave at full pay rather than at statutory paternity pay levels.

Leave enhancements

- Allowing all pregnant employees, regardless of length of service, to have a year's maternity leave.
- Giving the right to a year's adoption leave to staff from day one, rather than after 26 weeks' service.
- Allowing male employees to have additional unpaid leave of up to one year after the two weeks' paid leave. This may be of interest to individuals who intend to be the principal carer, after the mother has returned to work.

Whilst not all voluntary organisations will be able to offer additional pay, do consider whether you can provide additional unpaid leave to your employees. This is at no or minimal cost to your organisation, yet could be a very valuable benefit to the employee.

If you do intend to provide enhanced pay or leave, make sure you provide it to all staff, so that you do not discriminate.

If you do intend to provide enhanced pay or leave, make sure you provide it to all staff, so that you do not discriminate.

Parental leave

As well as maternity, paternity and adoption leave, parents (both mothers and fathers and including adoptive parents) have a legal entitlement to unpaid parental leave, if they have a year's service.

The maximum leave which can be taken in total is 13 weeks. The leave must be taken by the child's fifth birthday, or if the child is disabled, by their 18th birthday.

Leave can be taken in blocks of one week up to a maximum of four weeks' leave in a year (for each child). If the child is disabled, there is more flexibility: the four weeks' leave each year does not have to be taken in blocks of one week, but can be taken in shorter periods.

The employee must give 21 days' notice, prior to taking leave. You can postpone the leave for up to six months, if your business cannot cope with the employee's absence at that time. However, try to agree the leave at the time requested, if at all possible.

The employee has the right to return to their old job at the end of parental leave of four weeks or less.

Further information
- Working Families has a fact sheet which gives you more information about parental leave. You can download it from their website www.workingfamilies.org.uk, or call Working Families on 020 7253 7243.
- You can find further information on the DTI website at www.dti.gov.uk/er/parental_leave.htm.

Enhancements to parental leave

Here are some possible enhancements to parental leave you may wish to consider:

- If your organisation is able to do so, you may wish to provide a few days paid parental leave each year. Many parents may not otherwise be able to afford to take the leave.
- You could implement more flexibility, so that employees would be able to take their parental leave in blocks of less than one week, or to take more than four weeks each year.
- You could make parental leave available from the first day of employment, rather than after a year's service.
- You could widen the coverage of the leave, so that rather than just being parental leave, the leave would be available to all carers.

Emergency time off for dependants

All employees, regardless of their length of service, have a legal right to take a reasonable period of time off work to deal with an unexpected or sudden emergency involving a dependant and to make longer-term arrangements. Employees have a right not to be dismissed or victimised for exercising their right to time off. There is no legal right to payment for the time off.

The law does not say what is a reasonable amount of time, but in most cases, a short period of a few days should be sufficient to make arrangements.

A dependant might be:

- a husband, wife or partner
- a child or parent
- someone living with the employee as part of their family who is dependant on them.

An emergency is when someone who depends on the employee:

- is ill and needs their help;
- is involved in an accident or assaulted;
- needs them to arrange their longer term care;
- needs them to deal with an unexpected disruption or breakdown in care, such as a childminder or nurse failing to turn up;
- goes into labour;
- dies and there is a need to make funeral arrangements or attend the funeral.

> **Employees have a right not to be dismissed or victimised for exercising their right to time off.**

Employees must tell their employer the reason for their absence and how long they expect to be away from work, as soon as practicable. This need not be in writing.

Further information
- Working Families has a factsheet which tells you all about time off for dependants. It is downloadable from their website: www.workingfamilies.org.uk, or call Working Families on 020 7253 7243.
- You can find further information on the DTI website at www.dti.gov.uk/er/time_off_deps.htm

Enhancements to the right to time off for dependants

Many employers offer compassionate leave, whereby an employee is given a short amount of paid time off to deal with a personal situation. The personal situation could include the emergencies outlined above, as well as domestic emergencies such as a flood or electrical failure at home.

Paid compassionate leave of perhaps up to three or five days per year, could be given, with any additional requirement for leave being unpaid.

The right to request flexible working

Employees who are parents of children under the age of six or disabled children under the age of 18 have the right to apply to their employer for a flexible working arrangement. The request must be for the purposes of caring for the child. The request can cover hours of work, times of work and place of work, and could include:
- term-time only working
- decreasing weekly hours of work
- compressed working week
- job sharing
- a later start or finishing time
- working from home
- a request for flexi-time.

It might simply be a request to start and finish the working day 10 minutes later, in order to be able to drop a child off at school in the morning.

To qualify, the employee must:
- be the child's mother, father, adopter, guardian or foster parent, or be married to or be the partner of the child's mother, father, adopter, guardian or foster parent.

- have worked with their employer continuously for at least 26 weeks at the date the application is made.
- make the application no later than two weeks before the child's sixth birthday or 18th birthday in the case of a disabled child.
- not have made another application to work flexibly under this right during the past 12 months.

The right enables mothers and fathers to request to work flexibly. It does not provide an automatic right to work flexibly as there will always be circumstances when the employer is unable to accommodate the employee's desired work pattern.

The request must be made in writing. This request should provide all relevant details as to why such a change is being proposed and the details of how such an arrangement could operate. The employee can use a specific form to make their request; this is available from the DTI website www.dti.gov.uk/er/flexible.htm.

The process is as follows:
- Within 28 days of receiving the request, you must arrange to meet with the employee, so that you can both explore the proposed work pattern in depth, and discuss how best it might be accommodated. It also provides an opportunity to consider other alternative working patterns should there be problems in accommodating the work pattern outlined in the employee's application. The employee can, if they want, bring a colleague from your organisation with them to the meeting, as a companion.
- Within 14 days after the date of the meeting, you must write to the employee to either agree to a new work pattern and a start date; or to provide clear business grounds as to why the application cannot be accepted and set out the appeal procedure.
- If the employee wishes to appeal against the decision, he or she must do this within 14 days of being notified of it.
- Accepted applications will mean a permanent change to the employee's terms and conditions of employment unless otherwise agreed between both parties.

Further information
- See the fact sheet *Flexible Working and the Law* in the voluntary sector section of the Working Families website at www.workingfamilies.org.uk.
- You can also download information from the Department of Trade and Industry's website: www.dti.gov.uk/er/flexible.htm

Possible future changes to the right to request flexible working

At the time of writing, the Government had issued a consultation document on extending flexible working rights to carers of adults and parents of children over six years.

Enhancements to the right to request flexible working

Rather than limit the right to parents, you could give all employees the right to request flexible working.

You might also consider offering flexible working when recruiting people, or for existing staff who have less than 26 weeks' service. If a prospective employee must wait the statutory 26 weeks before being able to request flexible working, they may decide not to join you in the first place.

Other flexible working practices and support

The following practices and support are not legal requirements, but you could offer them to employees as enhancements.

Flexitime

A flexitime policy allows employees to choose their own working hours within certain limits.

There is a core time during each day when all full-time employees must be working, normally the busiest part of the day from 10am until around 4pm. Outside of the core time, employees can decide at what time they wish to start or finish, as long as they work the required number of hours per week. A small excess of time worked may be carried forward and taken as time off in lieu (TOIL) at a later date.

Flexitime can help employees to manage arrangements such as taking children to school or nursery or to follow interests or hobbies. Flexitime gives all employees more control over their working lives and as such can have a positive effect on morale.

Working from home ('teleworking')

More and more employees spend a proportion of their working week working from home. It is now much easier to work from home, with mobile phones, email links and teleconferencing.

Working from home avoids time spent travelling. It may mean that staff can deliver their children to school when they would otherwise not be able to do so. It may mean that you can recruit or retain a disabled worker who finds travelling difficult.

> Rather than limit the right to parents, you could give all employees the right to request flexible working.

Further information

The DTI website has information on working from home at: www.dti.gov.uk/er/individual/telework.pdf.

You can also look at the website www.flexibility.co.uk for further information.

Case study

The following case study outlines the benefits one organisation has gained from a 'teleworking' initiative.

Automobile Association (AA)

A teleworking initiative was launched in December 1997, initially consisting of 10 call-centre staff moving from an office-based environment to working from home. The pilot expanded in August 1998 to 25 staff, with further expansion planned.

The productivity of teleworkers was found to be 30 per cent higher than office-based staff. Sickness absence was very low and quality of performance very high. Apart from the benefits to the business of reduced absenteeism, increased employee productivity and commitment, the AA has benefited from greater flexibility to deal with unexpected peaks in customer demand.

Teleworkers have cited a variety of benefits: better quality time with family, a more relaxed working environment, reduced expenses and less time wasted in commuting and the associated stress of travelling to work. Several people who could only work part-time previously because of family commitments were able to extend their hours and to benefit from increased salaries.

This new way of working has led to new management practices. Teleworkers have regular one-to-ones with their managers, and monthly team meetings to stop any risk of isolation creeping in. Morale amongst the team is high. As well as the direct business benefits of the teleworking project, the AA believes it will assist people who had previously wanted to work, but had been unable to travel, or who had disabilities, family or caring commitments etc

Job-sharing

This is a contractual arrangement whereby two employees voluntarily share one full-time job between them. They also share the pay, the holidays and the benefits according to the number of hours each works. Job-sharers can share the job in a number of ways, for example:

- one week on, one week off
- mornings and afternoons
- one works Monday, Tuesday and Wednesday morning; the other works Wednesday afternoon, Thursday and Friday.

The hours worked by each job-sharer do not necessarily need to be the same. For example, one job-sharer might be contracted for two days and the other for three days.

Similarly, it may not be necessary to divide the job duties totally in all cases. Both job-sharers might be responsible for day to day work (and for keeping each other informed at handover times), but they might also have specific projects they work on individually, to suit their specific skills.

Each of the job-sharers should be employed on a permanent part-time contract. See chapter 4 for further information about employment contracts.

If one job-sharer leaves, the other job-sharer retains the right to employment in his or her own right. You could recruit a new job-sharer, or change the job into a part-time job.

Job-sharers should coordinate the whole job between them, with support from the manager. It is the job-sharers' responsibility to ensure that continuity is maintained throughout the week.

Jobs can be shared at all levels, including at senior levels.

Jobs can be shared at all levels, including at senior levels. Whilst there are additional costs involved in recruiting and training two workers for one job, there are several benefits:

- Two individuals typically bring a greater breadth of experience than one.
- A person working part-time may be more productive than they would if they were working a full week.
- It can be easier to cover periods of annual leave.

Career breaks

Under a career break scheme, an employee can negotiate long periods of time away from work. This may be for six months up to perhaps two years. The employee and employer keep in touch throughout the period and the employee's job is held for him/her until the date of return.

The advantage for employers is that the arrangement enables them to retain the skills of the experienced employee who, by taking the extended leave, would otherwise have had to forfeit his/her position.

Career breaks can be taken after maternity or other parental leave, or could be granted to allow an employee to take a qualification, or to travel the world.

Voluntary reduced time

Voluntary reduced time, or 'V-time', schemes allow employees to reduce their hours of work by an agreed percentage over a given period of time. V-time might be useful to help employees deal with a short to medium term domestic problem.

There is a right to return to full-time employment at the end of the period. Pay and benefits are reduced proportionately to the reduction in working hours.

This reduction can be achieved by either shortening the working day, the working week or taking block periods off during the year.

Term-time working

This is an arrangement that allows employees with children of school age to be given unpaid leave during school holidays. Such employees remain on permanent full or part-time contracts and typically, the salary is spread evenly throughout the year.

Further information on term-time only contracts is given in chapter 4.

Support with childcare

Employees with childcare problems can cost an employer money. For example:

- The employee may need to take time off to find suitable childcare.
- The employee may be less productive, due to the stress of childcare problems.
- The employee may leave, causing additional costs of recruiting and training a new employee.

There are some things that employers can do relatively cheaply to assist employees with childcare.

You could provide information. For example, Working Families publishes a book called *Balancing Home and Work*, which you can order from the Working Families website www.workingfamilies.co.uk, or call Working Families on 020 7253 7243.

You can obtain information on local registered childminders and nurseries from your local authority Under Eights Adviser.

You could provide childcare vouchers. Childcare vouchers have tax and National Insurance (NI) advantages for the employee and NI advantages for the employer. It is possible to provide childcare vouchers at no or minimal cost, because of the tax and NI savings. For further information, see chapter 6.

Case study

The following case study explains what one small charity has done to implement 'people friendly' working practices.

BIBIC (British Institute of Brain Injured Children)

BIBIC is a small national children's charity, which exists purely on voluntary financial contributions.

Previously the charity could have been described as having a long hours culture. Now, it regards itself as 'people friendly', and recently incorporated 'quality of life at home and at work' into its stated values. Consultation with staff on policies helps sustain culture changes. Hours worked and leave taken are monitored and BIBIC issues formal written reminders on leave to take.

BIBIC has introduced a range of employee options that were not previously available, or where they were, they were not formalised or functioning well.

Extended unpaid leave and generous paid compassionate leave are in place, which often becomes paid emergency dependency leave depending on circumstances. There is paid leave for medical and related appointments so that staff do not have to lie or take time off in lieu, and leave to attend training/study days if staff are contributing to the community outside their jobs (e.g. by being a school governor).

Mechanisms have been put in place to allow staff to work at home when necessary, e.g. loan of laptops.

Job sharing, self-employment, casual work and bank working options have provided additional resources for the charity in covering staff absences/training, whilst allowing staff to achieve personal objectives. Three key post holders: Finance Manager, Fundraising Manager and Trust Fundraiser, have joined BIBIC particularly because they could work from home part of the week. Flexitime has meant that the telephone is answered for an extra hour a day.

All options are in theory open to all levels of staff from day one.

A new willingness to respect and welcome all needs within the staff team has resulted in the successful appointment of several disabled adult volunteers. This has given staff a new perspective on social exclusion, and adult needs as well as children's. It has also given the volunteers a work opportunity and given BIBIC additional resources. Staff turnover is reported to have dropped significantly, leading to savings in recruitment costs.

This is an abbreviated case study from the Working Families website.

Checklist

- ✓ Know the basic legal rights of employees to all types of parental leave, emergency leave and flexible working.
- ✓ Consider how you can go beyond the requirements of the law to become a best-practice employer.
- ✓ If you offer more generous terms, make sure you offer them to all employees equally, to avoid possible discrimination.
- ✓ Make sure employees know what is available to them – unpublicised benefits are of little use!
- ✓ Build a culture of trust, so that employees have confidence in raising any problems with caring responsibilities.
- ✓ Conduct informal discussions to find out about the problems an employee may be dealing with, and to help resolve them.
- ✓ Develop systems at work that ensure employees are not disadvantaged by taking maternity/paternity/adoption leave. Implement effective systems to re-integrate them into the workplace.
- ✓ Train managers and supervisors to understand the organisation's provisions, the main legal obligations and their own responsibilities in implementing your policies.

Where to find out more

1. Working Families

The Working Families website has considerable resources on

all aspects of parental leave, family-friendly working and flexible working. It also has a specific voluntary sector section on its website. This section includes free fact sheets and an order form for a free Work Life Development Pack.

The following fact sheets are available:

Maternity fact sheet
Paternity fact sheet
Adoption fact sheet
Parental leave fact sheet
Time off for dependants fact sheet
Flexible working fact sheet

You can also get hard copies of the fact sheets, by contacting Working Families at:
1-3 Berry Street
London
EC1V 0AA
Tel: 020 7253 7243
Fax: 020 7253 6253
Website: www.workingfamilies.org.uk

2. The Department of Trade and Industry (DTI)

The DTI has information about the following areas on its website www.dti.gov.uk/er:

Maternity at www.dti.gov.uk/er/maternity.htm
Paternity at www.dti.gov.uk/er/paternity.htm
Adoption at www.dti.gov.uk/er/adoption.htm.
Parental leave at www.dti.gov.uk/er/parental_leave.htm
Time off for dependants at www.dti.gov.uk/er/time_off_deps.htm
The right to request flexible working at www.dti.gov.uk/er/flexible.htm.

3. The Department of Trade and Industry work-life balance website

The DTI has a specific website on work-life balance. The website contains guidance and case studies. Go to: http://164.36.164.20/work-lifebalance

4. askNCVO

www.askncvo.org.uk offers a wealth of free, practical, up-to-date advice on all aspects of running a charity or voluntary organisation. Hundreds of pages cover trusteeship, financial management, human resources and more.

5. Maternity Alliance

The Maternity Alliance is a national charity working to improve rights and services for pregnant women, new parents and their families. Its website has information on maternity benefits, work rights and tax credits.

Third Floor West
2-6 Northburgh Street
London EC1V 0AY

Information line: 020 7490 7638
Fax: 020 7014 1350
Email: office@maternityalliance.org.uk
Website: www.maternityalliance.org.uk

6. Acas

Acas has an advisory booklet called Parents at Work, available from its website at www.acas.org.uk/publications/B17.html

For more details on how to order Acas publications see page 36.

For information on specific individual cases, call the Acas helpline on 08457 47 47 47 or see their website www.acas.org.uk.

7. Health and Safety Executive

The Health and Safety Executive has produced a Guide for New and Expectant Mothers who work, available at www.hse.gov.uk/pubns/indg373.pdf, or call 08701 545500.

8. Inland Revenue

For information on the recovery of maternity, paternity or adoption pay, contact your local tax office or see the Inland Revenue website www.inlandrevenue.gov.uk

9 Grievance, discipline and poor performance

What this chapter is about

This chapter helps you deal more easily with what may seem to be the most difficult aspects of employing people: when disputes and differences arise. It covers the following areas:
- The legal position on dealing with disputes
- Drafting a grievance procedure
- Handling grievances
- Drafting a disciplinary procedure
- Rules
- Handling disciplinary matters
- Dealing with poor performance
- Mediation

The legal position – dealing with disputes

As of October 2004, new statutory procedures came into effect for resolving disputes at work.

The intention behind the law is to encourage employers and employees to talk first, before resorting to the law.

All employers and employees must follow a simple minimum three step procedure when dealing with most dismissals, disciplinary actions such as demotion or suspension without pay and grievances. If they do not follow the minimum procedures, there may be financial penalties, should the matter go to an Employment Tribunal.

The three step procedure, for both grievance and discipline cases, involves a written statement (step 1), a meeting (step 2) and an appeal if requested (step 3).

> The intention behind the law is to encourage employers and employees to talk first, before resorting to the law.

Step 1

In the case of a disciplinary matter, the employer must set out in writing to the employee the reasons why he or she is considering disciplinary action.

In the case of a grievance, the employee must set out in writing to the employer his or her grievance.

Step 2

The employer and employee must meet.

After the meeting, the employer must inform the employee of his or her decision and the right of appeal.

Step 3

An appeal meeting must occur if the employee requests it.

The employee must be informed of the outcome of the appeal.

Other requirements

The law also states other requirements in connection with the statutory process for grievances and discipline. It states that:

- Each step must be followed through without unreasonable delay.
- Both employee and employer must take reasonable steps to attend each meeting under the procedure and must have the opportunity to state their case.
- The meetings must be at a reasonable time and location.
- Both parties should have all the relevant information and have a chance to consider it prior to each meeting.
- The employee has the right to be accompanied by a colleague or trade union representative at the meetings.
- The appeal meeting should, where possible, be chaired by a manager more senior than the manager who took the decision at step 2.
- If the employee or their companion is disabled, the employer must make reasonable adjustments to enable them to participate fully.

Check your procedures

You must make sure that your grievance and disciplinary procedures meet the minimum statutory requirements. If they do not, you must amend them. If you have no disciplinary or grievance procedures in place, you must install at least the minimum procedures.

Part of your legal responsibility is that if you have changed your procedures as a result of the new legislation or at any point subsequently, you must inform your employees of their rights and of the procedures they must follow if involved in a grievance or disciplinary matter.

The Department of Trade and Industry has an example memo that you can use to inform employees of changes to your procedures, on its website at www.dti.gov.uk/er/memo.htm.

For new employees, you must tell them in their written statement of terms and conditions where they can find information about your organisation's grievance and disciplinary procedures.

The statutory procedures and Employment Tribunals

Grievances

Employees who have a grievance will have to use the three-step procedure and wait for 28 days, before they can make a claim to an employment tribunal. The 28 days is to allow you to respond, but you should aim to respond more quickly than that if you can.

If the employee fails to raise a grievance prior to making a claim to the Employment Tribunal, the Tribunal will not accept the claim. The employee will be advised by the Employment Tribunal to raise a grievance with their employer and wait 28 days for a written response before bringing the claim again. The Employment Tribunal may extend the deadline for the employee to bring a claim whilst this procedure is followed.

If the employee fails to follow the statutory minimum procedure before making a claim to an Employment Tribunal and the tribunal makes an award, that award may be reduced by between 10 per cent and 50 per cent. If you fail to follow the statutory minimum procedure, any award may be increased by between 10 per cent and 50 per cent.

Dismissal cases

If the employer fails to follow the statutory minimum procedure in a dismissal case, any dismissal will be automatically unfair. The dismissed employee will in these circumstances receive at least four weeks' pay. Any additional compensation for the employee will be increased by between 10 per cent and 50 per cent.

If the procedure is not completed because the employee did not follow the statutory minimum procedure, any ensuing award will be reduced by between 10 per cent and 50 per cent.

Note that an employee cannot normally take a case of unfair dismissal against you until he or she has been employed by you for a year or more. There are some important exceptions to this rule. Some dismissals are automatically unfair whenever they occur. For example, you cannot fairly dismiss a woman for becoming pregnant. If an employee is claiming that you have done this, she does not need a year's service to make an Employment Tribunal claim. However, an employee must have a year's service to bring an automatic unfair dismissal claim due to an employer's breach of the statutory disciplinary and dismissal procedures.

Modified two step procedure

For the vast majority of cases, you will need to follow the three step procedure.

There is however a modified two step procedure which may be used in certain cases.

The modified grievance procedure may apply in the case of a grievance if the employee is no longer working for you and:

- Both parties agree in writing that it should apply.
- Or it is not reasonably practicable for one or other party to carry out the standard procedure. This might be the case if, for example, one party has left the country or is seriously ill.

Step 1

The ex-employee sends a written statement of grievance to you.

Step 2

You write back to the ex-employee giving your response to the points raised.

The modified disciplinary procedure should only be used in a very small number of circumstances, such as a witnessed fight or theft, which might lead to a gross misconduct dismissal. In general, you are advised not to use the two step procedure and to follow the normal procedure outlined in your organisation's disciplinary procedure.

Step 1

You must put in writing the alleged misconduct that led you to dismiss the employee. You should include details of the evidence you relied on and the employee's right of appeal.

Step 2

If the employee wishes to appeal, you must arrange a meeting. You should give the employee your final decision after the meeting.

Circumstances where you do not need to follow the statutory procedures

You need only use the statutory procedures in discipline cases where you are considering taking serious disciplinary action that may result in dismissal (or demotion or suspension without full pay, if your contracts of employment allow for this). In the early stages of disciplinary action, you do not need to use the statutory procedures, although you should still follow your organisation's disciplinary procedure.

There are a few circumstances where the statutory procedures do not need to be followed at all. This might be the case if one party is abusive or violent, or where there are factors beyond the control of either party which make it impossible to proceed with the grievance (e.g. in the case of serious illness).

These circumstances would need to be very exceptional and you are advised to seek advice, for example from Acas, before deciding not to use the procedures at all.

If the employee fails to attend a meeting under the procedure, then the employer, taking account of the employee's right to be accompanied and any suggested dates, must rearrange the meeting once. If the second meeting falls through, neither party is under any further obligation to complete procedures. However, it is advisable to try to rearrange the meeting where possible.

Fairness and the statutory procedures

You should note that simply following the three step statutory procedures will not necessarily mean that an Employment Tribunal will find in your favour. Your actions must still be reasonable.

You are strongly advised to have grievance and disciplinary procedures that are fuller than the statutory minimum, so that everyone in the organisation is clear about how disciplinary and grievance matters will be handled.

Drafting a grievance procedure

An example of a grievance procedure which meets the requirements of the statutory three-step grievance procedure is reproduced below. You could adapt this for your organisation.

When drafting your procedure, make sure you consult with staff and managers before finalising it.

Model grievance procedure

> **1. Introduction**
> It is (organisation's) policy to ensure that employees with a grievance relating to their employment can use a procedure which can help to resolve grievances as quickly and as fairly as possible.
>
> **2. Principles**
> - Each step must be followed through without unreasonable delay.
> - Both employee and employer must take reasonable steps to attend each meeting under the procedure and will have the opportunity to state their case.
> - Meetings will be at a reasonable time and location.
> - All relevant information will be provided to both employer and employee in advance of any meeting under the procedure.

You are strongly advised to have grievance and disciplinary procedures that are fuller than the statutory minimum.

- The employee has the right to be accompanied by a colleague or trade union representative at the meetings at step 2 and step 3.
- The appeal meeting at step 3 will, where possible, be chaired by a manager more senior than the manager who took the decision at step 2, or by a trustee.
- If the employee or their companion is disabled, reasonable adjustments will be made to enable them to participate fully.
- Confidentiality will be maintained. Only those who need to know about the grievance will be informed.
- After the grievance and regardless of the outcome, both parties will endeavour to work together in a positive manner.

3. Informal discussions

If you have a grievance about your employment you should discuss it informally with your manager. It is hoped that the majority of concerns will be resolved at this stage.

4. Steps in the grievance procedure

Step 1 – written statement

If you feel that the matter has not been resolved through informal discussions, you should put your grievance in writing to your manager.

Step 2 – meeting

Your manager will arrange to meet with you and will aim to give you a written response within five working days. If this is not possible, he or she will inform you of the reason for the delay and when you can expect a response.

Step 3 – appeal

If you are not satisfied with the response, you may put your grievance in writing to your manager's manager, or to a trustee, if there is no more senior manager. That individual will arrange to meet with you and will give you a response within five working days. If this is not possible, he or she will inform you of the reason for the delay and when you can expect a response.

Step 3 is the final stage of the procedure and there is no further right of appeal.

Handling grievances

Dealing with matters as they arise

Try to have an open and approachable manner with employees. If they feel that they can raise matters of concern and that they will be listened to, they are likely to raise the concerns at an early stage, when it may be easier to find a resolution.

If an employee raises a matter, try and deal with it informally and quickly.

If the employee remains concerned, he or she may wish to set the grievance out in writing and give a copy to you as his or her manager.

Investigation

If you receive a formal grievance (whether against you personally or not), you will need to check the facts and the full reason why the employee is aggrieved.

You might check the facts in the grievance hearing itself. However, if the matter is complex, you may need to undertake a formal investigation, or you may need to ask someone independent to investigate. This could be someone from your organisation or, if your organisation is very small, you could ask someone external to the organisation to undertake the investigation.

The independent investigator will normally need to:

- Interview the person making the grievance.
- Interview the person against whom the grievance has been made (if the grievance is against another person).
- Interview anyone else who may have been involved (with due regard to confidentiality).
- Take formal, signed statements when interviewing.
- Review any documents relevant to the matter.
- Produce a brief and factual report on the findings of the investigation. The investigator should not include his or her own opinions in the report.

Below is an example report format.

CONFIDENTIAL INVESTIGATION REPORT – GRIEVANCE

Date investigation started: _____

Date finished: _____

Name of investigator: _____

Name of employee raising the grievance: _____

Details of the grievance raised_____

_____

_____

_____

Details of the investigation conducted (people interviewed, documents reviewed)

_____

_____

_____

Key findings of fact

_____

_____

_____

_____

Signature of investigator _____

Date _____

The findings of the investigator, plus notes of interviews, should be made available in advance of a grievance meeting to the following people:

- the manager who will hear the grievance
- the individual who raised the grievance
- the person against whom the grievance has been raised.

> **Document-ation should be received sufficiently in advance of the grievance meeting for those affected to be able to consider it.**

The documentation should be received sufficiently in advance of the grievance meeting for those affected to be able to consider it.

The grievance meeting ('hearing')

The meeting should be at a reasonable time and location and the employee should make all reasonable attempts to attend. The employee has a legal right to be accompanied by a colleague or trade union representative. If you wish, you can, as an alternative, allow the employee to be accompanied by a friend or family member. Note that the companion has the right to address the meeting, but cannot answer questions on the employee's behalf.

If the employee's companion cannot attend on the day stated, the provisions of section 10 of the Employment Relations Act 1999 apply. This provides that the employee must propose an alternative date within five days. If acceptable, you must then invite all parties to attend at this new time. You are obliged to rearrange the meeting once.

It is advisable for you to have another manager or a human resources specialist present, to assist you in decision making. One of you should take notes of the meeting, or you could arrange for a separate note-taker to attend. Accurate notes of the meeting should be retained.

You can conduct the grievance meeting as follows:

- Introduce the parties and explain the purpose of the meeting.
- Ask the employee to state his or her grievance. You should also ask the employee to state what outcome he or she would like. This can help employees to think about possible solutions, rather than just the problem.
- Ask the person against whom the grievance has been raised to respond.
- Ask questions about the issue, to gain a full understanding.
- Bring in any witnesses, if needed (the witnesses should only attend to answer questions and should then leave the meeting).
- Check that everyone involved feels they have had the opportunity to state their case fully.
- Adjourn the meeting so that you can think about what has been said. Discuss the matter with the person who attended to support you. Take further advice if needed.
- Bring the employee back to tell him or her of your decision, how you have come to that decision and that you will confirm it in writing. If you feel you cannot come to a decision that day, tell the employee when he or she can expect to receive your response in writing.
- Tell the employee that he or she has the right of appeal if dissatisfied with your decision and confirm this when you write.

Appeal

If the employee appeals against the decision, you should arrange a further meeting for the appeal to be heard. Where possible, a manager more senior than you should chair the appeal. If you are the most senior manager, a trustee could chair the appeal. If this is not possible, you should hear the appeal as impartially as possible.

The following format can be used for the appeal meeting:

- Introduce everyone and explain the purpose of the meeting.
- Explain what you understand to be the grievance and ask the employee to confirm this or to explain further.
- Ask the employee what he or she is still aggrieved about and why.

- Ask the employee what outcome he or she is looking for.
- Ask the manager who made the decision at stage 1 of the grievance procedure for information on why he/she made the decision he/she did.
- Ask if anyone has anything more they want to say.
- Adjourn the meeting to consider what has been said.
- Reconvene the meeting to inform the employee of your decision, how you have come to that decision and that you will confirm it in writing. If you need more time, inform the employee in writing on the following day of your decision.
- The employee should be clear that the decision is the final stage of the grievance procedure.

You should note that you should not overturn the decision at stage one simply because you would have taken a different decision. The important issue is whether or not you feel that the decision was a reasonable one for a manager to take, regardless of whether you personally would have taken this decision.

If you feel that the decision was indeed reasonable, you could still overturn it, if the employee brings additional information to the appeal meeting that was not available at the stage 1 meeting and if this information changes your perception of the matter.

Case study

One of the youth workers at the Westwich Association (WA) is aggrieved. He is unhappy that his youth worker colleague, who has just come back from maternity leave, has been given the right to base herself from home.
He has asked to base his work from home also, but has been refused.
He has raised a formal grievance, saying he has been discriminated against on the grounds of his gender.
From the general manager's point of view, she allowed the youth worker colleague to be based from home, after she received a request to do this. The request was made under the legal right to request flexible working (see chapter 8 for more information) and the general manager felt it was reasonable to agree in this case. The aggrieved youth worker has no right to request flexible working, because he does not have children under six years of age.
Anyway, the general manager would not agree to such a request. Whilst she can manage with one part-time youth worker being based at home, there would be insufficient

office cover for both youth workers to be out of the office. As far as she is concerned, this is not sex discrimination, she is simply following legal requirements.

The general manager and the employee follow WA's grievance procedure. The employee is still not happy and goes to appeal, which is heard by a trustee. Having listened to the points of view of all concerned, including the reasons why the employee is seeking to be based from home, the trustee's decision is that the employee be given some flexibility in working hours. The general manager is asked to consider the matter again and as a result comes up with a compromise proposal. The employee feels that he has been listened to and is prepared to work with the proposed arrangements.

Drafting a disciplinary procedure

You will need to draft your disciplinary procedure to suit your own organisation's needs.

Below is a model disciplinary procedure for small organisations, reproduced from the Acas advisory handbook *Discipline and grievances at work*, available for download from the internet at www.acas.org.uk/publications. You can use this model procedure as a basis for your own procedure.

When drafting or revising your procedure, make sure you consult with staff and managers before finalising it.

Acas model disciplinary procedure (small organisations)

1. Purpose and scope
The organisation's aim is to encourage improvement in individual conduct or performance. This procedure sets out the action which will be taken when disciplinary rules are breached.

2. Principles
a) The procedure is designed to establish the facts quickly and to deal consistently with disciplinary issues. No disciplinary action will be taken until the matter has been fully investigated.
b) At every stage employees will have the opportunity to state their case and be represented or accompanied, if they wish, at the hearings by a trade union representative or a work colleague.

c) An employee has the right to appeal against any disciplinary penalty.

3. The Procedure

Stage 1 – first warning

If conduct or performance is unsatisfactory, the employee will be given a written warning or performance note. Such warnings will be recorded, but disregarded after ... months of satisfactory service. The employee will also be informed that a final written warning may be considered if there is no sustained satisfactory improvement or change. (Where the first offence is sufficiently serious, for example because it is having, or is likely to have, a serious harmful effect on the organisation, it may be justifiable to move directly to a final written warning.)

Stage 2 – final written warning

If the offence is serious, or there is no improvement in standards, or if a further offence of a similar kind occurs, a final written warning will be given which will include the reason for the warning and a note that if no improvement results within ... months, action at Stage 3 will be taken.

Stage 3 – dismissal or action short of dismissal

If the conduct or performance has failed to improve, the employee may suffer demotion, disciplinary transfer, loss or seniority (as allowed in the contract) or dismissal.

Statutory discipline and dismissal procedure

If an employee faces dismissal – or action short of dismissal such as loss of pay or demotion – the minimum statutory procedure will be followed. This involves:

– *Step one:* a written note to the employee setting out the allegation and the basis for it.

– *Step two:* a meeting to consider and discuss the allegation.

– *Step three:* a right of appeal including an appeal meeting. The employee will be reminded of their right to be accompanied.

Gross misconduct

If, after investigation, it is confirmed that an employee has committed an offence of the following nature (the list is not exhaustive), the normal consequence will be dismissal without notice or payment in lieu of notice:

– theft, damage to property, fraud, incapacity for work due to being under the influence of alcohol or illegal drugs, physical violence, bullying and gross insubordination.

While the alleged gross misconduct is being investigated, the employee may be suspended, during which time he or she will be paid their normal pay rate. Any decision to dismiss will be taken by the employer only after full investigation.

Appeals
An employee who wishes to appeal against any disciplinary decision must do so to the named person in the organisation within five working days. The employer will hear the appeal and decide the case as impartially as possible.

Once the procedure has been written, you need to be sure that all employees are familiar with it and have access to a copy. You also need to be certain that all managers and supervisors are fully trained in its operation.

Rules

Acas advises that organisations should have disciplinary rules and that these should be clear and in writing. Consulting with employees when you develop the rules will help with acceptance and understanding.

Make sure that your managers understand the rules and that they enforce them consistently.

All employees should know about the rules and have access to a copy of them. If you have a staff handbook, you could include your rules in that document. Alternatively, in a small organisation, you might simply display your rules on the staff notice board.

You may need to make special effort to ensure that employees with little experience of working life, and employees for whom English is a second language, understand what is expected of them.

Below are some example subject areas for rules, drawn from the Acas advisory booklet on discipline and grievances at work, available from the internet at www.acas.org.uk/publications/H02.html.

You may need to make special effort to ensure that employees... understand what is expected of them.

Example subject areas for rules

Timekeeping
- arrival times
- lateness.

Absence
- authorising absence
- approval of holidays
- notification of absence

i) who the employee tells
ii) when they tell them
iii) the reasons for absence
iv) likely time of arrival/return
- rules on self-certification and doctor's certificates.

Health and safety
- personal appearance – any special requirements regarding, for example, protective clothing, hygiene or the wearing of jewellery (employers should be aware that any such requirement must be solely on the basis of health or safety, and should not discriminate between sexes or on the basis of race, disability, sexual orientation or religion or belief)
- smoking policy
- special hazards/machinery/chemicals
- policies on alcohol, drug or other substance abuse.

Use of organisation facilities
- private telephone calls
- computers, email and the internet
- company premises outside working hours
- equipment.

Discrimination, bullying and harassment
- equal opportunities
- rules/stance on harassment relating to race, sex, disability, sexual orientation, religion or belief.

Gross misconduct
The types of conduct that might be considered as 'gross misconduct' (this is misconduct that is so serious that it may justify dismissal without notice).

Handling disciplinary matters

The aim in any disciplinary matter should be to improve conduct or performance. Go into each situation with this in mind, rather than thinking about dismissal.

Informal action

Informal action is when a manager raises a concern with an employee about his or her conduct or performance. It is prior to the formal disciplinary procedure.

When someone is not performing well or their conduct is of concern, deal with it at the time. A 'quiet word' in private may be all that is needed to set the employee back on track. Follow up any concerns in regular supervision and appraisal meetings (see chapter 7 for further information). Make sure that the individual understands the concern about his or her performance or conduct and knows what to do to rectify it.

You should always listen to what the employee has to say in response to your concerns. There may be a particular problem that is causing the poor performance. Here is an example from the Acas *Advisory Booklet on Discipline and Grievances at Work*.

> **Example**
> A valued and generally reliable employee is late for work on a number of occasions, causing difficulty for other staff who have to provide cover.
> You talk to the employee on his own and he reveals that he has recently split up with his wife and he now has to take the children to school on the way to work. You agree an adjustment to his start and finish times and make arrangements for cover which solves the problem.

Following the disciplinary procedure

If the poor performance or misconduct continues, or is so serious as to warrant more serious action, you will need to instigate the disciplinary procedure. Here is an example from the Acas advisory booklet on discipline and grievances at work.

> **Example – failure to improve**
> A member of the accounts staff makes a number of mistakes on invoices. You bring the mistakes to his attention, make sure he has had the right training and impress on him the need for accuracy but the mistakes continue.
> You invite the employee to a disciplinary meeting and

inform him of his right to be accompanied by a colleague or employee representative. At the meeting the employee does not give a satisfactory explanation for the mistakes so you decide to issue an improvement note setting out: the problem, the improvement required, the timescale for improvement, the support available and a review date. You inform the employee that a failure to improve may lead to a final written warning.

Investigation

The above examples of lateness and inaccuracy are not likely to require a major amount of investigation. However, in some circumstances, such as alleged fraud or abuse, you may need to suspend the employee on full pay and organise a thorough investigation, before convening a disciplinary hearing. You should explain to the employee that suspension is a neutral act to allow investigation – it does not imply guilt.

It may be appropriate for a separate manager, if not someone external to the organisation, to undertake such an investigation.

Make sure that the investigation is undertaken quickly. It is very stressful to be on suspension awaiting a disciplinary hearing.

The principles of investigating a disciplinary matter are the same as those outlined earlier in this chapter for grievance hearings. The investigator will normally need to:

- Interview the person who made the allegation.
- Interview the person against whom the allegation has been made.
- Interview anyone else who may have been involved (with due regard to confidentiality).
- Take formal, signed statements when interviewing.
- Review any documents relevant to the matter.
- Produce a brief and factual report on the findings of the investigation. The investigator should not include his or her own opinions in the report.

Below is an example format for the report.

> **You should explain to the employee that suspension is a neutral act to allow investigation – it does not imply guilt.**

CONFIDENTIAL INVESTIGATION REPORT – GRIEVANCE

Date investigation started: _____
Date finished: _____
Name of investigator: _____
Name of employee against whom the allegation has been raised: _____
Details of the allegation _____
_____
_____
_____
_____

Details of the investigation conducted (people interviewed, documents reviewed)
_____
_____
_____

Key findings of fact
_____
_____
_____

Signature of investigator _____
Date _____

The findings of the investigator, plus notes of interviews/witness statements should be made available to the following people:
- the manager who will hear the disciplinary matter
- the person against whom the allegations have been made.

The documentation should be received sufficiently in advance of the disciplinary meeting for those affected to be able to consider it.

If you are contemplating dismissal, it is particularly important to give this information to the employee in advance. You also need to set out in advance exactly what the employee has done, or failed to do, that may result in disciplinary action or dismissal. The law does not allow you to present this information only at the hearing.

The disciplinary meeting

The meeting should be at a reasonable time and location and the employee should make all reasonable attempts to attend. The employee has a legal right to be accompanied by a colleague or trade union representative. Tell the employee in advance of this right. If you wish, you can, as an alternative, allow the employee to be accompanied by a friend or family member. Note that the companion has the right to address the meeting, but cannot answer questions on the employee's behalf.

If the employee's companion cannot attend on the day stated, the provisions of section 10 of the Employment Relations Act 1999 apply. This provides that the employee must propose an alternative date within five days. If acceptable, you must then invite all parties to attend at this new time. You are obliged to rearrange the meeting once.

It is advisable for you to have another manager or a human resources specialist present, to assist you in decision making and to take notes of the meeting. Accurate notes of the meeting should be retained.

It is advisable for you to have another manager or a human resources specialist present.

You can conduct the disciplinary meeting as follows:

- Start by introducing those present and by explaining the format of the meeting.
- Explain your understanding of the allegation.
- Unless the matter is very straightforward, such as poor timekeeping, in which case you can gather the facts yourself, a separate manager should normally have conducted an investigation into the matter. You should ask that manager to present his or her findings to the hearing.
- Ask the employee to comment on what is said. You should give the employee full opportunity to present his/her side of the story and to say anything he/she wishes to.
- If needed, bring in witnesses and allow all parties to question them on their evidence.
- Ask the investigating manager to sum up.
- Ask the employee to sum up.
- Summarise your understanding of the facts (but do not give your views about the facts at this stage).
- Adjourn the meeting to consider the matter in private. Discuss it with the person who attended the meeting to support you. Take advice from a human resources practitioner if needed.
- Reconvene the meeting to give your decision and confirm this in writing. If you need more time, reconvene the meeting to tell the employee that you will give your decision in writing on the following day or as soon afterwards as you can. Inform the employee of his/her right to appeal.
- Throughout the hearing, make sure you demonstrate an open mind and keep your approach formal and polite.

Coming to a decision

In coming to a decision, you should consider:

- Taking all matters into account, including the thoroughness of the investigation and on the balance of probabilities, is the case against the employee proven?
- If you feel that the case against the employee is not proven, no disciplinary penalty should be imposed.
- If you feel that the case is proven, then you should consider:
- What is a reasonable penalty in this circumstance? In considering this, review your disciplinary procedure and the rules of your organisation. Consider any similar cases in the organisation in the past and what action was taken.
- Are there any mitigating circumstances which might make it appropriate to lessen the penalty?
- Does the employee already have current disciplinary warnings?

- If you are considering dismissal, what is the reason? The reason must be one allowed by the law, that is:
  - capability or qualifications of the employee
  - conduct of the employee
  - redundancy
  - contravention of a duty or restriction
  - some other substantial reason

In normal circumstances, you should not dismiss an employee unless you have previously given one or more warnings. The exception to this is in cases of gross misconduct (i.e. very serious matters such as theft, fighting, assault or neglect of service users), where you may dismiss summarily without prior warnings and without pay in lieu of notice.

In normal circumstances, you should not dismiss an employee unless you have previously given one or more warnings.

The appeal meeting

If the employee wants to appeal against your decision, he or she should do so in writing. If possible a manager more senior than you or one or more trustees should hold the appeal hearing.

The employee may be accompanied at the meeting by a colleague or trade union representative or, if your procedures allow, a friend or family member.

Here is a format for the appeal meeting:

- The person chairing the appeal should explain the purpose and format of the appeal.
- The employee should be given the opportunity to explain the grounds for his or her appeal.
- The person chairing the appeal should ask for clarification if required from the manager who took the original decision.
- Witnesses may be brought in if necessary, but a full re-hearing of the case should normally be avoided.
- Once all parties have said what they wish to about the matter, the hearing should be adjourned.
- The person chairing the appeal should consider all the matters raised and then reconvene the meeting to inform the employee of his/her decision. This should be confirmed in writing. If more time is needed, the employee should be told this and a decision should follow in writing as soon as possible afterwards. The employee should be informed that there is no further right of appeal.

If the employee wants to appeal against your decision, he or she should do so in writing.

Coming to a decision – appeals

The person hearing the appeal must consider whether, in all the circumstances, the original decision was a reasonable management decision to take and whether the procedure was

189

followed appropriately.

The person hearing the appeal should set aside whether he/she would have taken a different decision in the circumstances. The only thing to be assessed is whether the original decision was within the range of reasonable management decisions.

The person hearing the appeal should also consider whether any new evidence has been presented that may change the decision. If this is the case, he or she should consider it carefully, before confirming or overturning the original decision.

Dealing with poor performance

Matters of poor performance/incapability should be dealt with under the disciplinary procedure, but they may need particularly sensitive handling.

In all cases, you should:

- Ask the employee for an explanation and check the explanation if possible.
- If the reason is lack of the required skill, give the employee training and support to achieve the required performance level within a reasonable period.
- Consider finding the employee suitable alternative work, with his or her agreement.
- Explore all options with the employee, but you should still make sure that the employee understands that his or her performance is not acceptable – so give warnings under the disciplinary procedure as appropriate.
- If, ultimately, the employee's performance does not improve and there is no possibility to redeploy the employee, or he/she does not agree to this, you can dismiss the employee on the grounds of capability. However, a dismissal without prior warnings under the disciplinary procedure is unlikely to be found to be fair.
- Consider whether the job content has changed so significantly that you are actually dealing with a situation of redundancy (i.e. the requirement for work of a particular type has diminished or disappeared) rather than a matter of capability. In this case, discuss with the employee treating this situation as a redundancy matter.

Problem situations

In general, if you are not sure what to do, take advice, because grievance, discipline and disciplinary matters can be difficult to deal with. In particular, if the employee raises a grievance at the

In general, if you are not sure what to do, take advice

same time as you are undertaking disciplinary action, you should take advice on how to proceed.

Mediation

Mediation is a voluntary, confidential process, where a neutral third party helps individuals in dispute to work out where are the areas of difference, how they can find common ground and how they can reach a settlement.

Effective mediation can avoid costly employment tribunals, if a work relationship can be repaired.

Mediation can be used as an alternative to following the grievance procedure, if both parties agree. You could consider including a clause such as the following in your grievance procedure:

'As an alternative to following the grievance procedure, and if both parties agree, the matter may be referred to mediation. An independent mediator will assist parties to find a solution that is acceptable to all.'

If you would like to know more about mediation, you could refer to the NCVO publication called *You're not listening to me!* which contains lots of practical advice. In addition, the Centre for Effective Dispute Resolution (CEDR), in partnership with NCVO, operates a subsidised mediation service for the voluntary and community sector. To find out more about the publication or the mediation service, contact the NCVO HelpDesk on 0800 2 798 798 or textphone 0800 01 888 111 or email helpdesk@ncvo-vol.org.uk. Alternatively, Acas can either train mediators or can attend themselves to undertake the mediation. Contact the Acas helpline on 08457 47 47 47 to find out more.

Checklist

- ✓ Make sure your grievance and disciplinary procedures comply with the statutory minimum procedures.
- ✓ Draft disciplinary rules, so that staff know what is expected of them. Make sure all staff have access to a copy of the rules.
- ✓ Follow principles of fairness and reasonableness in dealing with any grievance or disciplinary matter. Always follow your procedures.
- ✓ Consider the use of mediation to deal with disputes, where appropriate.
- ✓ Seek human resources or legal advice when in doubt.

Where to find out more

1. Acas

The following Acas publications may be of use:

A self-help tool to producing grievance and disciplinary procedures, at the Acas website www.acas.org.uk/publications/g02.html

The Acas Advisory Handbook Discipline and Grievances at Work, available at www.acas.org.uk/publications/H02.html

The Acas Code of Practice on Disciplinary and Grievance Procedures www.acas.org.uk/publications/pdf/CP01.pdf

For specific questions, you can contact the Acas helpline tel: 08457 47 47 47 or textphone 08456 06 16 00

2. The Department of Trade and Industry (DTI)

If you go to the DTI web page www.dti.gov.uk/er/resolvingdisputes, you can find several documents about the statutory dispute resolution procedures. There is also a useful publication targeted at smaller employers, called *Disciplinary, dismissal and grievance procedures, guidance for employers*. This publication includes standard letters that you can use in disciplinary cases.

3. askNCVO

www.askncvo.org.uk offers a wealth of free, practical, up-to-date advice on all aspects of running a charity or voluntary organisation. Hundreds of pages cover trusteeship, financial management, human resources and more.

4. Business Link

The Business Link website has a section on its website about dealing with grievances and disciplinary matters.

Go to www.businesslink.gov.uk and search under grievance and discipline.

10 Managing absence

What this chapter is about

High levels of absence can be a problem for any organisation. If you are a small employer with little flexibility to reallocate work, employee absence can be especially difficult to deal with. Quite apart from the operational problems, high levels of employee absence can affect morale. It can also be costly: the Chartered Institute of Personnel and Development 2004 employer survey found that the average cost of absence per employee per year was £567.

This chapter covers:
- Legal requirements
- Maximising staff attendance
- Notification and certification requirements
- Recording and analysing absence
- Return to work interviews
- Employee absence as a conduct matter
- Employee absence as a capability matter
- Accessing medical records
- Absence and employees with disabilities
- Terminating employment due to ill health
- Developing a sickness absence policy.

This chapter does not deal with *payments* of statutory or occupational sick pay. These are covered in chapter 6.

Legal requirements

There are certain legal requirements that affect the management of employee absence.

Disability Discrimination Act 1995 (DDA)
The DDA says that if an employee has a disability, you must make reasonable adjustments so that the employee is not treated less favourably than other employees.

Health and Safety at Work Act (HSWA) 1974

Under the Health and Safety at Work Act, you have a responsibility to protect the health and safety of your employees. If your employee is more vulnerable to physical or psychological risk on return to work because of his or her illness, injury or disability, you have an extra responsibility to protect him or her.

Employment Rights Act 1996 and Employment Act 2002 (Dispute Regulations) 2004

If you feel that you need to dismiss an employee on the grounds of ill health, you must follow the statutory minimum dismissal procedure. You must also follow a fair procedure.

Data Protection Act 1998

If an absence record contains specific medical information relating to an employee, this is deemed sensitive data and you must gain the employee's consent to process it. You can achieve this via a general clause in the written statement of terms and conditions of employment (see chapter 4).

Maximising staff attendance

Employees who have high motivation and job satisfaction are likely to have better attendance.

Employees who have high motivation and job satisfaction are likely to have better attendance. Acas comments that 'although some absence is outside management's control, levels of absence can be reduced when positive policies are introduced to improve working conditions and increase workers' motivation to attend work.'

There are certain things that all employers can do to encourage a work environment which maximises staff attendance. Here are some suggestions:

- Provide good physical working conditions and high health and safety standards.
- Try and provide interesting and varied work, where staff are given responsibility to take decisions about their work.
- Encourage teamworking.
- Give new starters, particularly younger employees, thorough induction training.
- Have effective policies and practices on equality and discrimination.
- Give as much flexibility as you can, so that employees can fulfil work as well as domestic responsibilities.
- Support staff through difficult periods, to help them to maximise attendance. For example, you could agree with them a temporary reduction in hours or you could pay for a course of counselling.

In general, implement the suggestions in this Good Guide!

Notification and certification requirements

You should make clear to your employees how they need to notify you if they are not well enough to come into work. On their return, you should ask them to produce a self-certificate for absences of seven days or less; and a doctor's certificate for absences of more than seven days. You should make clear that failure to adhere to your organisation's certification and notification requirements, or unauthorised absence, will be treated as a disciplinary offence.

Below is an example statement on certification and notification requirements.

Westwich Association sickness absence certification and notification

If you are unable to attend work due to sickness, you must call to speak with your immediate manager, no later than the time that you would be due to start work. If your immediate manager is not available, you should ask to speak with the general manager.

You should keep in contact with your manager on a daily basis, or less than this if agreed with your manager.

On your return to work, and if your absence is for seven days or less, you must fill in a self-certification form and pass it to your manager. A form is available on the shared drive on the computer network, or from the administrator. If you are absent for more than seven days, you must complete a self-certification form and provide a doctor's certificate. If your absence is for more than 14 days, you must send in medical certificates regularly during your absence.

If you fail to adhere to the above requirements, or if your absence is unauthorised, the matter may be treated as a potential disciplinary offence.

Here is an example self-certificate form that you could adapt for use in your organisation. Alternatively, you can use form SC2 which is available from social security offices or from www.inlandrevenue.gov.uk/forms/sc2.pdf.

The Westwich Association
Self-certificate
Note – this form must be completed for ALL periods of sickness. For a period of sickness lasting more than seven calendar days in a row, a medical certificate is also required.

Name: _____

Date illness began (including non-working days): _____

Date you were better (including non-working days): _____

First date of absence from work: _____

Date of return to work: _____

Reason for absence: _____

_____ Did you attend hospital   Yes/No
_____   clinic   Yes/No
_____   doctor   Yes/No
Please briefly describe symptoms:

_____ Did you receive medication
_____ from your doctor   Yes/No
Give details of any accident:

_____ Did you purchase medication
_____ from a chemist   Yes/No

I understand that if I provide inaccurate or false information about my absence it may, depending on the circumstances, be treated as gross misconduct and result in my summary dismissal from the organisation.

Signature _____ Date _____
I confirm that the employee was absent from work on the above dates.

Date of return to work interview _____

Manager's Signature _____ Date _____

Recording and analysing absence

If your employees tend to have only occasional days off sick, and you pay them full pay for such days, you may get into a habit of not recording these absences. However, problems can arise if:
- the 'odd day off sick' becomes a regular thing
- or short term sickness becomes a longer-term situation.

If you do not keep records from the beginning, it will be more difficult to check the details of an employee's sickness absence. Further, you are legally required to keep records on levels and dates of absence and sickness, for Statutory Sick Pay purposes. You will not be able to do this unless you keep accurate records.

You can adopt a simple record system for each of your employees. The following recording forms are adapted from the Acas advisory booklet on *Personnel Data and Record Keeping*. The advisory booklet is available for download at www.acas.org.uk/publications/b03.html.

If you do not keep records from the beginning, it will be more difficult to check the details of an employee's sickness absence.

Individual record of absence

Employee name								
Week no	Absent					Sick pay due in week/month	Sick pay running total	Comments
	M	T	W	Th	F			
1								
2								
3								
4								
5								
6								
7								
8								
9								
10								
11								
12								
Etc								

Monthly summary of absence

Employee name	Date in month																	
	1	2	3	4	5	6	7	etc	21	22	23	24	25	26	27	28	29	30	31

A= authorised absence
U = unauthorised absence
S = certified sickness
US = uncertified sickness
L = lateness

Time lost to sickness

You can assess the percentage of time lost due to sickness each year in your organisation. This can be helpful in assessing year on year trends and checking whether or not you have a problem.

You could use the following formula:

$$\frac{\text{Total absence days}}{\text{Total available days in the period}} \times 100$$

So, for example, if the total days lost to absence over the year was 82 and the total working days available to your organisation was 2,600 (i.e. working days excluding weekends/rest days and holidays), then the formula would be:

$$\frac{82}{2,600} \times 100$$

This would give the percentage of time lost to absence as three per cent.

You might then check your percentage absence rate against other organisations, to see how serious the problem is and to decide whether special action is needed. You may be able to get figures for other organisations through local employers' groups or your local Council for Voluntary Services (CVS).

As a guide to national figures on absence, the Chartered Institute of Personnel and Development 2004 employer survey found the following:

- the average level of sickness absence was 3.9 per cent
- the most commonly quoted target figure for absence was 3 per cent
- 59 per cent of absence was accounted for by spells of less than five days.

You can analyse your absence in different ways, to find out whether most of your absence is due to long-term sickness, short-term absence or unauthorised absence and lateness. You should discount any periods of pregnancy-related illness when contemplating taking action over someone's absence record.

For further ways of analysing and measuring absence, see the Acas advisory handbook *Absence and Labour Turnover* available for download from the Acas website at www.acas.org.uk/publications/B04.html.

Return to work interviews

A 'return to work interview' is a meeting that you, as a manager, hold with your employee when he or she returns to work after sickness, either after a single day off or after a longer period. The

Chartered Institute of Personnel and Development Employer Survey 2004 states that return to work interviews are judged to be one of the most effective management actions in increasing employee attendance.

The aims of a return to work interview are:
- to support the employee back into the workplace
- to ensure that the employee is fit to return to work
- and to discuss if any reasonable adjustments need to be considered.

A possible format for the meeting is:
- Check that the employee is feeling better.
- Receive the self-certificate or doctor's certificate from him or her.
- Tell them that they have been missed.
- Tell them about any workplace developments.
- Check what work priorities they have.
- Help them re-prioritise if needed.
- Go through their attendance record if there are any areas of concern. Follow up, as outlined in the sections below, as needed.

Employee absence as a conduct matter

On occasions, you may find that there is no acceptable reason for absences and they do not improve after an informal discussion. Regular days 'off sick', combined with frequent lateness and poor timekeeping can be disruptive to an organisation and are particularly concerning when the absence appears to be due to a lack of commitment on behalf of the employee.

Frequently, a discussion in a return to work interview or in another meeting about absence can be all that is needed to improve attendance levels. It is the fact that the employee's attendance has been noticed that makes the change.

However, if there is no improvement, you should treat the matter as a conduct rather than a capability issue and deal with it under the disciplinary procedure. See chapter 9 for information on dealing with disciplinary matters.

Employee absence as a capability matter

Where an employee either suffers from regular short-term illnesses or long-term ill health, you should treat the absence as a capability matter and proceed with sensitivity.

You should:
- Monitor the employee's absence record.
- Consult regularly with the employee about their health and the support you can give them to improve their attendance or return to work.
- Set time limits on assessing the situation and tell the employee.
- Let them know if their job is at risk, and why.
- Obtain medical reports, seeking the employee's consent first.
- Consider adjustments to the employee's work or work environment.
- Only consider dismissal as a last resort, after exploring all other avenues with the employee. See the section below on termination of employment.

How you deal with the matter will depend on the situation. Below are some examples.

Example 1 – long-term absence with a relatively clear end date

David has broken his leg and it is anticipated that he will be off sick for two months. A full recovery is anticipated. David's manager takes the following actions:
- Keeps in contact with David.
- Pays occupational sick pay (to which David is entitled for 9 weeks at full pay, in any 12 month period).
- Towards the end of David's sick leave and in agreement with David, passes him some work which he is able to do from home.

Example 2 – longterm ill health with no clear date for improvement

Julie has long-term ill health problems which have led to increasing periods of time off work. It is uncertain as to whether she will be able to return to her previous duties. Her manager:
- Keeps in regular contact.
- Ensure Julie receives her Occupational Sick Pay entitlement.
- Seeks Julie's agreement to gaining a medical report.
Once the medical report has been received, her manager arranges a formal meeting with Julie. Julie's statutory right is to be accompanied by a work colleague or trade union representative but in this circumstance and bearing in mind

Julie's ill health, her manager agrees that her partner
should accompany her.

At the meeting, Julie and her manager review the medical
report and discuss all available options, including reducing
her hours of work on a permanent basis, phasing her
return to work or making adjustments to the work.
Redeployment to a different job is also discussed, although
Julie's manager makes clear that no alternative job is
currently available.

The Doctor's report has indicated that some improvement
may be anticipated in around two months' time, so Julie
and her manager agree that a further report will be sought
then and another formal meeting arranged. The manager
lets Julie know that all reasonable adjustments will be
explored to get her back to work but that ultimately, her
job is at risk if she is unable to return within another three
months. This is because of the operational difficulties
caused by her absence.

Julie's manager confirms the outcome of the meeting in
writing and keeps in touch with Julie, prior to the next
formal meeting. She also suggests that Julie comes in to see
colleagues at lunchtimes when she can, in order to keep in
touch.

If, after the next formal meeting, there is no improvement,
Julie's manager will need to consider whether termination
of Julie's employment is reasonable and necessary. If it is,
Julie's manager will need to follow the statutory dismissal
procedure (outlined later in this chapter).

Example 3 – short-term absence (adapted from a case study from Acas)

Chas has suffered from lower back pain, on and off for
several years, leading to spells of short term certificated
absence. He is currently absent due to his bad back and is
awaiting physiotherapy.

His manager has kept in touch with him each week and
has encouraged him to call into work for a chat and to
keep in touch both with what is happening at work and
with his colleagues.

Chas's wait for physiotherapy will be a few weeks and
there are problems covering his work. The manager has
talked to Chas about this problem and his health and they
agree that he should be examined by an independent

occupational health practitioner for advice on the best course of action.

After speaking to the occupational practitioner, Chas agrees to return to work for a few hours each day on a temporary basis until he completes the course of physiotherapy.

As he finds it painful to sit or stand for long periods, adjustments are made to accommodate this. Arrangements are made to make the journey to and from work as easy as possible by allowing him to start and finish outside the rush hours and reserving a parking place near his place of work. The manager and Chas review his work area and job and establish that the chair provided for him does not provide enough support. A more supportive chair is provided. His colleagues agree to help with any lifting required in the job. During this ongoing process, the organisation also increases awareness of back injuries, among its staff, by distributing relevant leaflets, providing training on the manual handling of materials and carrying out risk assessments on each job.

Accessing medical records

Where an employee has a health problem preventing him or her from attending work, you will need medical information on the employee's fitness to work now and in the future. This will help you in determining your duty of care (for example, to make reasonable adjustments if there is a disability). You can obtain a medical report from the employee's GP and if relevant, their consultant. As an alternative or in addition, you may wish to have the employee examined by an independent occupational health practitioner.

Seeking consent

In accordance with the Access to Medical Reports Act 1998, the employee is entitled to withhold consent to your obtaining a medical report on them. If the employee gives consent, he or she is entitled to see the report before it is sent to you.

If the employee refuses to give access to medical records or to see an independent occupational health practitioner, then you are entitled to make a decision on employment based on the facts available to you.

In some circumstances, more than one report may be needed, especially if the employee is off sick for an extended period, or the employee disputes the contents of the first report.

Process

You should draft a consent form for the employee to sign, making it clear that they are giving consent to their GP to supply a medical report. You should send the consent form to the GP along with a list of questions relating to the illness/absence and details of the role of the employee in your organisation. The more information that is supplied to the GP, the more likely it is they will be able to make an assessment and comment on the suitability of the role and any reasonable adjustments.

Retaining the services of a medical advisor

One option you might consider is to retain the services of an independent occupational health practitioner on a sessional basis. If you want to appoint an occupational health practitioner, you could contact the Faculty of Occupational Medicine, 6 St Andrew's Place, Regent's Park, London, NW1 4LB, tel: 020 7317 5890. www.facoccmed.ac.uk.

Making decisions based on medical reports

You might take one of several options, upon receipt of a medical report:

- To re-organise or re-design the job to enable the employee to continue to carry out their work. Financial support for any adjustments may be available from the Government's Access to Work scheme. You can find out information about Access to Work from the Disability Employment Adviser at your local Jobcentre Plus.
- To consider finding alternative work for the employee.
- To take no action, either pending a further medical report after a set period of time, or because there is a set return date which is reasonable.
- To consider termination of employment, on the grounds of ill health and after consultation with the employee. If you are considering termination, you must follow the procedures outlined in the section later in this chapter on termination of employment due to ill health.

Absence and employees with disabilities

The Disability Discrimination Act 1995 says that if an employee has a disability, you are under an obligation to make reasonable adjustments to allow the employee to undertake his or her job. The adjustments you agree will depend on the requirements of the individual.

Even if the employee does not have a disability, it is still good practice if you make adjustments to enable each employee to maximise their attendance.

For example, if an employee with Multiple Sclerosis has periods when he or she is not able to work, a possible adjustment might be to allow the employee to work on the basis of annual hours – so that there is more flexibility on when the work must be undertaken.

Even if the employee does not have a disability, it is still good practice, and will benefit your organisation, if you make adjustments to enable each employee to maximise their attendance.

Some examples suggested by the Health and Safety Executive are:

Adjustments to working arrangements:
- allowing a phased return to work
- changing individual's working hours
- providing help with transport to and from work
- arranging home working
- allowing an employee to be absent from work for rehabilitation treatment.

Adjustments to premises:
- moving tasks to more accessible areas
- making alterations to the premises.

Adjustments to a job:
- providing new or modifying existing equipment and tools
- modifying work furniture
- providing additional training
- modifying instructions or reference manuals
- modifying work patterns and management systems
- arranging telephone conferences to reduce travel
- providing a buddy or mentor
- providing supervision
- reallocating work within the sick employee's team
- providing alternative work.

Consult with the employee to find out what adjustments may assist. You could also seek the advice of the Disability Employment Adviser at your local Jobcentre Plus.

Terminating employment due to ill health

Long-term absence or frequent persistent short-term absence can be very difficult to deal with in a small organisation. You will be trying to keep the employee's job open but on the other hand, you may need to replace the employee to get the job done.

At some point, the time may come when you are not able to hold open employment for any longer, because of the employee's inability to do the job and because adjustments are not practicable.

If this is the case, and even if the employee is disabled, it may be fair for you to dismiss the employee.

Dismissals due to ill health can be complex. You are advised to take advice from an employment lawyer or human resources specialist.

Remember that the employee is unwell and will be more vulnerable than usual. You will need to proceed with great care and sensitivity.

If termination of the employee's contract is contemplated, or other actions such as a move to a lesser job, you must have given prior warnings and you must follow the minimum statutory procedure under the Statutory Dispute Regulations from the Employment Act 2002. This involves:

Step 1
A written note to the member of staff, setting out the fact that termination of the employee's contract is contemplated and the basis for it, i.e. absence from work.

Step 2
A meeting to discuss the matter, after which a decision should be taken.

Step 3
A right of appeal against any decision taken at step 2. The appeal should normally be heard by a more senior manager, or if there is none, a trustee or trustees not previously involved in the matter.

The member of staff should be given full opportunity to state his or her point of view at both the step 2 meeting and any appeal. He or she should be informed prior to the meetings of his/her right to be accompanied by a colleague or trade union representative. As an alternative, you may want to give the employee the right to be accompanied by a friend or family member.

You should note that in addition to the minimum statutory procedure, you must also adopt a fair procedure. Your reason for dismissal must be genuine (i.e. capability) and you must be reasonable in treating this as a reason for dismissal.

Should termination of employment result, the employee should be given paid notice, in accordance with the requirements of his or her employment contract.

> Dismissals due to ill health can be complex. You are advised to take advice from an employment lawyer or human resources specialist.

Developing a sickness absence policy

It is a good
idea to have a
sickness
absence
policy, so that
staff know
what is
expected of
them.

It is a good idea to have a sickness absence policy, so that staff know what is expected of them, the support and payments they will have when off sick and what may happen if they do not adhere to the requirements of the policy.

The policy could cover the following areas:

A statement of intent

This would clarify that your organisation aims to provide payments above the level of Statutory Sick Pay (SSP), if it can, for employees who are sick.

It could also explain that your organisation's policy is to support staff who may be on long term sick leave, to make adjustments to work or premises to accommodate individuals and to hold jobs open wherever possible.

Notification and certification requirements

This would explain what you expect staff to do if they are not able to come to work, and what certificates they must produce. The consequences of not complying with the system should be spelled out.

Return to work interviews

Your policy on return to work interviews.

Sickness payments

Details of any occupational sick pay, over and above SSP.

Frequent short-term absence

Your procedures in the case of frequent short-term absence.

Long-term absence

Your procedures in the case of long-term absence.

Referral to a medical specialist

Circumstances where you may refer an employee to a medical specialist.

Reference to other areas of support

A reference to other time off to which employees may be entitled (such as for emergencies involving dependants, parental leave) – see chapter 8 for more information.

Checklist

✓ Establish clear notification and certification procedures for cases of employee absence.

✓ Keep records of absence. Analyse your records periodically to check for problems or trends. Any sickness that indicates stress/anxiety/depression could be logged, so that a stress audit of the organisation could be carried out.

✓ Implement a system of return to work interviews.

✓ If employee absence is a misconduct matter, deal with it under the disciplinary procedure.

✓ If an employee is suffering from long-term ill health or regular short-term illnesses, take the following steps:
  • Consult with the employee about their absence, their return and any reasonable adjustments.
  • Set time limits for assessing the situation.
  • Let the employee know if their job is at risk and why.
  • Obtain medical reports.
  • Consider adjustments.

✓ Follow the minimum statutory dismissal procedures if you are contemplating dismissing an employee on the grounds of ill health.

✓ Develop a policy on managing sickness absence.

Where to find out more

1. Acas

The following Acas advisory booklets may be useful:
Advisory Booklet on Absence and Labour Turnover
www.acas.org.uk/publications/B04.html
Personnel Data and Record Keeping
www.acas.org.uk/publications/b03.html

Acas also has a free online learning package to help small organisations to manage workplace absence. Go to www.acas.org.uk/elearning/.

You can contact Acas for advice on 08457 47 47 47 or textphone 08456 06 16 00.

For more details of how to order Acas Publications see page 36.

2. askNCVO

www.askncvo.org.uk offers a wealth of free, practical, up-to-date advice on all aspects of running a charity or voluntary organisation. Hundreds of pages cover trusteeship, financial management, human resources and more.

3. Business Link

The Business Link website has some information on managing absence. Go to www.businesslink.gov.uk and in the search field, enter 'managing absence.'

4. Health and Safety Executive (HSE)

The HSE has a section on managing absence on its website. Go to www.hse.gov.uk/sicknessabsence/.

| | Health and safety

What this chapter is about

This chapter gives an overview of what you as an employer will need to know and do about health and safety.

The following areas are covered:

- Your health and safety obligations
- Drafting a health and safety policy
- The role of directors
- The Working Time Regulations
- Stress at work
- Smoking

Your health and safety obligations

Your main health and safety obligations are outlined below.

General duties of employers

The Health & Safety at Work Act 1974 places a general duty on you as employer to ensure the health, safety and welfare of employees and others who may be affected by the actions of the Company, so far as is reasonably practical. The phrase "so far as is reasonably practicable" appears throughout much of Health and Safety legislation and in simple terms means that amount of cost, time, trouble and effort involved must be proportional to the level of risk.

The general duties extend to:

- Providing safe equipment and safe systems of work.
- Ensuring that articles and substances are used, handled, stored and transported safely.
- Providing information, instruction, training and supervision necessary to ensure the health and safety of employees.
- Providing safe workplaces with safe means of entering and leaving the workplace.
- Providing a healthy work environment with adequate welfare facilities.

Produce a health and safety policy

Under the Health and Safety at Work Act 1974, you must have a written, up to date health and safety policy if you employ five or more people. The policy must be brought to the attention of all employees and be easily accessible. Failure to have a policy in place is an offence and could lead to a fine.

See later in this chapter for information about writing a policy.

Failure to have a policy in place is an offence and could lead to a fine.

Carry out risk assessments

The Management of Health and Safety at Work Regulations 1999 say that you must undertake a suitable and sufficient assessment of risks to both employees and others who may be affected by their work activities. A risk assessment is a vigilant examination of what could cause harm to people so that you can assess if you have taken enough precautions, or should take more.

If you employ five or more people, you should record the significant findings of your risk assessments.

It is a legal requirement for you to also undertake special risk assessments on young persons (anyone under 18) and any woman who is pregnant or breastfeeding.

You can download information about risk assessments from the Health and Safety Executive (HSE) website at www.hse.gov.uk/pubns/indg218.pdf, or contact HSE Books on 01787 881 165 for a hard copy.

Another useful HSE document is *5 Steps to Risk Assessment* which can be downloaded from www.hse.gov.uk/pubns/indg163.pdf or obtained from HSE Books as above.

Register with the local enforcing authority for health and safety

To register with your local authority, use form OSR1, available from the Health and Safety website at www.hse.gov.uk/contact/faqs/newbusiness.htm.

Display a current certificate of Employers' Liability Insurance

You can find out more information from the leaflet Employers' Liability (Compulsory Insurance) Act 1969: a guide for employers. You can download this leaflet at www.hse.gov.uk/contact/faqs/newbusiness.htm or contact HSE Books for a hard copy.

Display the Health and Safety Law poster

The law says that a Health and Safety Law poster must be displayed at all times giving information to employees about health, safety and welfare. Names and locations of safety representatives and health and safety responsibilities need to be inserted onto the pro-forma poster. You can obtain a copy of the pro-forma poster from HSE Books by calling 01787 881 165 or going to its website at www.hsebooks.com.

Report certain injuries, diseases and dangerous occurrences
Under the Reporting of Injuries, Diseases and Dangerous Occurrences Regulations 1995 (RIDDOR), you must report certain work-related health and safety incidents.
The reportable instances are:
- Deaths, including the death of an employee within one year of being injured as the result of a notifiable accident.
- Major injuries.
- Where an employee or self-employed person has an accident resulting in them being off work for more than three days.
- Any gas incident.
- Injuries to members of the public that require them to go to hospital.
- Work-related diseases.
- Specified dangerous occurrences that could potentially have resulted in death, injury or ill health.

You can find out further information about reporting arrangements from the HSE publication about RIDDOR, downloadable at www.hse.gov.uk/pubns/hse31.pdf, or you can order it from HSE Books.

Maintain accident records
If you employ more than 10 people, you must keep accident records at the workplace. These must be kept for at least three years.
Accident records have to comply with the Data Protection Act 1998 and you must therefore not allow personal details and information to be seen by anyone reading or making an entry in an accident book. A way of doing this is to have tear-out pages. The Health and Safety Executive has published an Accident Book with pages which can be retained separately. It is available from HSE Books.

Provide first aid facilities
The Health and Safety (First Aid) Regulations 1981 require you to make adequate and appropriate provision for first aid. For further information, see the Health and Safety Executive booklet about first aid, at www.hse.gov.uk/pubns/indg214.pdf, or obtain it from HSE Books.

Consult with your employees about health and safety matters

If you have a recognised trade union, then you must consult with the safety representatives appointed by the union.

If the trade union requests it, you must set up a safety committee.

You must also consult with employees not covered by trade union safety representatives.

If there is no recognised trade union, you can consult with employees either individually or via representatives.

All representatives must be given reasonable training, time off with pay, facilities and help to enable to them to undertake their role.

For further information, see the leaflet *Consulting Employees on Health and Safety*, available for download at www.hse.gov.uk/pubns/indg232.pdf or from HSE books.

Provide a safe and healthy work place

Under the Workplace (Health, Safety and Welfare) Regulations 1992, there are a number of requirements covering matters such as the provision of adequate space for employees, maintenance of the workplace, conditions of floors, safe access routes, and control of temperature, lighting, ventilation and cleanliness.

This is the regulation that states that there must be adequate welfare facilities in place, drinking water available, places for hanging clothing etc.

The regulations also provide that non-smokers should be allocated separate rest areas from smokers. For further information, see the HSE booklet on *Workplace health, safety and welfare* at www.hse.gov.uk/pubns/indg244.pdf, or order it from HSE Books.

Ensure minimum standards for the use of machines and equipment

Under the Provision and Use of Work Equipment Regulations 1998, you must ensure minimum standards for the use of machines and equipment with regard to suitability, maintenance and inspection.

Further, you must ensure that employees have received sufficient information, instruction and training before using any equipment and that only authorised people are allowed to use the equipment.

Where guards or covers are fitted to guard against contact with dangerous parts, you must ensure that the guards or covers are fitted at all times.

You can download a guide to these regulations at www.hse.gov.uk/pubns/indg291.pdf, or order it from HSE Books.

Manual handling

The Manual Handling Operations Regulations 1992 state that, wherever possible, you should aim to avoid the need for employees to undertake manual handling operations.

If manual handling cannot be avoided, then the operations must be assessed and risks of injury eliminated or reduced by using mechanical means wherever practicable. Failing this, the risk assessment should identify other options such as redesign of task/layout, limiting size of loads, team lifting, training in safe lifting techniques etc.

You need to be aware that the HSE recommends a maximum lifting weight of 25kg for a man and 16kg for a woman, but these limits vary depending upon circumstances. The overriding requirement is that employees should not be required to lift anything that they feel is beyond their capability.

You can download a guide to these regulations www.hse.gov.uk/pubns/indg143.pdf, or order it from HSE Books.

> The overriding requirement is that employees should not be required to lift anything that they feel is beyond their capability.

Provide protective clothing/equipment

The Personal Protective Equipment at Work Regulations 1992 state that you must provide protective clothing or equipment to control those health and safety risks that cannot be adequately controlled by other means or as a backup to other control measures. Personal Protective Equipment (PPE) must always be considered a last resort.

You must assess and select suitable equipment taking into account the individual, compatibility with other PPE, comfort and any other additional risks the PPE may introduce.

You must provide PPE free of charge and provide information, instruction and training in the use, maintenance and storage of PPE.

You can download a guide to these regulations at www.hse.gov.uk/pubns/indg174.pdf, or order it from HSE Books.

Ensure safe use of VDUs

The Health & Safety (Display Screen Equipment) Regulations 1992 introduced measures to prevent repetitive strain injury, musculo-skeletal disorders, fatigue and eye problems when using VDUs (visual display units).

You must make a suitable and sufficient assessment of each workstation and surrounding work environment, together with the individual, to identify any specific risks to the individual. The assessment will highlight areas for improvement.

You must also give free eyesight tests on request, ensure that VDU operators have sufficient breaks from using the equipment and provide health and safety information about the hazards and safe use of the equipment to each VDU operator.

You can download a guide to these regulations at: www.hse.gov.uk/pubns/indg36.pdf, or order it from HSE Books.

Use of hazardous substances

You are required to carry out risk assessments for the handling, storage and use of hazardous substances as required by the Control of Substances Hazardous to Health Regulations (COSHHR) 2005.

In the first instance you must establish whether a substance is hazardous by looking at the label or obtaining the safety data sheet for the substance.

The COSHHR assessment will establish: who might be affected by the substance and how; the level of risk; and the required control measures necessary to eliminate or reduce the level of risk.

The safety data sheet must be retained and be accessible in an emergency. This contains useful information about the hazards, health effects, control measures, first aid, storage, disposal etc.

A guide to the regulations can be downloaded from www.coshh-essentials.org.uk or the HSE.

Assess risks relating to electricity

The Electricity at Work Regulations 1989 place a duty on you to control risks associated with the use of electricity in the premises. This includes fixed installations and portable appliances such as heaters, kettles and microwaves.

You must ensure that electrical equipment is suitable for the task, regularly inspected and properly maintained (i.e. Portable Appliance Testing). Steps should be taken to avoid electrical overloading as this can leads to fires.

All electrical work in the premises must only be undertaken by a competent person.

You can download a guide to these regulations at www.hse.gov.uk/pubns/indg231.pdf, or order it from HSE Books.

Fire certificates

The Fire Precautions Act 1971 states that certain types of workplace must have fire certificates which are issued by the fire authority. In general, fire certificates are required when there are more than 20 persons working in the premises at any one time, or there are more than 10 persons on a floor other than the ground floor.

However, it is anticipated that this regulation will be repealed in 2005, to be replaced by the Regulatory Reform (Fire Safety)

Order. The outcome will be that fire certificates are no longer required. The onus will be on the employer or person in control of the site to undertake a fire risk assessment of the premises.

Fire precautions and fire risk assessment

You must ensure that a fire risk assessment is undertaken and, where there are five or more employees, the significant findings of the risk assessment must be documented.

The fire risk assessment must take into consideration: the means of escape; signs and notices; emergency lighting; fire alarms; fire extinguishers; fire doors and compartments; fire evacuation procedures; staff training; and fire drills etc.

For further information on workplace fire safety, see www.hse.gov.uk/fireandexplosion/spdfire.htm.

Not discriminate against your employees on health and safety grounds

Under the provisions in the Employment Rights Act 1996, employees are protected from dismissal or victimisation by an employer for a health and safety related reason, (e.g. bringing to the employer's attention matters which potentially breach health and safety regulations).

Employees who act as health and safety representatives must not be dismissed or subjected to a detriment for carrying out or proposing to carry out duties in connection with preventing or reducing risks to health and safety at work.

If a dismissal occurs for any of the above reasons, the dismissal will be automatically unfair.

Drafting a health and safety policy/plan

If you have more than five employees, you must have a health and safety policy. This should show who will do what, when and how they will do it.

You also need to carry out risk assessments to identify any risks and record the outcome of the assessments.

You can combine the policy and risk assessment into an annual (or more frequent if required) health and safety plan. An example is given below.

When you draw up or review your plan, you should discuss it with your employees or their health and safety representatives.

The Royal Society for the Prevention of Accidents (RoSPA), suggests the following practical steps you should take to draw up your plan.

How to draw up a health and safety plan

Start with a single sheet of A4 paper.
Write it in your own words and make it fit your company's needs.
Divide it up into sections:
On one side, in simple terms, write down your overall health and safety objectives (see below).
Next outline responsibilities (from director level down to the newest recruit).
Then outline the arrangements you have in place for achieving a safe and healthy working environment (for example, carrying out risk assessments
providing necessary training and information; monitoring health and safety performance; accident/incident reporting; first aid; general fire safety; obtaining professional advice; and so on).
Now turn the sheet over and on the other side write down the results of your risk assessments, detailing hazards, what could happen and any rules or control measures that need to be in place with appendices giving other useful information.
Don't make the plan any longer than it needs to be. Keep it as simple as possible.
Remember, if it is to be of any value at all, it has to be a working document which your employees will actually refer to and read.
When you have drafted your plan, ensure that it is signed and dated by the director or chief executive as the person with overall responsibility for formulating, implementing and developing the policy.
You need to set aside time to explain your plan to your staff, explaining the contribution of managers and every member of the team to its successful development and the formulation and implementation of procedures.

Remember, it has to be a working document which your employees will actually refer to and read.

The example health and safety plan/policy below is from the Royal Society for the Prevention of Accidents (RoSPA), at its website at www.rospa.com/occupationalsafety/smallfirms/sheet6.htm.

Example health and safety plan

The Go-ahead Manufacturing Company: Health and Safety Action Plan
PART A. What we're trying to do
We aim to:
- avoid accidents and damage to people's health and cutting corners on health and safety to try and save time and money;
- ensure that we pay as much attention to health and safety as any other key business objective;
- always follow safe systems of work;
- avoid buying in unsafe products;
- work to legal requirements as a minimum standard to be achieved;
- always insist on high standards of health and safety when dealing with others; and
- strive for continuous improvement in health and safety performance.

How we're going to do it.
We will always:
- make sure we consider health and safety whenever we plan anything (however small);
- identify hazards, assess risks to see whether our control measures are adequate or need to be improved and (see below);
- set ourselves measurable health and safety standards and targets with dates for implementation;
- monitor how well we are achieving them (for example, through inspection) and record results;
- report and record all accidents and incidents and investigate them to see why we have not been able to prevent them;
- consult everyone to get their views about possible health and safety problems and solutions;
- communicate all necessary health and safety information;
- provide necessary training for everyone so they can meet their health and safety responsibilities;
- get advice from outside competent specialists whenever we need it;
- meet basic workplace welfare requirements, have appropriate first aid and fire precautions and employers liability insurance;
- and make time every three months to see how we're doing, record our findings, and, where necessary, set new targets for improvement.

Who is responsible for what?
- Josephine Soap, as managing director, has overall responsibility for health and safety in the company.
- Joe Soap and Tom Thumb, as supervisors must make sure safe systems of work are always followed and carry out regular monitoring.
- Every member of staff must co-operate in following safe procedures, report problems and make suggestions for improvements.
- Our contractors and suppliers must provide us with all necessary safe information and co-operate with our health and safety requirements.

Signed
Josephine Soap, Managing Director. 1/06/2005

PART B. The Go-ahead Manufacturing Company Record of Risk Assessments		
Hazards	Risks	Control Measures
What could cause harm? Machinery? Chemicals? Manual handling? Electricity etc?	What could happen? How bad could it be? How likely is it? Who could be affected?	What do we need to do to prevent harm? Is it adequate?
	What is the risk level, high medium or low?	Do we need to do more? If so, by when?

Directors' responsibilities

The Health and Safety Commission has published guidance on the health and safety responsibilities of board directors of all types of organisation.

The guidance may be relied upon in court as an example of good practice, and health and safety inspectors may use it as a point of reference when carrying out inspections.

The guidance lists five main action points:

- The board should accept formally and publicly a collective role in providing health and safety leadership in their organisation.
- Each member of the board should accept his/her individual role in providing health and safety leadership for the organisation.
- The board should ensure that all board decisions reflect health and safety intentions as articulated in an organisational health and safety policy statement.
- The board should recognise its role in the act of engaging the active participation of workers and improving health and safety.
- The board should ensure it is kept informed of and alert to the relevant health and safety risk management issues; the Health and Safety Executive recommends that a member of the board should be designated health and safety director for this purpose.

For further information, see the publication *Directors' responsibilities for health and safety*, available for download from the HSE website at www.hse.gov.uk/pubns/indg343.pdf, or from HSE Books.

The Working Time Regulations

The Working Time Regulations 1998 (as amended) place certain restrictions on the working time of employees and make certain requirements of employers in terms of rest breaks and paid annual leave. The Regulations implement the provisions of the European Working Time Directive. The Health and Safety Executive (HSE) is responsible for enforcement of the Regulations. It is a criminal offence for an employer to fail to comply with the provisions of the Working Time Regulations.

The Regulations apply not only to employees but also to the wider category of 'workers'. See chapter 4 for further information about the differences between a 'worker' and an 'employee'.

Working time

Under the Regulations, 'working time' means any period during which the individual is working, is at the employer's disposal and is carrying out their activities or duties.

> 'Working time' means any period during which the individual is working, is at the employer's disposal and is carrying out their activities or duties.

Working time includes:

- any period during which the employee is receiving training in connection with the job;
- travel time during the working day (e.g. the journey between two work places or clients);
- time spent waiting at the place of work for work to be allocated;
- time spent working away from home;
- time on call at the workplace.

Working time does not include:

- the journey to or from the workplace and home;
- time resting at the end of the working day, even if the worker is required to stay away from home overnight;
- time spent 'on call' when away from the workplace and not carrying out duties.

There have been two European Court of Justice cases, Simap and Jaegar, which have changed the UK's original interpretation of the Working Time Regulations in that they have specified that time spent 'on call' at the work place is in fact working time, even if the employee is not actually working. These cases have direct effect in the UK and have caused considerable concern. For example, if you run residential care homes, the whole period of time members of staff spend at a 'sleep in' will be considered to be 'working time'. This means that these staff may be working in excess of the maximum 48 hours average and may not be having sufficient rest breaks (see below).

The European Commission proposed to introduce a third category of 'inactive time' to address the problem caused by the

SIMAP and Jaegar cases, but at the time of writing, this had been rejected by European Parliament MEPs.

For the latest information, see www.dti.gov.uk/er/work_time_regs/index.htm. The law is changing quickly in this area, so it is worth checking.

The '48 hour week'

The Working Time Regulations state that employees must not work, on average over a 17 week period (26 weeks in some circumstances) more than 48 hours per week. These working hours include any overtime.

If you require an employee to work more than the average 48 hours, the employee must first sign an 'opt out', formally agreeing to this.

Please note that, at the time of writing this publication, the European Commission's (EC) draft legislation was undergoing consultation with Member States and it stated that the averaging period should be 12 months and that the circumstances where opt outs are permitted will be changed. You may wish to check the latest situation.

Employees must not be pressured to sign an opt-out agreement. If they have opted out, they may opt in again, subject to a maximum of three months' notice.

Keeping records

You are not required to keep a record of employees' working hours, but you must keep a record of the names of those who have opted out of the 48 hour average working week.

The right to rest breaks

Workers have a legal right to the following rest breaks:
- An uninterrupted rest break of 20 minutes, if a worker's daily working time is more than six hours. The rest break may be unpaid.
- A daily rest period of 11 consecutive hours.
- An uninterrupted weekly rest period of not less than 24 hours, although this can be aggregated to one uninterrupted rest period of 48 hours over a 14 day period.

Night work

A night worker is someone who normally works at least three hours at night time. 'Night time' is defined between 11pm and 6am, although workers and employers may agree to vary this.

Night workers should not work more than eight hours daily on average, including overtime where it is part of a night worker's normal hours of work.

Nightly working time is calculated over 17 weeks, but can be longer in some situations.

A night worker cannot opt-out of the night work limit.

Exempt workers

Managing executives whose working time is 'unmeasured' are exempt from the Working Time Regulations.

There are certain other exemptions. For example, shift workers are exempted from the right to daily and weekly rest periods, but must be afforded adequate 'compensatory rest' within a reasonable time.

Annual leave

The Regulations say that you must give your workers and employees a minimum of 20 days' paid leave annually (pro-rated for those working part-time). The 20 day requirement includes the eight UK public and bank holidays. You must not give pay in lieu of the 20 day's annual leave, except when the employee leaves your employment.

'Rolling up' holiday pay

If you have workers or employees who work on a casual or irregular, part-time basis, it may be complicated to work out their entitlement to paid annual leave.

Some employers get round this by adding a monetary amount of holiday pay to each hour worked. This is referred to as 'rolling up' holiday pay.

There have been several cases which have considered whether 'rolling up' holiday pay is legal. The current position is that it is legal, provided that you adhere to the guidelines below, set out by the Employment Appeal Tribunal in MBP Structures v Munro.

- The rolled up holiday pay has to be expressly agreed and incorporated into the contract of employment.
- The percentage amount of holiday pay should be clearly identified in the contract and ideally also in the payslip, as a separate element.
- The rolled up holiday pay must be a real addition to the hourly rate of pay – you can't just split the existing hourly rate into pay and holiday pay.
- You should keep records of holidays taken, to ensure that individuals are taking rest and you should take reasonable steps to ensure that individuals take their holiday before the end of the holiday year.

Holiday pay on leaving

The normal rules under the Working Time Regulations are:

- that a worker has no right to carry untaken holiday forward to the next year;
- and if they do not take holiday, they cannot claim pay in lieu;
- but once employment has ended, the worker is entitled to holiday pay for holiday they have not taken.

Annual leave requests

Unless the individual's contract of employment states otherwise, the default legal requirement is that an employee must provide notice of twice as many days as the length of leave that is to be taken, in advance of the first day of leave requested. For example, if an employee requests two weeks of annual leave, he or she must give four weeks' notice prior to the first day on which the leave was due to start.

If you can't agree to the request for leave, you must inform the employee of this a period of time in advance that is equal to the amount of leave requested. So if two weeks is requested, you must tell the employee at least two weeks in advance if you intend to reject the leave.

Young workers

There are different provisions that regulate the working time of young workers (i.e. those over school leaving age but under 18). In summary, these provisions are as follows:

- a limit on the hours of work to eight per day;
- a maximum working week of 40 hours;
- an uninterrupted rest break of 30 minutes where the normal working day is more than four and a half hours;
- a rest period of not less than 48 hours in a seven day period. This cannot be aggregated over a 14 day period;
- no provision for averaging weekly working time over a reference period;
- no opt-out;
- restrictions on night work – young workers should not ordinarily work at night, although there are certain exceptions.

Collective agreements and workforce agreements

The Working Time Regulations allow for 'collective agreements' or 'workforce agreements', which may modify or exclude certain provisions of the Working Time Regulations. A collective agreement is an agreement between an employer and a trade union. A workforce agreement is an agreement between an employer and employee representatives, or if the employer has less than 20 workers, between the employer and the majority of workers.

Employers and workers can agree that night work limits and rights to rest breaks may be varied, with the workers receiving 'compensatory rest'. They may also agree to extend the averaging period for the 48 hour week up to 52 weeks. [Note: this is likely to change with the EC proposals to 52 weeks in all circumstances.]

For further information on the Working Time Regulations, see the Department for Trade and Industry website: www.dti.gov.uk/er/work_time_regs/.

Stress at work

One part of your responsibility to provide a safe and healthy work environment is to ensure that work is not overly stressful. A certain amount of pressure helps people to achieve their best, but too much stress can be damaging to health and can lead to lower productivity and higher sickness absence.

Stress audit

To find out whether stress is a problem in your organisation, you could undertake a stress audit. Basically, this involves talking to staff about their jobs and gaining an understanding from them as to what they find stressful and why, and what they do not find stressful and why. You could use the Health and Safety Executive Management Standards for stress to assist you in the audit. You can find the standards at www.hse.gov.uk/stress/standards.

Once you have completed the audit, you can determine a plan of action if needed.

Tackling the causes of workplace stress

The following is advice taken from the Business Link website. You can find this by going to www.businesslink.gov.uk and searching under 'stress.'

> **Dealing with workplace stress**
> Once you've identified possible stress problems in your business, you can then take steps to tackle the causes.
> If overwork is a problem, consider how you might reduce people's workload. Ensure targets are challenging but realistic. Help people to prioritise work, cutting out unnecessary tasks and providing time-management training if necessary. Encourage delegation of work where possible, and try to delegate work yourself.
> Make sure staff take their holiday entitlement – and take your own.

One part of your responsibility to provide a safe and healthy work environment is to ensure that work is not overly stressful.

Check individuals are well-matched to the jobs you give them. Make sure your recruitment and selection procedures help you to achieve this.

Make sure every employee has a well-defined role – and that they know what this is.

Review people's performance so they know how they're doing. Reviews also allow you to get feedback from employees about potential problems and identify any training they may need.

Where possible give employees more autonomy, allowing them to plan their work schedule and decide how to tackle problems.

Adopt a management style that encourages employees to discuss problems with you. Provide them with opportunities to express ideas about their work.

Keep staff informed about your business direction and make sure you tell them about significant changes to the business.

Ensure you have effective discipline and grievance procedures to tackle bullying and harassment.

Encourage employees to achieve a better work-life balance. Take a sympathetic approach to any personal problems employees may have – a relationship break-up or family illness. Discuss with the individual what support may help them. This might be a period of time off, or a period of more flexible working.

Good management practice

Lots of the good management practice described elsewhere in this guide will help to ensure that employee stress levels do not go undetected. For example: see the guidelines on induction and probation at chapter 5; staff supervision at chapter 7; diversity and non-discrimination at chapter 2; and work-life balance at chapter 8.

Case law and stress

There have been some Employment Tribunal cases in recent years concerning employee stress. In some cases, employees have been awarded significant sums in compensation where an employer has failed to take steps to protect the employee's psychological health and safety. Case law indicates the following:

- Unless the employer knows of a particular problem or vulnerability, it is usually entitled to assume that an employee can withstand normal job pressures.
- No occupation should be regarded as intrinsically dangerous to health.

- To trigger an employer's duty to take steps, the indications of likely harm to the employee's health must be obvious enough for the reasonable employer to realise that something should be done.
- Where an employer offers a confidential advice service with referral to counselling, it is unlikely to be in breach of its duty.

Personal stress

Make sure you also deal with your own stress if you need to. The Business Link website has some practical suggestions about dealing with your own stress. See www.businesslink.gov.uk/ and search under 'stress.'

> Make sure you also deal with your own stress if you need to.

Guides on managing stress

The Health and Safety Executive (HSE) has a guide to workplace stress, which you can download at www.hse.gov.uk/pubns/indg281.pdf, or order from HSE Books. Acas also has a guide about stress, which you can download at www.acas.org.uk/publications/b11.html#7 or order from Acas Publications, tel: 08702 42 90 90.

Case study

The following case study is taken from the HSE website.

Tackling stress at a care home

Background
Care-giving in old people's homes involves providing assistance with activities of daily living (walking, bathing, feeding, etc) and emotional support (companionship) for residents who often have reduced physical or mental capacity.

Problem
Physical and mental demands on staff are high. The home in question was originally designed for residents who were relatively independent, however as residents have aged, their dependency levels have naturally increased and some now require much greater support. As a result, staff have reported considerable physical and mental strain and there has been a marked increase in the rate of sickness absence from stress-related illnesses, such as depression and anxiety.

Assessing the risks and finding solutions

Workers, managers, safety representatives and specialist staff discussed the issue through the home's health and safety committee. It was found that there were predictable patterns in demands on care-givers, which allowed the following measures to be brought in:

- Work schedules were adjusted to increase staff numbers during hours of peak demand.
- The roles of auxiliary nursing staff were clarified to ensure that both they and specialist staff knew their responsibilities and needs regarding support.
- Greater power to make decisions was given to certain groups of workers.

Results

Care staff reported a more manageable workload, an increase in perceived support from management and other care-givers, and greater ownership of their work. Although some had greater responsibilities, this was welcomed as a positive development.

The success of these interventions has also contributed to a substantial reduction in stress-related sickness absence. Problems of work overload and constrained resources have been reduced by targeting resources at particularly busy areas or times.

Consulting with and involving staff and their representatives 'on the ground', was a simple way of ensuring that this was done effectively and fairly.

Smoking

You have a legal duty to protect the health of your employees and this includes preventing passive smoking.

The Health and Safety Executive (HSE) has produced a booklet entitled *Passive Smoking at Work*. You can download this from the HSE website at www.hse.gov.uk/pubns/indg63.pdf, or call the HSE information line (see the end of this chapter) to request a copy.

The booklet recommends that all employers should introduce a policy on smoking at work, following consultation with employees, and it gives guidance on what the policy should achieve.

Here is the smoking policy introduced by Westwich Association:

Smoking policy
It is the policy of the Westwich Association not to permit smoking within its premises, except where specified. This policy has been introduced after consultation with all employees and volunteers, to protect the health and safety of all and to allow for an unpolluted working environment. If you wish to smoke, you may do so in the specified rest room and outside the main building. Smoking is not permitted in the toilets. Any employee or volunteer found to be in breach of these rules may be subject to disciplinary action.

Checklist

The following checklist is adapted from www.healthandsafetyinfo.org.uk, which is a dedicated website from Unison for employees in the community and voluntary sector.

- ✓ Have you got an up to date health and safety policy?
- ✓ Have staff been notified of the policy?
- ✓ Do you display the statutory Health and Safety notice in your premises?
- ✓ How do you consult with staff on health and safety matters?
- ✓ Do all staff get health and safety training at induction?
- ✓ Are staff given training on specific risks they might face such as manual handling and violence?
- ✓ Have you done risk assessments on every aspect of your operations?
- ✓ Are they up to date?
- ✓ Have you acted on the results of the risk assessments?
- ✓ Have risk assessments included manual handing, chemical and stress risks?
- ✓ Have you undertaken a stress audit?
- ✓ Do you have safety data sheets for all potentially dangerous materials you use – including cleaning fluids?
- ✓ Are all chemicals clearly marked?
- ✓ Have all VDU users had an ergonomic assessment?
- ✓ Have all VDU users been offered free eye tests?
- ✓ Is all electrical equipment tested regularly?
- ✓ Are gas appliances checked regularly?
- ✓ Do you have first aiders?
- ✓ Do you have sufficient first aid boxes?
- ✓ Are all work surfaces, walls and floors kept tidy and clean?
- ✓ Are floors and stairs free from obstruction and non-slip?
- ✓ Is the temperature comfortable all year?
- ✓ Is there sufficient space for staff?

✓ Are there sufficient toilets, washing facilities and other facilities?

✓ Is there sufficient ventilation?

✓ Do you have a smoking policy that protects workers from passive smoking?

✓ Are there clear and sufficient fire signs and instructions?

✓ Do you have regular fire drills?

✓ Are fire alarms and smoke detectors checked regularly?

✓ Are all reportable accidents and occurrences recorded and reported?

✓ Do you have an accident book?

✓ Have you got employers Liability Insurance?

✓ Have you got a member of your management committee who has been designated as a champion of health & safety?

✓ Have all managers and management committee members received health and safety training?

✓ Do you comply with the requirements of the Working Time Regulations?

Where to find out more

I. Acas

The following publications can be downloaded from the Acas website:

An Advisory Booklet on Stress at Work

An Advisory Booklet on Heath and Employment. The booklet includes sections on smoking, alcohol, drugs, stress and AIDS. For more details of how to order Acas publications see page 36.

For specific questions, you can contact the Acas helpline tel: 08457 47 47 47 or textphone: 08456 06 16 00.

2. The Department for Trade and Industry (DTI)

You can download a guide to the Working Time Regulations at www.dti.gov.uk/er/work_time_regs/.

3. askNCVO

www.askncvo.org.uk offers a wealth of free, practical, up-to-date advice on all aspects of running a charity or voluntary organisation. Hundreds of pages cover trusteeship, financial management, human resources and more.

4. Business Link

The Business Link website has a section on its website about health and safety. The information on the Business Link website has been developed in conjunction with the Health and Safety

Executive, specifically for small/medium-sized employers.

Go to www.businesslink.gov.uk and search under 'health and safety.'

5. The Health and Safety Executive (HSE)

The HSE has a wealth of information on all aspects of health and safety at work.

You could start by looking at its webpage on Getting started for small businesses at www.hse.gov.uk/smallbusinesses/getting started.htm.

You could also order its *Health and Safety Starter Pack* which contains most of the basic health and safety advice you need to help your organisation comply with the law and protect its employees. The pack (available from HSE Books, see below) includes copies of the HSE *Accident Book*, the *Health and Safety Law Poster*, and the publication *Essentials of Health and Safety at Work*.

There are a large number of free leaflets that can be downloaded from the HSE website, or ordered from HSE books, including:

INDG259 *An Introduction to Health and Safety*

INDG218 *A Guide to Risk Assessment Requirements: common provisions in health and safety law*

INDG291 *A Guide to the Provision and Use of Work Equipment Regulations*

INDG136 COSHH: *a brief guide to the regulations*

INDG214 *First Aid at Work – your questions answered*

INDG347 *Basic Advice on First Aid at Work*

INDG143 *Manual Handling*

INDG174 *Personal Protective Equipment*

INDG244 *Workplace, Health, Safety and Welfare, a guide for managers*

INDG229 *Using Work Equipment Safely*

INDG36 *Working with VDU's*

INDG345 *Health and Safety Training – What you need to know*

HSE31 *RIDDOR Explained*

INDG232 *Consulting Employees on Health and Safety*

INDG293 *Welfare at Work – A guide to welfare arrangements*

You can order a publication from HSE books on 01787 881 165, or via the website.

For any question about health and safety, you can call the HSE Infoline on 08701 545 500.

Health and Safety Executive
Information Centre
Broad Lane
Sheffield
S3 7HQ

HSE Books
PO Box 1999
Sudbury
Suffolk
CO10 6FS

6. Royal Society for the Prevention of Accidents (RoSPA)

RoSPA has a small firms advice pack at www.rospa.com/occupationalsafety/smallfirms/index.htm

You can contact them at:

RoSPA Head Office
RoSPA House
Edgbaston Park
353 Bristol Road
Edgbaston
Birmingham B5 7ST

Tel: 0121 248 2000
Fax: 0121 248 2001
Email: help@rospa.com

7. Unison health and safety website

Unison has a dedicated website for employers in the community and voluntary sector: www.healthandsafetyinfo.org.uk.

8. The Fire Protection Association (FPA)

For information about fire precautions visit the FPA website: www.thefpa.co.uk/default.asp or contact the FPA:

London Road
Moreton-in-Marsh
Gloucestershire GL56 0RH

Tel: 01608 812 500

12 Employee relations

What this chapter is about

The subject of 'employee relations' covers the relationships between an employer and its employees. It is about individual relationships as well as group ('collective') relationships. It may involve communication, consultation or collective bargaining. These are defined by Acas (in its guide to the Information and Consultation Regulations) as follows:

Communication is concerned with the interchange of information and ideas.

Consultation goes beyond this and involves managers actively seeking and then taking account of the views of employees before making a decision.

Collective bargaining is the process by which employers and recognised trade unions seek to reach agreement through negotiation on issues such as pay and terms and conditions of employment. It is quite different from consultation where the responsibility for decision making remains with management.

This chapter covers the following areas:

- Communicating and consulting with your employees
- Staff surveys
- Trade unions and collective bargaining
- Other forms of collective employee relations
- The Information and Consultation Regulations
- Public interest disclosure ('whistleblowing')

Communicating and consulting with your employees

Employees who feel that little notice is taken of them at work, that they are not appreciated or that their views and comments are not heard, are likely to feel less positive about their work and be less productive.

Conversely, effective communication and consultation are likely to have the following benefits:

- Avoidance of misunderstandings, because staff will

understand the organisation, its performance and constraints.
- Better individual performance, because employees will understand what they need to achieve, how and why.
- Greater support for management decisions, because employees will have been more involved in decision taking.
- Better management decisions, because of employee involvement.
- Fewer staff grievances

Below are some practical steps you could take to ensure that you are communicating and consulting appropriately with your employees.

Hold face-to-face meetings
Have regular team meetings and one-to-one meetings.

Chapter 7 gives more information about one-to-one staff supervision meetings.

Communicate in writing
Written communication may be via a notice board, email, a staff newsletter, your intranet (if you have one) or a staff handbook.

If staff in your organisation are based in more than one work location, written communication will be especially important.

Undertake group communication and consultation
Unless your organisation is very small (e.g. under 50 employees), it is helpful to communicate and consult not only with individuals but also with staff representatives or trade union representatives. Collective consultation and communication can help with joint learning and problem solving. In addition, collective consultation allows you to make 'workforce agreements' on the application of some aspects of the law, notably the Working Time Regulations (see chapter 11).

Collective consultation and communication can help with joint learning and problem solving.

Good practice in communication and consultation
- Try and act in an open manner, with an 'open door' policy and frequent informal discussions with staff.
- Encourage staff to give their views and suggestions.
- Hear what they have to say with an open mind. If your decision is to do nothing, say why. If you have taken up a suggestion, make sure that you tell staff that you have done this and thank the person who suggested it.
- Make sure that your communications reach all staff, including part-time staff, staff who work from home and other staff who may be overlooked.
- As a general principle, be generous in your communication. You cannot over-communicate!

Legal requirements

As an employer, you are required to:

- Consult employee representatives over planned collective redundancies and transfers of undertakings (Trade Union and Labour Relations (Consolidation) Act 1992 and Transfer of Undertakings (Protection of Employment) (Amendment) Regulations 1987).
- Consult safety representatives of recognised trade unions (Safety Representatives and Safety Committees Regulations (SRSCR) 1977).
- Consult on health and safety with any employees not in groups covered by trade union representatives. You can choose to consult them directly or through elected representatives (Health and Safety (Consultation with Employees) Regulations (HSCER) 1996).
- Include in your annual report action that has been taken to inform, consult and involve employees (Companies Act 1985), if you have more than 250 employees.
- Provide information and consult in certain circumstances (Information and Consultation Regulations 2004). Further information about information and consultation obligations is given later in this chapter.

Staff surveys

One method of finding out what your staff think is to undertake a staff attitude survey. Staff surveys may be administered by an external organisation, so that your staff are able to give their opinions in a confidential manner. The external organisation will also be able to benchmark the results of your staff survey with similar organisations. Staff may express opinions to an external organisation that they may not otherwise give.

If yours is a very small organisation, you probably won't need to undertake a formal survey, but you may find it useful to hold a meeting, perhaps facilitated by an external person, in which staff are asked to give their views about your organisation.

The areas covered in a staff survey might include:

- the organisation as a place to work
- equality and fairness
- communication
- opportunities for consultation
- job satisfaction
- appraisal and supervision
- opportunities for development
- pay and benefits
- any other areas staff wish to highlight.

Give staff feedback about the outcome of the survey and tell them what you intend to do as a result. Make sure you do what you say you will do, or the whole process is likely to lose credibility.

Below is an example survey that you could use as a basis for your own staff survey.

Example staff sample

[Organisation] is keen to be a good employer, with good employment procedures and practices.

We want to make sure that we are treating everyone in a fair, honest and open manner.

Please could you answer the following questions, to help us assess how well we are doing.

Please tick the relevant box, to indicate how you rate [organisation's] practice in each of the areas listed.

	Very Fair	Mostly Fair	Often Unfair	Very Unfair	Don't Know
Recruitment and selection					
Training and development					
Induction and probation					
Internal career progression					
Pay and benefits					
Performance review					
Communication and consultation					
Accessibility of buildings					
Opportunities to work flexibly					
Other adjustments made to accommodate individuals					
Handling of disciplinary matters					
Handling of grievance and harassment matters					
Day to day decisions managers make					

Please now provide comments in the box below to support the above answers. Could you give:

• examples of what we have done well
• examples of what we have done less well
• your suggestions on how we could improve.

Thank you for your time please now return this survey to _____ in the envelope provided. You do not need to put your name on the survey and your responses will be treated in confidence.

Trade unions and collective bargaining

A trade union is an organisation which exists to support its members at work.

A trade union may be recognised in a workplace, which means that the employer agrees to negotiate about certain items. What is negotiated depends on the contents of a recognition agreement. Typically, recognition covers negotiation on pay, conditions of employment, training and health and safety. Recognition agreements may be informal, but a formal, written agreement helps avoid misunderstandings.

The negotiations between union and employer are called collective bargaining and the employees who are covered by collective bargaining are called a bargaining unit.

Individual employees are free to choose to be a member or not of a trade union. A dismissal which is found to be on the grounds of trade union membership or non-membership is automatically unfair, regardless of an individual's length of service.

Even if no union is recognised in a particular workplace, individual employees have the right to be accompanied by a union representative in formal grievance or disciplinary meetings.

Unions normally also provide benefits to members in addition to their collective bargaining and representational role. They may provide discounted services and products as well as financial and legal advice.

> Even if no union is recognised in a particular workplace, individual employees have the right to be accompanied by a union representative in formal grievance or disciplinary meetings.

Trade union recognition – voluntary basis

Union recognition can occur on a voluntary basis. This means that the employer and union agree to recognition without using any legal procedures.

Organisations and unions wanting to set up a recognition agreement can gain support from Acas (see contact details at the end of this chapter).

If you are considering voluntary recognition of a trade union, consult carefully with your employees to see if this is what they want. If the majority of employees are members of a particular union, it may make sense to set up a recognition agreement. However, if only a few employees are members of the union, then it would not normally be appropriate to recognise the union, as they would only represent the minority of your workforce.

Trade union recognition – statutory basis

A trade union can make an application for statutory recognition provided that you, together with any associated employers, employ 21 workers or more.

The union must first submit to you a written request for recognition and you have 10 days from receipt to start negotiations or to refuse the request.

If you refuse the request or no agreement is reached, the union can apply to the Central Arbitration Committee (CAC). The union must be able to show that 10 per cent of workers in your organisation (or in a particular part of it – a 'bargaining unit') belong to the union and that the majority are likely to favour recognition. If it cannot show this, its application will not be accepted.

The CAC will issue a declaration that the union is recognised for the bargaining unit in question, if:

- the employer accepts that the union enjoys the support of a majority of the workforce;
- or the CAC is satisfied that more than 50 per cent of the bargaining unit are members of the union seeking recognition.

If the CAC cannot issue a declaration, it will arrange for a secret ballot of the bargaining unit to be conducted. The union must have support of a majority of those voting in the ballot and at least 40 per cent of those entitled to vote to achieve recognition.

The union must wait three years before making a new application if it fails.

Rights of recognised trade unions

A number of statutory rights arise when a trade union is recognised, including:

- the right to receive certain information from you for collective bargaining purposes;
- the right to receive information on health and safety and occupational pension schemes;
- the right to paid time off for officials for trade union duties, training and activities;
- the right to reasonable time off (which need not be paid) for trade union members during working hours to take part in the activities of the union;
- the right to be consulted if your organisation proposes to dismiss as redundant 20 or more employees over a period of 90 days or less;
- the right to be consulted and informed about any transfer of the business and, in certain circumstances, the right to be recognised by the new employer;
- the right to appoint a safety representative;

- rights for Union Learning Representatives to reasonable paid time off to carry out their duties and to undergo training.

In addition, if a union has been recognised by the statutory recognition route (as opposed to voluntary recognition), then there is a legal right to:
- collective bargaining about pay, hours, and holidays – as a minimum;
- consultation on training;
- not to be derecognised for at least three years.

Content of recognition agreements

The recognition agreement should set out procedural arrangements for bargaining.

Whilst collective bargaining agreements are not normally legal documents, the outcome of collective bargaining (such as a pay increase) may be incorporated into employees' contracts of employments and in this way becomes legally enforceable.

Here is an example collective bargaining agreement:

Sample recognition and procedural agreement

Recognition and procedural agreement between
_____ Nursing Home
_____ and Unison, 1 Mabledon
Place, London WC1H 9AJ

1. Definition of terms
In this Agreement:
The Nursing Home – refers to Nursing Home and
Subsidiaries
The Union refers to Unison
Staff refers to all employees of the Nursing Home

2. Commmencement date
This Agreement commences on _____

3. Objectives
3.1 In drawing up this Agreement, the Nursing Home and
   the Union recognise that the Nursing Home exists to
   serve its patients. The purpose of this Agreement is to
   ensure that employment practices in the Nursing Home
   are conducted to the highest possible standards within
   the resources available, and that equal opportunities

---

are offered to employees or prospective employees and that the treatment of staff will be fair and equitable in all matters of dispute.

4. General principles

4.1 The Nursing Home and the Union accept that the terms of this Agreement are binding in honour upon them but do not constitute a legally enforceable agreement.

4.2 The Union recognises the Nursing Home's responsibility to plan, organise and manage the work of the Nursing Home in order to achieve the best possible results in pursuing its overall aims and objectives.

4.3 The Nursing Home recognises the Union's responsibility to represent the interests of its members and to work for improved conditions of employment for them.

4.4 The Nursing Home and the Union recognise their common interest and joint purpose in furthering the aims and objectives of the Nursing Home and in achieving reasonable solutions to all matters which concern them. Both parties declare their common objective to maintain good industrial relations.

5. Union representation

5.1 The Nursing Home recognises Unison as the Trade Union with which it will consult and negotiate on all matters set out in Clause 8.2. of this Agreement.

5.2 The Nursing Home will inform all new employees of this Agreement and will encourage them to join the union and provide facilities for them to talk to a representative as part of their induction procedure.

5.3 The Nursing Home accepts that the Union's Members will elect mutually agreeable representatives in accordance with their Union Rules to act as their spokespersons in representing their interests.

5.4 The Union agrees to inform the Nursing Home of the names of all elected representatives in writing within five working days of their election and to inform the Nursing Home in writing of any subsequent changes, each time within five working days of the change having taken place. Persons whose names have been notified to the Nursing Home shall be the sole representatives of the Unison membership.

5.5 The Nursing Home recognises that Union representatives fulfil an important role and that the discharge of their duties as Union representatives will in no way prejudice their career prospects or employment with the Nursing Home.

6. Union meetings and other facilities

6.1 Meetings of Union Members may be held on the Nursing Home premises outside working hours and there shall be no restriction on the frequency or duration of such meetings.

6.2 Union meetings may be held on the Nursing Home premises inside working hours provided that prior consent for such meetings shall be obtained from the Nursing Home by the Union. Such consent shall not be unreasonably withheld. The Union shall provide the Nursing Home with a timetable of regular Union meetings or give at least three working days notice of the intention to hold a meeting as appropriate.

6.3 The Nursing Home agrees to provide reasonable and defined facilities to the Union representatives to enable them to discharge their duties including the provision of a notice board and reasonable use of telephones, photocopiers and computers.

6.4 Subject to at least seven days notice and the agreement of the Nursing Home, Union representatives will be granted special leave without loss of pay to attend training courses run by the Union or other appropriate bodies which are relevant to the discharge of their Union duties.

6.5 Union representatives will be permitted to take reasonable paid time off during working hours to enable them to carry out their duties under this Agreement as provided for under the Trade Union and Labour Relations (Consolidation) Act 1992.

6.6 Subject to reasonable prior notice and the consent of the Nursing Home which shall not unreasonably be withheld, Union representatives will be permitted reasonable time off during working hours for the purpose of taking part in Trade Union activity as defined under the Trade Union and Labour Relations (Consolidation) Act 1992.

6.7 Subject to reasonable prior notice, employees who are Union Learning Representatives may take reasonable time off during working hours to fulfil their role.

6.8 In all other respects, elected Union representatives shall conform to the same working conditions as all the employees.

7. Check-off system
7.1 It is agreed that a check-off system will operate whereby the Nursing Home will deduct Union dues from the salaries of Union Members and pay them to the Union each month with a schedule of payments.
7.2 The Union will co-operate with management in devising and implementing a system to secure the completion of authorisation forms for deduction of subscriptions from salaries. The Union will also afford full co-operation to management in advising members of any increase in subscriptions.

8. Joint negotiating facility
8.1 The Nursing Home and the Union agree to set up a joint Negotiating Committee consisting of representatives of both sides.
8.2 The joint Negotiating Committee shall be governed by a written constitution which should cover such areas as:
Hours of work
Holiday and sickness arrangements
Pensions
Overall salary structure
Pay awards
Health and safety
Equal opportunities policies
New technology
Training and recruitment
Staff amenities
Redundancy and redeployment
Disciplinary and grievance procedures
Any other item which both sides agree to refer.

9. Grievance and discipline
9.1 The Nursing Home recognises the Union's right to represent the interests of all or any of its members at any stages during grievance and disciplinary procedures and to call in Union representatives who are not employees of the Nursing Home wherever this is considered appropriate.
9.2 The Nursing Home undertakes to inform the Union representatives immediately of the name of any Unison

staff member faced with disciplinary action to enable the Union to make appropriate arrangements for representation. This information will be limited to the name of the member only.

9.3 Union representatives will be permitted to spend reasonable paid time inside working hours to discuss grievance or disciplinary matters with affected employees.

10. Variations
10.1 This Agreement may be amended at any time with the consent of both parties.

11. Termination
11.1 The Agreement shall not terminate except by mutual consent.

for Unison
SIGNED _____
DATE _____

for Nursing Home
SIGNED _____
DATE _____

Statutory derecognition
In certain circumstances, an employer may wish to derecognise a union.

There are two main grounds for derecognition:
- the employer no longer has a workforce of 21 or more workers;
- the union no longer has enough support from workers in the bargaining unit – the group of workers the union represents.

There are certain procedures which must be followed in cases of statutory derecognition. For further information, see www.dti.gov.uk/er/recognition.htm.

Other forms of collective employee relations

Organisations which do not recognise trade unions may have one of the following:
- Staff committee
- Joint committee

A staff committee is made up of staff representatives elected from amongst the workforce. Depending on the make-up and size of the organisation, there may be more than one committee in an organisation.

A staff committee may meet as frequently as needed, such as monthly, quarterly or biannually.

While management may consult staff representatives on a staff committee, they are under no obligation to act on what they say. This is different from the negotiation that will take place with a recognised trade union.

A staff committee will not normally have independent resources of its own, or access to external expertise. This means it will rely on you as an employer to provide employee relations and employment law advice. Not only is this an additional demand on time and resources, it means the committee is not truly independent. You would also have to arrange training for the staff representatives.

A joint committee is a consultation committee that includes union and non-union representatives. A joint committee may be set up when management do not wish to enter into a recognition agreement with a union. This may be because there is not enough employee support for full recognition, or where the majority of employees are not union members.

A joint committee may be set up when management do not wish to enter into a recognition agreement with a union.

The Information and Consultation Regulations

The Information and Consultation of Employees Regulations 2004 came into effect in the UK on 6 April 2005, for organisations with at least 150 employees.

The Regulations come into effect on 6 April 2007 for organisations with at least 100 employees and on April 2008 for organisations with at least 50 employees.

The Regulations require employers to inform and consult employees in certain circumstances, although the requirement to inform and consult does not operate automatically. It is triggered either by a valid request from employees for an Information and Consultation (I&C) agreement, or by employers choosing to start the process themselves. A 'valid request' from employees consists of a request (or a series of cumulative requests made over a six month period) by at least 10 per cent of the employees in the organisation (subject to a minimum of 15 and a maximum of 2,500 employees).

If a valid request is received, an employer must enter into negotiations with the workforce on how and on what the employer will inform and consult its workforce in the future. If within six months, an agreement has not been reached, a statutory default agreement will come into play. This will have to include the standard information and consultation provisions set out in the Regulations. The standard provisions are that employers will need to inform and consult with employee representatives about:

- the organisation's economic situation;
- employment prospects;
- decisions likely to lead to substantial changes in work organisation or contractual relations, including redundancies and transfers;

Pre-existing agreements

If there is already a pre-existing agreement approved by employees on information and consultation with the workforce and if a valid employee request is received for a new agreement, the employer may ballot the workforce to ascertain whether it endorses the request by employees. If the employer chooses not to ballot the workforce, they will come under the obligation to negotiate a new agreement.

Where a ballot is held, and 40 per cent of the workforce and a majority of those who vote, endorses the employee request, the employer would come under the obligation to negotiate a new agreement. Where less than 40 per cent of the workforce or a minority of those voting endorse the employee request, the employer does not come under an obligation to negotiate a new agreement, and a three-year moratorium on further employee requests would begin.

To be valid a pre-existing agreement must:

- Be in writing.
- Cover all the employees in the undertaking.
- Set out how the employer will inform and consult the employees or their representatives. The legislation does not impose any requirements or set any restrictions, on the method, frequency, timing or subject matter of the information and consultation arrangements set up under pre-existing agreements.
- Be approved by the employees. This would include support indicated by a simple majority among those voting in a ballot of the workforce; a majority of the workforce expressing support through signatures; or the agreement of representatives of employees (including trade union and other appropriate representatives) who represent a majority of the workforce.

Protection for information and consultation representatives

An employee who is an information and consultation representative will be able to:

- claim automatic unfair dismissal if dismissed for carrying out their duties (or in connection with being a candidate for the post);
- complain to an employment tribunal if they suffer a detriment related to their duties.

The Department of Trade and Industry (DTI) has produced more detailed guidance on the legislation which is available at: www.dti.gov.uk/er/consultation/proposal.htm.

Acas has also produced some good practice advice which is intended to help organisations develop and maintain effective information and consultation arrangements. It is available at www.acas.org.uk/services/ic.html.

Public interest disclosure ('whistle blowing')

The Public Interest Disclosure Act 1998 gives legal protection from detriment, to workers who 'blow the whistle' about wrong-doing in their organisations. The term 'workers' includes not only employees but also contractors providing services, most agency workers, home workers and trainees on vocational and work experience schemes.

Detriment may take a number of forms, such as denial of promotion, facilities or training opportunities which the employer would otherwise have offered. It could also include dismissal.

Employees who are protected by the provisions may make a claim for unfair dismissal to an Employment Tribunal if they feel they were dismissed for making a protected disclosure. If the dismissal is indeed found to be due to making a protected disclosure, it is automatically unfair. Compensation is unlimited and there is no qualifying length of service to make a claim.

The legislation does not give protection to whistleblowers in all circumstances. It applies where workers follow certain procedures laid down by law, in respect of the disclosure of specific types of malpractice.

Protected disclosures

A disclosure will be 'protected' if in the reasonable belief of the individual, it concerns one or more of the following:

- a criminal offence
- a failure to comply with a legal obligation
- a miscarriage of justice

- the endangering of an individual's health and safety
- damage to the environment
- deliberate concealment of information relating to any of the above.

The behaviour that gives rise to the concern does not have to take place within the UK.

Qualifying for protection

In order for the employee to qualify for protection, the following must apply:

- Disclosure to the employer will be protected, provided that it is made in good faith and the whistleblower has a reasonable suspicion that the alleged malpractice has occurred, is occurring, or is likely to occur.
- Disclosure to a regulator (e.g. Health and Safety Executive, Environment Agency, OFWAT) will be protected where, in addition, the whistleblower honestly and reasonably believes that the information and any allegation in it are substantially true.
- Disclosure to other bodies is protected if, in addition to the tests for regulatory disclosures, it is reasonable in all the circumstances and is not made for personal gain. The whistleblower must also meet one or other of the following further preconditions, if disclosing to other bodies:
  - they reasonably believed that they would be victimised if they raised the matter internally
  - they reasonably believed that the disclosure related to a criminal offence and was thus a 'qualifying disclosure'
  - there was no prescribed regulator and they reasonably believed the evidence was likely to be concealed or destroyed
  - the concern had already been raised with the employer or a prescribed regulator
  - the concern is of an 'exceptionally serious' nature
  - they had suffered an identifiable detriment.

In addition, the disclosure itself must be 'reasonable'. In deciding the reasonableness of the disclosure, a Tribunal will consider all the circumstances. This will include the identity of the person to whom the disclosure was made, the seriousness of the concern, whether the risk or danger remains, and whether the disclosure breached a duty of confidence which the employer owed a third party.

Internal procedures

A clear procedure for raising concerns about the organisation can allay fears from both managers and employees that the raising of a serious concern may be mishandled. The employee may be concerned about repercussions on his or her employment and the employer may be concerned about adverse publicity that could result.

A climate of open communication, supported by a clear procedure for dealing with concerns can encourage employees to raise concerns and help ensure that such concerns are dealt with effectively.

Further information about public interest disclosure is available from the Department of Trade and Industry website at www.dti.gov.uk/er/individual/pidguide-pl502.htm.

You can also find information on whistle blowing at the Public Concern at Work website: www.pcaw.co.uk.

Checklist

✓ Establish regular verbal and written communication and consultation with your employees.

✓ Encourage staff to give their views. Make sure they know their views are valued and taken into account.

✓ Seek feedback from your employees about working in your organisation. Consider undertaking a staff survey.

✓ Recognise a trade union where the majority of your workforce are in favour, ideally following a voluntary, rather than a statutory process.

✓ Establish a clear recognition agreement between your organisation and the trade union.

✓ Give to recognised trade unions the rights afforded to them by law.

✓ As an alternative to trade union recognition (and unless your organisation is very small), consider establishing a staff committee or joint committee.

✓ Adhere to the requirements of the Information and Consultation Regulations. Consider developing with your employees an Information and Consultation agreement, if you do not have one already.

✓ Do not discriminate against individuals on the grounds of trade union membership or non-membership, or on the grounds of being an information and consultation representative. This is illegal.

✓ Make clear to employees, ideally via a brief procedure, how they can raise concerns ('whistleblow') if they identify wrong doing.

Where to find out more

1. Acas
The following publications can be downloaded from the Acas website:
A leaflet on communicating with your employees
An advisory booklet about communication and consultation
An advisory booklet on representation at work
Information about trade unions and representation

For more details of how to order Acas publications see page 36.
For specific questions, you can contact the Acas helpline tel: 08457 47 47 47 or text phone 08456 06 16 00.

2. The Department of Trade and Industry (DTI)
The DTI employment website, www.dti.gov.uk/er has the following guidance:
General information about employee consultation
A guide to disclosures in the public interest

3. askNCVO
www.askncvo.org.uk offers a wealth of free, practical, up-to-date advice on all aspects of running a charity or voluntary organisation. Hundreds of pages cover trusteeship, financial management, human resources and more.

4. Business Link
Business Link has a section on employee representatives and trade unions at www.businesslink.gov.uk

5. TUC
There is a 'union finder' on www.tuc.org.uk.

Trades Union Congress
Congress House
Great Russell Street
London
WC1B 3LS
Tel: 020 7636 4030
Fax: 020 7636 0632

6. Public Concern at Work (for 'whistleblowing' concerns)

Public Concern at Work
Suite 306
16 Baldwins Gardens
London EC1N 7RJ

Tel: 020 7404 6609
Fax: 020 7404 6576

Website: www.pcaw.co.uk
Email: whistle@pcaw.co.uk

13 Redundancy

What this chapter is about

As far as possible, you will want to ensure job security for your employees. However, sometimes this may not be possible and you may need to make staff redundant.

This chapter explains the various aspects of redundancy.

It covers:

- Legal definition of redundancy
- Collective consultation
- Individual consultation
- Measures to avoid or minimise redundancy
- Selection process
- Suitable alternative employment
- Voluntary redundancy
- Statutory dismissal procedures
- Notice of redundancy
- Redundancy payments
- Assistance with job seeking
- Leaving before the expiry of notice
- Enhanced redundancy provisions
- Disabled employees
- Employees on fixed term contracts

Whilst this chapter gives an overview of how to handle redundancies, please note that redundancy is one of the most complex areas of people management and you may wish to take specialist advice.

> Redundancy is one of the most complex areas of people management and you may wish to take specialist advice.

Legal definition of redundancy

The law says that a redundancy occurs when:

- the employer has ceased, or intends to cease, to carry on the business for the purposes of which the employee was so employed;
- or the employer has ceased, or intends to cease, to carry on the business in the place where the employee was so

employed;

- or the requirements of the business for employees to carry out work of a particular kind has ceased or diminished or are expected to cease or diminish;
- or the requirements of the business for the employees to carry out work of a particular kind, in the place where they were so employed, has ceased or diminished or are expected to cease or diminish.

Collective consultation

'Collective consultation' means consulting with employee representatives.

Section 188(1) of the Trade Union Labour Relations (Consolidation) Act states:

'Where an employer is proposing to dismiss as redundant 20 or more employees at one establishment within a period of 90 days or less, the employer shall consult about the dismissals all the persons who are appropriate representatives of any of the employees who may be affected by the proposed dismissals or may be affected by measures taken in connection with those dismissals.'

You should note that even if you do not end up dismissing 20 employees as redundant, if there is a possibility that this number may end up redundant, you should still undertake collective consultation.

Timing of collective consultation

The law says that the consultation should begin in 'good time', that is:

- at least 30 days before the first dismissal, if between 20 and 99 employees are to be dismissed within a 90-day period
- at least 90 days before the first dismissal if 100 or more employees are to be dismissed.

Electing representatives

If the affected employees are represented by an independent trade union recognised for collective bargaining purposes, you must inform and consult an authorised official of that union. This may be, for example, a shop steward, a district union official or, if appropriate, a national or regional official. You are not required to inform and consult any other employee representatives in such circumstances, but you can do if you wish.

If your organisation does not recognise a trade union, you will need to consult either with existing representatives (for example, from a staff council) or new ones specially elected for the purpose. If you want to consult with existing representatives, their remit and method of election or appointment must give them suitable authority from the employees concerned.

There are certain rules on the way the elections must be handled. For further information on these rules, you can refer to document number PL833 *Redundancy Consultation and Notification*, available from the Department of Trade and Industry website www.dti.gov.uk.

If you give your employees the opportunity to elect representatives and they fail to do so, then you have fulfilled your obligations and may simply consult with the employees direct.

Fairness

Consultation must be 'fair', that is, you should meet with the representatives while the redundancy proposals are still at an early stage. They should then be given enough information on the proposed redundancies and enough time to digest it before making an informed response. You must genuinely consider their response.

Content of consultation

The following information must be disclosed in writing to employee representatives:

- the reasons for the proposals;
- the numbers and descriptions of employees it is proposed to dismiss as redundant;
- the total number of employees of any such description employed by the employer at the establishment in question;
- the proposed method of selecting the employees who may be dismissed;
- the proposed method of carrying out the dismissals, taking account of any agreed procedure, including the period over which the dismissals are to take effect;
- the proposed method of calculating any redundancy payments, other than those required by law, that you propose to make.

You could also provide information on:

- arrangements for reasonable time off with pay to seek alternative work;
- assistance with job seeking, such as access to computers, help with writing CVs or completing application forms.

> If you give your employees the opportunity to elect representatives and they fail to do so, then you have fulfilled your obligations

There is a legal onus on you to take all reasonable measures to avoid the need for redundancies.

The outcome of consultation

You are not obliged to agree with or implement the employee representatives' response, but the law does require you to consult 'with a view to reaching an agreement'. There is also a legal onus on you to take all reasonable measures to avoid the need for redundancies.

Informing the Department of Trade and Industry

If you intend to make 20 or more employees redundant, you must also notify the Department of Trade and Industry (DTI) in writing. Form HR1 is available from your local Jobcentre Plus for this purpose.

The reason for this advance notification is so that the DTI has an opportunity to provide help in finding alternative work or retraining for the employees who may be made redundant.

Notification does not mean the redundancies will necessarily take place, but simply that you foresee a situation where redundancies are likely.

The minimum time limits for notification are:

- At least 30 days before the first dismissal if between 20 and 99 employees are to be dismissed within a 90-day period.
- At least 90 days before the first dismissal if 100 or more employees are to be dismissed within a 90-day period.

If you do not notify the DTI in advance of making 20 or more employees redundant, you may incur a fine.

Individual consultation

Regardless of whether you have undertaken collective consultation as outlined above, you must always consult individually with affected employees. If you do not, your redundancy may be found to be unfair if you are taken to an Employment Tribunal.

The law says that where possible, you should undertake consultation when the proposals are still in their formative stage.

- You should provide adequate information on which affected employees can respond.
- You should give a reasonable time (e.g. at least two weeks) for the consultation process.
- You should give conscientious consideration to any points raised.

Quite apart from the legal requirements, there are good practice reasons to consult; the Acas *Guide to Redundancy Handling* (available at www.acas.org.uk/publications/b08.html) states:

'The purpose of consultation is to provide as early an opportunity as practicable for all concerned to share the problem and explore the options. It can stimulate better co-operation between managers and employees, reduce uncertainty and lead to better decision making ... representatives or individual employees may be able to suggest acceptable alternative ways of tackling the problem or, if the redundancies are inevitable, ways of minimising hardship.'

Subject of consultation

Individual consultation needs to cover the same areas as collective consultation.

It is good practice to put your consultation in writing, as well as meeting with employees to consult with them.

Who to consult with

You should consult primarily with those whose jobs may be made redundant. However, you should also consult about your proposals with anyone else who may be affected, such as the managers of those who may be made redundant.

Make sure you don't forget people who are absent from work, such as employees on maternity leave or long term sick leave.

Remember also that redundancy can affect the morale of those who aren't being made redundant. You may want to consider ways you can reassure these employees about their future in your organisation.

> **It is good practice to put your consultation in writing, as well as meeting with employees to consult with them.**
>
> **Redundancy can affect the morale of those who aren't being made redundant.**

Case study

Here is how the Westwich Association undertook consultation concerning a potential redundancy situation.

The Westwich Association (WA) had for some time employed a part-time book keeper. The Treasurer, a qualified accountant, had taken responsibility on a voluntary basis for producing management and annual accounts.

As WA grew, the Treasurer became unable to keep undertaking this work. WA felt that it would need to pay for accountancy support instead.

Having considered various options, WA felt that the most appropriate option might be to appoint a part-time financial accountant, who would prepare management and annual accounts as well as undertake all book keeping.

253

Because funding was limited, it would not be able to keep on a separate book keeper.

WA therefore entered into a consultation process with the book keeper about the proposed change and the impact on his job.

First, the general manager met with the book keeper to explain the situation. She made sure that she met him mid-week, rather than on Friday afternoon, so that he could discuss the situation further with her at work on the following day, if he wished.

She explained:

- That WA proposed to replace his current post with a more senior post of accountant.
- The reasons for the proposal – that there was a need for accountancy support to ensure that WA's accounting processes were appropriate.
- That should the proposal go ahead, the book keeper could apply for the higher position, but if he were unsuccessful and there were no other suitable alternative employment, his post would be redundant and statutory redundancy pay would be payable.
- The proposed timescale for change.

At the end of the meeting, she gave the book keeper a letter containing the information she had talked through with him. Here is the letter:

Dear Paul

Consultation on redundancy of your post

I write to let you know that Westwich Association is proposing a restructuring of the way that financial management and administration is conducted. Up to now, you have undertaken book keeping work, with our Treasurer having responsibility, on a voluntary basis, for producing management and annual accounts. Our Treasurer is no longer able to fulfil this role.

This proposed restructuring will directly affect you, as the proposal is to replace your role with the role of Financial Accountant. This post would prepare management and annual accounts as well as undertake all book keeping. Because our funding is limited, we would not be able to keep on a separate book keeper.

I must stress that at this stage, no firm decisions have been made. This letter is intended to start a formal consultation process with you. You may have thoughts on how we could achieve our objective in different ways and we are genuinely keen to hear these.

Should the proposal go ahead, you will be given the opportunity to apply for the financial accountant post and we would discuss with you reasonable training to achieve the requirements of the role.

Should you be unsuccessful in applying for the accountant post, you would be entitled to redundancy pay at statutory levels.

I and the trustees would like your response within two weeks of today, i.e. (date). I am happy to discuss the matter with you at any time during the two week consultation period.

At the end of the two weeks, we will take a decision on how to proceed. Should the proposal to replace your job go ahead, we will continue to consult with you throughout the process.

I appreciate that this is an uncertain time and would like to take this opportunity to thank you for all the good work you do. This proposal is in no way connected with the quality of your work.

Yours sincerely

Freda Platt
general manager

Measures to avoid or minimise redundancy

You should make every effort to avoid or minimise redundancies. For example, if you know your funding will decrease and you will need to reduce the number of paid staff, you could:

- Restrict the recruitment of permanent employees, either to new or to vacant posts.
- Reduce the use of temporary employees.
- Fill vacancies, where possible, from amongst existing employees.
- Reduce (with agreement) the hours of work of existing employees.

Make sure you consult with employees about your plans to minimise redundancies. They may have some useful suggestions.

Selection process

If, having taken steps to avoid or minimise redundancies, the number of employees still exceeds requirements, redundancy may occur.

If there is only one post that you propose to make redundant, for example because the funding for that post is coming to an end, then it will normally be clear that the person in that post should be redundant.

In other circumstances, such as if you have two staff doing the same job and in the future you only need one, you will need to apply selection criteria.

You should have clear and published selection criteria for redundancy.

You should have clear and published selection criteria for redundancy. Selection criteria might simply be along the lines of an assessment of the suitability of an individual's skills, experience and potential for the remaining posts. You might also take into account the individual's disciplinary record or attendance record. However, if you take into account attendance, care should be taken to exclude any periods of absence that relate to maternity or disability.

Some organisations select individuals for redundancy on the basis of 'last in, first out.' If you are considering taking this approach, review the composition of your workforce carefully to ensure that this would not be discriminatory. Female employees tend to take more breaks in employment than male employees, and therefore tend to have shorter service with an employer.

Do not use part-time status as a selection criteria. This would be discriminatory against part-time workers and could also amount to sex discrimination.

Do not discriminate against an employee who is pregnant. Apply exactly the same selection criteria as for other employees. If an employee is on maternity leave, make sure that you still include her in the selection process.

Suitable alternative employment

Where possible, try and redeploy otherwise redundant employees to suitable alternative work in your organisation. If you employ only a few people, there may be few opportunities for alternative employment, but make sure you still consider all available options with each affected employee.

If there is alternative employment, it will be considered to be 'suitable alternative employment' if it is at broadly the same level, with similar duties, hours and terms and conditions.

If you can offer alternative employment, you need to put the offer in writing, showing how the new employment differs from the old. You need to make the offer before the employment under the previous contract ends. In accordance with the law, the new job should start either immediately after the end of the old job or after an interval of not more than four weeks.

Any employee who is under notice of redundancy has a legal right to a trial period of four weeks in the alternative job. The trial period begins when the previous contract has ended.

The effect of the trial period is to give the employee a chance to decide whether the new job is suitable without necessarily losing the right to a redundancy payment. This trial period can be extended for retraining purposes by an agreement which is in writing, specifies the date on which the trial period ends and sets out the employee's terms and conditions after it ends.

As the employer, you should also use the trial period to assess the employee's suitability. Should either of you feel that the employee is unsuitable or the employee feel that the post is unsuitable, the employee will normally preserve the right to the redundancy payment under the old contract.

However, if the employee unreasonably refuses the alternative employment (either before the trial period or at any time during it), he or she may lose any entitlement to redundancy pay. Unreasonable refusal might be where the difference between the old and new jobs is negligible or where the employee rejects the changes a new job might involve, before investigating whether they are feasible.

If the only available alternative employment is at a lower salary level, then the employee should still be offered it, if he or she has the relevant skills and knowledge. The employee may prefer this to redundancy. However, a refusal to take the lower paid job would be reasonable and the employee would still be entitled to redundancy pay.

Voluntary redundancy

Sometimes in a redundancy situation, an employer may ask for volunteers for redundancy or individuals may come forward to volunteer for redundancy.

You can agree to voluntary redundancy if the remaining workforce has the skills and experience you need for the organisation in the future. However, if the skills of the person volunteering are still required in the organisation, and no one else has these skills, you would be reasonable to refuse the request for voluntary redundancy.

You can agree to voluntary redundancy if the remaining workforce has the skills and experience you need for the organisation in the future.

257

Statutory dismissal procedure

If, **after** consultation, you feel that certain redundancies are necessary, you must follow the statutory dismissal procedure:

Step one – written statement
You must send or give a letter to the employee, stating that it is proposed to make him or her redundant and the reasons for this, and inviting the employee to a meeting to discuss the situation. You must give reasonable notice of the date of the meeting.

Step two – meeting
You should give the employee the opportunity to state his or her point of view at the meeting.

The employee must take all reasonable steps to attend the meeting.

After the meeting, you should:
- inform the employee about any decision (which will either be to retain the employee or to issue a notice of redundancy);
- offer the employee the right of appeal;
- confirm your decision and the right of appeal in writing.

Step three – appeal
The employee must inform you if he/she wishes to appeal on the grounds of unfair selection for redundancy. You can set a reasonable time limit for receipt of the appeal e.g. five working days from the date of your letter confirming the outcome of step 2.

You should then:
- Invite the employee to attend a further meeting.
- Arrange for the appeal meeting to be chaired by another manager (more senior if possible) or a panel of trustees who were not involved in the original decision to dismiss on grounds of redundancy.
- Give the employee the opportunity to state his or her view at the meeting.
- Adjourn the meeting to consider what the employee has said.
- Communicate the final decision to the employee in writing, after the meeting and not at the end of the meeting. This means you have time to consider all information carefully and there is less pressure and likelihood of a reactive decision.

The law says that in following the above three-step process:
- Each step and action should be taken without unreasonable delay.

- The timing and location of meetings should be reasonable.
- Meetings should allow both employer and employee to explain their cases.
- The employee may be accompanied at both the original and the appeal meeting by a colleague or trade union representative. If you wish, you may allow the employee to bring a friend or family member instead of a colleague or trade union representative.

Notice of redundancy

If, having met with the employee in accordance with the statutory procedure and as outlined above, you decide to confirm the employee's redundancy, you will need to issue the employee with written notice of redundancy. You can issue this notice, even if the employee has appealed against the redundancy and the appeal meeting has not yet taken place.

This notice should state the employee's last day of service with your organisation and the redundancy payments that will be made (see next section in this chapter). The employee is entitled to the statutory notice of one week's notice after one month's service up to two years, then two weeks' notice after two years, three weeks' notice after three years, and so on up to a maximum of 12 weeks' notice after 12 years service.

If it is not possible for notice to be given, pay in lieu of any unexpired period of notice can be added to the final redundancy payment. Pay in lieu of notice is, according to current legislation, free of tax and National Insurance, provided that there is no provision for pay in lieu in the contract of employment. If however the employee's contract of employment specifically states that pay in lieu may be given instead of actual notice, then the payment is deemed to be a contractual payment and as such is subject to tax and National Insurance.

Redundancy payments

Statutory redundancy pay is payable to employees who have at least two years' service. Service before the age of 18 does not count.

Statutory redundancy pay is not payable to any employee:
- Who is offered suitable alternative employment before the date on which redundancy is due to take place but unreasonably refuses that employment.
- Whose service ends on or after their 65th birthday.
- Who works for an organisation with a normal retiring age lower than 65 and has reached that age.

You must fund the payments from your organisation's funds; the Government does not reimburse you for these payments.

Amount of payment

Payment is as follows, for each complete year of service, up to a maximum of 20 yearss:

- For each year of service at age 18 or over but under 22 – half a week's pay.
- For each year of service at age 22 but under 41 – one week's pay.
- For each year of service at age 41 or over but under 65 – one and a half weeks' pay.

Where an employee is within 12 months of age 65, the statutory redundancy entitlement is reduced by one twelfth for each complete month after the employee's 64th birthday.

A week's pay

The Government says that the maximum payable as a week's pay is £280 (as at February 2005). This means that employers do not by law have to pay more than £280, even if the employee's weekly pay is more than this (however, some organisations choose to pay more, see section below on enhanced redundancy provisions).

If an employee's weekly pay is less than £280, then you should pay this lesser amount.

You should calculate a week's pay based on the employee's contractual entitlement at the date on which you give the minimum notice to which the employee is entitled.

You can use a 'ready reckoner' for calculating redundancy payments if you go to the Department of Trade and Industry website at the following address: www.dti.gov.uk/er/redundancy/ready.htm.

Redundancy payments are, according to current legislation, free of tax and National Insurance up to a maximum of £30,000.

Holidays accrued but not yet taken should also be paid on termination of employment. Holiday pay is subject to tax and National Insurance.

Assistance with job seeking

Employees who are under notice of redundancy and have been continuously employed for at least two years have a legal right to reasonable time off to look for work or to arrange for training for new employment.

Leaving before the expiry of notice

The law states that during an individual's period of contractual or statutory notice, they can write to their employer to say that they wish to leave early. The employer needs to write back within seven days and either agree (in which case redundancy payments would be made) or state that it is not operationally feasible for the employee to leave early.

So, for example, if the individual has five years' service, he or she would be entitled, under law, to five weeks' notice. His or her contract may say less or more than this (e.g. four weeks or eight weeks). The higher of these notice periods is the one that needs to be taken into account.

If an individual wishes to leave early during a period of extended redundancy notice (for example, if you are giving more notice of redundancy than their contract or statute requires) then there is no entitlement to receive redundancy pay.

Enhanced redundancy provisions

You could consider enhancing your redundancy provisions beyond legal requirements in the following ways:

- Offer employees the opportunity for collective consultation, even where not legally required.
- Offer longer than four weeks as a trial period in suitable alternative employment, if the employee wishes.
- If you are going through the statutory dismissal procedures, allow the employee to be accompanied by a friend or family member, as an alternative to the legal right to be accompanied by a colleague or trade union representative.
- Give as long notice of redundancy as possible – longer than statutory or contractual requirements where you can.
- Allow all employees, including those with less than two years' service, to have time off for job seeking.
- Contact other employers with a view to canvassing for any vacancies which may be suitable for the redundant employees.
- Contact the local job centre to inform them of the skills and abilities of your redundant employees.
- Consider providing redundancy guidance/counselling, which might include: guidance on how to find another job; advice on completion of application forms; and guidance on attending interviews.
- Make enhanced redundancy payments if you can. For example, you could give one week's actual pay per year of service, rather than only paying up to the statutory

maximum for a week's pay.
- Be as flexible as possible in allowing staff to leave, with no loss of redundancy pay, before the expiry of notice.

Disabled employees

If a disabled
person may
be affected by
redundancy,
you may need
to make
adjustments
to your
redundancy
and redeploy-
ment
processes.

If a disabled person may be affected by redundancy, you may need to make adjustments to your redundancy and redeployment processes. You will need to consult with the disabled employee and if needed take advice. Here are some examples of what you may need to do.

Make adjustments to the consultation process

If one of your employees is visually impaired, for example, you may need to provide the consultation document in larger text or on a tape.

If one of your employees has a learning disability, you may need to ensure that the language you use is accessible and you may need to provide the consultation document on tape. You may also need to arrange for a supporter to assist the employee during the consultation process.

Make adjustments to the selection process

If you have an employee with chronic fatigue syndrome (ME), you may need to adjust the selection process so that the individual can rest between, for example, an interview and a written test.

Make adjustments to any possible alternative job

You will need to consider a disabled person's suitability for an alternative job AFTER any reasonable adjustments have been applied. It would not be appropriate, for example, to disallow a disabled employee who could not drive, if adjustments could be made to the job or the way the job was carried out, to remove the requirement to drive.

Employees on fixed-term contracts

Termination
of a
fixed-term
contract
is also
considered to
be a
redundancy
situation in
law.

You should note that the termination of a fixed-term contract is also considered to be a redundancy situation in law. You may have fixed-term contracts where, for example, you have limited funding for a particular project.

Consultation on redundancy in this circumstance may be less than in other cases, because the employee will be aware that the term of his or her post is coming to an end. However, you will still need to consult with the employee about matters such as:
- any ideas they have for keeping the post going
- possible alternative employment
- any ways of minimising hardship to them.

262

You will also need to follow the statutory dismissal procedure and, if the employee has two years' service or more, you must pay redundancy payments. The only exception to paying redundancy payments is if the employee is on a fixed-term contract entered into in July 2002 or earlier and the contract contains a 'redundancy waiver' clause.

You can find a case study about the termination of a fixed term contract in chapter 4.

Checklist

- ✓ Give early warning of possible redundancy situations. Consult collectively where the law requires. Always consult with individuals.
- ✓ Select fairly for redundancy based on published criteria. Ensure selection for redundancy does not discriminate directly or indirectly against a particular group of employees based on their gender, maternity status, religion, race colour, ethnic or national origins, disability, age or sexual orientation.
- ✓ Consider ways to minimise or avoid redundancies, for example by reducing the use of temporary staff, redeployment or reducing (with agreement) hours of work.
- ✓ Consider whether any suitable alternative employment exists and if so, offer it to otherwise redundant employees.
- ✓ Provide redundancy guidance/counselling, if possible, for employees selected for redundancy.
- ✓ Accept voluntary redundancies where possible.
- ✓ Follow statutory dismissal procedures when making staff redundant.
- ✓ Give employees selected for redundancy their notice entitlement.
- ✓ Make redundancy payments where applicable.
- ✓ Allow employees under notice of redundancy to leave early if possible.
- ✓ Make suitable and reasonable adjustments throughout the process for disabled employees.
- ✓ Prepare p45 certificate for all departing employees.

Where to find out more

Try the following free sources of information.

1.Acas

Acas has an advisory booklet, called *Redundancy Handling*. You can download this from www.acas.org.uk/publications/b08.html. For more details of how to order Acas publications see page 36.

For specific queries as you go through the redundancy process, you can call Acas on their helpline tel 08457 47 47 47 or textphone 08456 06 16 00.

2.The Department for Trade and Industry (DTI)

There are several documents on redundancy on the DTI website: www.dti.gov.uk/er/redundancy.htm.

You can also use the DTI redundancy ready reckoner to work out the redundancy payments due to your employees. The ready reckoner is at www.dti.gov.uk/er/redundancy/ready.htm.

3. askNCVO

www.askncvo.org.uk offers a wealth of free, practical, up-to-date advice on all aspects of running a charity or voluntary organisation. Hundreds of pages cover trusteeship, financial management, human resources and more.

4. Business link

Business Link, www.businesslink.gov.uk has information on its website about redundancy. Go to their website and enter 'redundancy' in the search field.

5.The Inland Revenue

For information on the tax treatment of redundancy, go to the Inland Revenue website section on Income Tax and Redundancy, at www.inlandrevenue.gov.uk/pdfs/ir143.htm.

Alternatively, you can call the Inland Revenue employers' helpline on 0845 7143 143.

14 Essential policies and employment documentation

What this chapter is about

The benefit of clear employment documentation is that all employees know what is expected of them and all managers know the procedure for dealing with particular situations. It is easier to achieve consistency of approach across an organisation if there are clear policies and procedures.

However, the number and type of policies you have is likely to be commensurate with the size of your organisation. If you have under 10 employees, it is easier to adopt a consistent approach without formal policies. Once you have 30 or more employees, you are likely to need a number of written policies.

This chapter explains:

- The employment documentation that all employers should have as a minimum
- Additional documentation that you may feel you need to have as your organisation grows
- A format for your employment policies
- What you could include in a staff handbook
- Consulting and communicating about your employment documentation.

Essential minimum documentation

The following is essential documentation that you should give to each employee:

A written statement of terms and conditions
It is a legal requirement to issue a written statement of terms and conditions to each employee, within two months of the employee starting. For further information, see chapter 4.

A grievance procedure
You must implement and publish to your employees at least the

statutory minimum procedure. For further information, see chapter 9.

A disciplinary procedure

You must implement and publish to your employees at least the statutory minimum procedure, but you are advised to have a fuller procedure, based for example on Acas guidelines. For further information, see chapter 9.

A health and safety policy

If you have more than five employees, you are legally required to have a health and safety policy. For further information, see chapter 11.

Health and safety poster

You must display a health and safety poster at all times, giving information about health, safety and welfare. For further information, see chapter 11.

Pensions information

From the time that you appoint your fifth employee, you must provide access to a Stakeholder Pension scheme, and give written information on this scheme. For further information, see chapter 6.

Equality and diversity policy

There is no legal requirement to have an equality and diversity policy, but you are advised to do so, to help you ensure that your workforce is representative of the community you serve.

Funders may also require a statement of your policy on equality and diversity.

For further information, see chapter 2.

Rules

You should publicise brief rules, covering matters such as making personal phone calls, confidentiality, non-harassment, data protection and use of computers. For further information, see chapter 9.

Sickness absence arrangements

You will need to specify in writing what procedures employees need to follow if they are sick. For further information, see chapter 10.

Annual leave arrangements

You will need to inform your employees in writing about booking and notification procedures for annual leave. For information about statutory requirements with regard to annual leave, see chapter 11.

Additional documentation

As your organisation, grows, you may find it useful to have some or all of the following documentation:
- application form, monitoring form other standard recruitment documentation (see chapter 3);
- induction procedure (see chapter 5);
- probation procedure (see chapter 5);
- salary review policy (see chapter 6);
- staff supervision and appraisal policy (see chapter 7);
- standard staff supervision and appraisal forms (see chapter 7);
- learning and development policy (see chapter 7);
- learning and development plan (see chapter 7);
- maternity, paternity, adoption and parental leave policies (see chapter 8);
- policy on compassionate leave and emergency domestic leave (see chapter 8);
- policy on requesting flexible working for parents of young children (see chapter 8);
- whistleblowing policy (see chapter 12);
- absence policy (see chapter 10);
- redundancy policy (see chapter 13).

A format for your employment policies

Below is an example format for your employment policies.

Policy statement
Include here a brief statement of your organisation's stance concerning the policy area.

Scope
Explain here to whom the policy applies and in what circumstances.

Policy details
Here you can put the details of how your policy will work in practice.

Responsibilities under the policy
The responsibilities of managers and employees in implementing the policy should be stated here.

Date
State the date the policy was drafted.

Staff handbooks

Many employers produce a staff handbook for their employees. Staff handbooks take many forms, but a popular approach is to set out the main areas of employment in brief in the staff handbook, with cross-references to the full policies and where to find them.

Example

The Westwich Association staff handbook – contents

Introduction to Westwich Association
A letter of introduction from the chair of the trustees

About the organisation
Brief history, mission, current and future plans

Joining Westwich Association
Induction and probation
Performance reviews and supervision meetings
Staff benefits

Working at Westwich Association
Equality and diversity
Harassment and bullying
Pay and payment method
Overtime
Flexitime
Parental rights
Sickness absence reporting and sick pay
Annual leave entitlement
Arrangements for public holidays
Taking time off for religious festivals
Compassionate leave and emergency domestic leave
Health and safety
Fire
Accidents

Rules and expectations
Drugs and alcohol
Smoking
Use of computers during personal time
Use of the organisation's facilities
Computer security

Use of the internet
Confidentiality
Expenses
Acceptance of personal gifts

Dealing with problems
Grievance procedure
Disciplinary procedure
Whistleblowing
Complaints

Leaving employment
Redundancy
Giving notice
Return of Association property

Consulting and communicating about your employment documentation

Your new employment documentation is likely to be much more readily accepted if you consult and communicate with staff as you draft it. If you recognise trade unions, you should also consult with them.

Your staff will be able to tell you how things work in practice, and where things could be improved. You can build these comments into your policies and procedures.

You should also consider whether any proposed new policy may make a significant change to the existing terms and conditions of employment of your staff. It if does, then you will need the agreement of your staff before you can make the change. You cannot change terms without individual employees' agreement (see chapter 4).

Make sure that all your employees have access to your employment policies. You could display your policies on notice boards, include them in a staff handbook, or add them to your organisation's shared computer drive or intranet.

Make sure that all your employees have access to your employment policies.

Checklist

- ✓ Make sure you have all the essential documentation outlined in this chapter.
- ✓ Introduce new policies as your organisation grows and as needed.

✓ Review existing policies from other organisations, to assist you with drafting your own policies.
✓ Consult with your employees about any new documentation you want to introduce. Gain their agreement if there is a significant change to terms and conditions.
✓ Communicate all your policies – make sure all staff have access to them.

Where to find out more

When drafting your policies, you could use the following sources of information:

- Ask other organisations for a copy of their policies, to use as a basis for your own.
- Ask your local Council for Voluntary Services to give you any example policies they may have. You can find their contact details in your local telephone directory or by looking on the National Association of Councils for Voluntary Services website at www.nacvs.org.uk.
- Review the NCVO HR Bank. Go to www.askNCVO.org.uk and enter in the search field 'NCVO HR Bank'. You will find here several example documents. You can obtain copies of further documents by writing to: HR Bank, Workforce Development, NCVO, Regent's Wharf, 8 All Saints Street, London N1 9RL.
- Use this publication, referring to the web links indicated at the end of each chapter, to gain the latest information.

15 Volunteers and employment

What this chapter is about

In this chapter, you can find out about:
- Things to think about if you are thinking of taking on volunteers.
- The legal difference between a volunteer, an employee and a worker.
- How you can make sure that the non-employee status of your volunteers is clear.
- Some key information about taking on and managing volunteers.
- Where you can go for further information about managing volunteers.

This chapter does not give comprehensive guidance about all aspects of managing volunteers, because the focus of this guide is employment. However, reference is made to other sources of information and publications about volunteers.

Some of the information from this chapter is reproduced or adapted, with thanks, from much more extensive information provided by Volunteering England on its website www.volunteering.org.uk.

Considering taking on a volunteer?

If you are thinking of taking on one or more volunteers, here is a brief overview of some of the things you should consider:
- Are you ready for volunteers?
- Do you have a volunteer policy in place?
- How will you recruit?
- How will you induct volunteers?
- What ongoing training do you need to provide?
- Who will be responsible for supervising them?
- Have you taken health and safety into account?
- How will you deal with volunteer expenses?
- How will you deal with any problems?

There is lots of support available to help you think through these issues. As a first step, try looking at the Volunteering England website: www.volunteering.org.uk, or tel: 0845 305 6979 or email: information@volunteeringengland.org.uk.

The legal difference between a volunteer, an employee and a worker

Volunteers:
- Support your organisation because they want to – there is no contract obliging them to do so.
- Do not have a contract of employment.
- Are not paid for what they do.

Employees:
- Have a contract of employment, that is, the employee agrees to work in return for 'consideration', i.e. pay and other terms and conditions.
- Must come to work in accordance with the terms of their contract.
- Are paid to work.

Workers:
- Have a lesser status than employees, but do have a contract to provide work for an organisation.
- Are generally engaged on a casual, 'as and when' basis.

Employees enjoy many legal rights that have already been covered in this guide, such as protection against unfair dismissal, redundancy and discrimination on various grounds. Employees also have a right to parental leave, sick pay, a minimum wage and holidays. Workers do not have as many rights, but do have the right to paid annual leave and to the minimum wage. Further information on employees and workers is contained in chapter 4.

Volunteers do not have any of these rights. However, you still need to be just as careful in your recruitment and treatment of volunteers as you do with paid staff. You will need to interview them to make sure they are suitable.

You should be aware that the Protection of Children Act and the Care Standards Act apply to volunteers as well as paid employees. This means that if volunteers may have regular or substantial contact with children or with vulnerable adults, you must seek Criminal Records Bureau checks ('Disclosures') on them (see chapter 3 for further information).

Although volunteers are not directly covered by health and

safety legislation, you do have a duty of care to them. This means that you need to apply the same high standards of health and safety to your volunteers as to any paid employee (see chapter 11).

Making clear the status of your volunteers

Problems can arise if the status of your volunteer becomes unclear. A volunteer might become an employee or a 'worker' if you do not make their status clear.

Volunteers have in the past made Employment Tribunal claims for unfair dismissal and for employment rights such as the minimum wage.

Here are a number of tips on what you can do to make clear the status of your volunteers:

Problems can arise if the status of your volunteer becomes unclear.

Application form
- Don't use the same application form as you use for paid employees – it will probably make reference to 'employment', which is misleading when you are looking for volunteers not employees.
- You may not need an application form at all. Consider whether you may be able to get the information you need when you meet the volunteer in person (this approach may also widen your pool of potential volunteers, as some volunteers may be put off by an application form or may have limited written English skills).

Volunteer agreement
- It can be useful to have a volunteer agreement, because it sets out what volunteers can expect from the organisation and what the organisation expects from its volunteers.
- Don't try to adapt the contract of employment that you may use for paid employees! Instead, use a volunteer agreement and base it on one of the model agreements provide by Volunteering England (see below for details).
- Avoid any form of obligation or contractual language. Any hint of obligation – volunteers agreeing to volunteer for the next six months, for example – runs the risk of the document being seen as contractual.
- Talk of hopes and expectations, with the understanding that volunteers are free to come and go. For example, if you need volunteers to stay with you for a period, you could state 'we hope that you can stay with us for at least three months, for you, us and our clients to make the most of the volunteering opportunity. However, you are of course free to leave at any

time.' This is better than saying 'you must volunteer with us for at least three months.'

- Explain in the agreement that your organisation will pay volunteer expenses, provide adequate training and supervision, carry out adequate risk assessments, and treat volunteers in accordance with its equal opportunities policy.
- Explain in the agreement that volunteers are expected to follow the rules and procedures of the organisation, and meet time commitments, giving adequate notice if this is not possible.
- Consider putting some sort of disclaimer in the agreement, such as: 'this agreement reflects the hopes and intentions of the volunteer and the voluntary organisation, and is not contractually binding in any way on either party.'

A volunteer policy

- A volunteer policy can help clarify exactly why volunteers are being used within an organisation, and how they will work alongside paid staff and how they can expect to be treated by the organisation.
- If yours is very small organisation, where everything is done on a face-to-face level, you may not need a volunteer policy. However, once the organisation starts to get larger, consider producing a volunteer policy to help ensure consistency and good practice.

Volunteer expenses

- It may seem easier to pay volunteers a flat rate, rather than reimbursing actual receipted expenses, but by doing this you are putting both your organisation and the volunteer at risk. Volunteers on benefit may lose part of their benefit if they receive anything over and above what they have actually spent. So, for instance, if your flat rate is £5 a day, but they have only spent £3.50, the entire sum may be seen to be income and could affect their benefits. The Inland Revenue also views money over and above actual out-of-pocket expenses as taxable income.
- You may also find that if you pay a flat rate you are inadvertently creating a contract of employment, because the volunteers may be seen as working in return for a sum that exceeds their actual expenses – no matter by how little. Such a sum is called, in legal terms, a 'consideration.' By creating a contract you could make the volunteer a 'worker.' If this is the case, they may be entitled to rights such as paid annual leave and the National Minimum Wage. It is also

possible that they could be considered to be an 'employee', in which case there are also additional rights such as the right not to be unfairly dismissed and other rights of employees listed in chapter 1.

- You must therefore take receipts and keep records so that you can prove that any money you have paid out is an actual reimbursement.
- Volunteers paid cash for subsistence (the practice with almost all residential volunteering) do not qualify for the minimum wage if they have been recruited through another charity or similar body.

Paying an honorarium

- An honorarium is a lump sum amount of money that may be given as a 'thank you'.
- It is only acceptable to pay an honorarium if it is totally unexpected and there is no precedent surrounding it. However, if it can be proved that there was an expectation that the payment would be made in return for a certain piece of work, length of service, or on leaving the organisation; then the payment would not be an honorarium, would be taxable and would indicate that the individual had employee status.
- It is best to be extremely wary about paying honoraria. As well as the possibility of creating a contract it may cause other problems. Benefits Offices generally see honoraria as a payment and may well dock the money off an individual's benefits.
- Instead of paying out honoraria organisations could make sure volunteers are able to claim expenses for meals, travel and care costs and that spare money is invested in making volunteer roles more rewarding. For example, offering more training (relevant to the job), social activities, extra resources, tools to make the organisation more accessible.

Grievance and disciplinary procedures

- It is generally better to have separate grievance and disciplinary procedures for volunteers. You may wish to make the procedures for volunteers simpler, so that they are accessible and so that volunteers fully understand where they are in the process. You can look on the website of Volunteering England for advice on drafting these.
- Having different policies also helps to clarify the non-employee status of volunteers. While Employment Tribunals will be looking mainly for evidence of payments from the

> It is only acceptable to pay an honorarium if it is totally unexpected and there is no precedent surrounding it.

organisation and obligation on the part of the volunteer, one part of lessening risk is to create a clear distinction within the organisation between paid staff and volunteers.

- Having different procedures does not mean giving volunteers a lesser status, it simply recognises that they have different needs to those of paid staff.

Providing training

- Following clarification in a recent tribunal decision, training is unlikely to be regarded as a 'consideration', but organisations should avoid giving training that is not relevant to the volunteer's role, as such a perk may be regarded as a form of payment. This might be the case if, for example, you pay for a volunteer gardener to go on computer training.
- As training must be necessary for the volunteer role to not count as a consideration, it is important to make sure that any training is open to all volunteers and that being eligible for training is not reliant on them having volunteered for a set period of time.

Case study

Amit has been a volunteer at Westwich Association (WA) for about nine years. He started by making teas and coffees and now undertakes the majority of the administration (mail-outs, newsletters and all responses to queries). He comes to the WA premises each Monday, Wednesday and Friday between 9.00am and 12.30pm.

The arrangement suits Amit, because, despite occasional part-time jobs, he has not been able to secure regular paid employment. Going to WA gives him a sense of purpose and a feeling of 'giving something back.' WA has also been very supportive to him in his search for employment. For example on one occasion, it paid for a week-long advanced driving course, to assist him in his application to become a lorry driver.

The management committee has, over the years, come to rely on Amit. In fact, the committee has changed in the nine years of Amit's volunteering and no one is quite sure how he started or what arrangements are in place. There is nothing in writing between Amit and WA.

Amit is not very accurate, but no one has liked to mention this to him, given all the support he gives WA.

There is a long-standing unwritten agreement that Amit will be given a cash 'allowance' of £10 per day as a 'thank you' for his work. He takes holiday for about six weeks per year and he doesn't receive the allowance when on holiday.

The treasurer of the management committee is new. He thinks that WA has now grown to such a size that a full-time paid administrator is needed.

The management committee discuss this with Amit. Amit decides to apply for the administrator job, but is not appointed. The committee tells him that it would be pleased if he would still undertake some other volunteering, but Amit feels his work has been taken away. He stops volunteering at WA.

A week later, WA receives an Employment Tribunal application from Amit. He is claiming: constructive unfair dismissal; breach of the Minimum Wage Act; failure to pay holiday pay; failure to issue a written statement of terms and conditions of employment.

Some points to consider
- Amit has received £30 per week from WA for some time. This is not paid to reimburse receipted expenses; it is simply an 'allowance'.
- It is possible that the £30 per week could be considered to be a 'consideration' in return for work undertaken, as could the payment for training which was not relevant to the volunteering.
- It is quite possible that an Employment Tribunal could find that Amit was in reality an employee. If they were to find that he was an employee, it is possible that Amit's Employment Tribunal claims could succeed.
- Alternatively, an employment tribunal may find that Amit is not an employee, but is a 'worker.' In this case, Amit's claims for minimum wage and holiday pay may succeed.
- Do you have any volunteering arrangements that are unclear and need to be reviewed?

Recruiting volunteers as employees

There is nothing to stop you from recruiting a volunteer as a paid employee. However, it may be poor equal opportunities practice to recruit only from within, especially if your existing volunteers are not representative of your local community. Volunteers may come to expect they will be guaranteed paid work, as it becomes available. This can affect volunteers' motives for volunteering and lead to people volunteering just to obtain paid work, like an unpaid apprentice. This again runs against equal opportunities, as not everyone is able to volunteer.

It is important to have a clear policy on this issue. If there is inconsistency, volunteers may have false hopes or expectations, or carry resentment that one volunteer was selected out of several.

Some organisations simply advertise all posts externally, encouraging volunteers to apply. Others have internal recruitment procedures, similarly encouraging volunteers to apply alongside paid staff. If no suitable candidate is found, the post is then advertised externally.

There are advantages and disadvantages to both approaches. External recruitment is purer in terms of equal opportunities, while internal recruitment allows staff and volunteers to develop within an organisation.

Checklist

- ✓ Use volunteer application forms not employment application forms.
- ✓ Use volunteer agreements not employment contracts.
- ✓ Avoid contractual language – speak of 'hopes' and 'expectations'.
- ✓ Draft a volunteer policy.
- ✓ Pay expenses against receipts.
- ✓ Only pay honoraria if they are totally unexpected, with no precedent surrounding them.
- ✓ Provide training that is relevant to the voluntary work you need doing.

Where to find out more

Volunteering England
Volunteering England offers a range of services designed to help and support everyone who works with volunteers.

Its website has:
- A programme of professional level training for people who manage volunteers.
- A useful 'Frequently asked questions' section.
- Information about important aspects of recruiting and managing volunteers, such as health and safety, impact on benefits and seeking criminal records checks.
- Sample volunteer agreements.
- Details of an extensive range of publications.

You can contact Volunteering England as follows:
  Information line: 0800 028 3304
  (Mon to Fri 10.30am-12.30pm and 2pm- 4pm)
  Tel: (London & Birmingham): 0845 305 6979
  Fax (London): 020 7520 8910
  Fax (Birmingham): 0121 633 4043
  Email: information@volunteeringengland.org.uk
  Website: www.volunteering.org.uk

  Volunteering England (London)
  Regent's Wharf
  8 All Saints Street
  London N1 9RL

  Volunteering England (Birmingham)
  New Oxford House
  16 Waterloo Street
  Birmingham B2 5UG